DIRECTIONS IN DEVELOPMENT

Reducing Poverty through Growth and Social Policy Reform in Russia

DIRECTIONS IN DEVELOPMENT

Reducing Poverty through Growth and Social Policy Reform in Russia

Poverty Reduction and Economic Management Unit
Europe and Central Asia Region

Radwan Shaban

Hiromi Asaoka • Bob Barnes • Vladimir Drebentsov
John Langenbrunner • Zurab Sajaia • James Stevens • David Tarr
Emil Tesliuc • Olga Shabalina • Ruslan Yemtsov

THE WORLD BANK
Washington, D.C.

1818 H Street, NW
Washington, DC 20433
Telephone: 202-473-1000
Internet: www.worldbank.org
E-mail: feedback@worldbank.org

1 2 3 4 09 08 07 06

ISBN-10: 0-8213-6340-9
ISBN-13: 978-0-8213-6340-9
eISBN: 0-8213-6341-7
DOI: 10.1596/978-0-8213-6340-9

Library of Congress Cataloging-in-Publication Data

Reducing poverty through growth and social policy reform in Russia.
p. cm. — (Directions in development)
This report has been prepared by a World Bank multi-sector team led by Radwan Shaban ... and others.
Includes bibliographical references.
ISBN 0-8213-6340-9
1. Poverty—Russia (Federation) 2. Russia (Federation)—Economic conditions—1991-3. Russia (Federation)—Social policy. I. Sha'ban, Radwan 'Ali. II. Directions in development (Washington, D.C.)

HC340.12.Z9P67 2005
362.5'0947'09049—dc22

2005049914

Cover photos: ITAR TASS
Cover design: Drew Fasick

Contents

Appendixes

Boxes

Figures

Tables

Abbreviations

Currency Unit (as of May 11, 2004)
1 RUB = $0.028
$1.00 = 28.95 RUB

cif	cost, insurance, and freight
CIS	Commonwealth of Independent States
DECDG	Development Data Group
DECRG	Development Research Group
DFID	Department for International Development (United Kingdom)
EASPR	Poverty Reduction and Economic Management Unit, East Asia and Pacific Region
ECSHD	Human Development Unit, Europe and Central Asia Region
ECSPE	Poverty Reduction and Economic Management Unit, Europe and Central Asia Region
EU	European Union
FDI	foreign direct investment
FSSS	Federal Service for State Statistics
GDP	gross domestic product
Goskomstat	State Committee of the Russian Federation for Statistics
GRP	gross regional product
HDNSP	Social Protection Team, Human Development Network
HRSCE	Client Engagement and Team Learning Unit, Human Resources Network
HRSLO	Leadership and Organization Effectiveness Unit, Human Resources Network
ILO	International Labour Organization
LSE	London School of Economics
MFN	Most Favored Nation
NOBUS	National Survey of Household Welfare and Program Participation

OECD	Organisation for Economic Co-operation and Development
PEGR	poverty equivalent growth rate
PPP	purchasing power parity
PRMPR	Poverty Reduction Group, Poverty Reduction and Economic Management Network
RLMS	Russia Longitudinal Monitoring Survey
SASHD	Human Development Unit, South Asia Region
SPIDER	Stockholm-Petersburg Institutional Development in Education and Research
UKDA	United Kingdom Data Archive
VCIOM	Russian Public Opinion Survey Center
WIDER	World Institute for Development Economics Research
WTO	World Trade Organization

Acknowledgments

This report was prepared by a World Bank multisector team led by Radwan Shaban (ECSPE) and consisting of Hiromi Asaoka (ECSHD), Bob Barnes (consultant), Vladimir Drebentsov (ECSPE), John Langenbrunner (ECSHD), Zurab Sajaia (consultant), James Stevens (ECSHD), David Tarr (DECRG), Emil Tesliuc (HDNSP), Olga Shabalina (DECDG), and Ruslan Yemtsov (ECSPE). It draws extensively on analytical work by international and local consultants, namely: Sergei Aivazian, Jeff Alwang, Chris Ash, Alexandr Baturin, Tamara Chernysheva, Andre Decoster, Irina Denisova, Franziska Gassman, John Gibson, Olesia Grabilina, Nanak Kakwani, Graham Kalton, Ekaterina Kozerenko, Marina Liborakina, Vladimir Litvinov, Ludmila Migranova, Gad Nathan, Alexander Poduzov, Lidia Prokofieva, Alexander Puzanov, Yana Roshtchina, Oleg Shakhnazarov, Alexei Shevykov, Sergey Smirnov, Sergey Sourkov, Alan Thompson, and Vladislav Zharomsky. Additional papers and inputs were made by World Bank staff Martin Ravallion, Michael Lokshin, James Anderson, Alexander Morozov, and Olga Antimonova. Very valuable contributions to the report were made in papers by Russian researchers Anastasiya Alexandrova, Tatyana Bandyukova, Tatyana Bogomolova, Tatyana Chetvernina, Svetlana Gerasimova, Elena Grishina, Elena Ivanova, Evgenia Kolomak, Irina Korchagina, Svetlana Lomonosova, Anna Lukyanova, Alexander Razumov, Galina Rodionova, Vera Tapilina, and Mariya Yagodkina. Their papers were chosen from proposals submitted for background papers on various aspects of poverty in Russia. Guidance for the background papers was provided by Vladimir Drebentsov (Senior Economist, World Bank); Vladimir Gimpelson (Director of the Labor Survey Center of the State University, Higher School of Economics, Moscow); Lilia Ovtcharova (Research Director, Independent Institute for Social Policy, Moscow); and Svetlana Misikhina (Social Protection Expert, International Labour Organization, Moscow Office).

Peer reviewers Giovanna Prennushi (PRMPR), Tamar Manuelyan Atinc (EASPR), and Jill Fletcher (DFID) offered valuable guidance and advice at various stages of the analysis and writing. Christine Jones (consultant) provided valuable and detailed comments on an early draft of the report. Special thanks to Julian Schweitzer (SASHD) for his unwavering support and encouragement for developing the programmatic collaborative work. The report was prepared under the guidance of Asad Alam, Cheryl Gray, Daniela Gressani, Pradeep Mitra, and Debbie Wetzel. The support of Arup Banerji and Mamta Murthi is also appreciated. Emily Evershed and Barbara Karni edited the report. Usha Khanna and Victoria Levin provided additional editorial help. Helena Makarenko was instrumental in the administrative preparation and production of the report, with the support of Judy Wiltshire, Rosario Hablero, Ekaterina Kuznetsova, Natalia Shagalina, and Sergey Karakin. This book version of the report was produced with the invaluable help of Paola Scalabrin, Samiha Sobhan, Melissa Edeburn, and Aziz Gokdemir in the World Bank's Office of the Publisher.

The DFID team that provided expert advice and contributions to the report consisted of Jill Fletcher, Statistical Advisor; Vardan Marashlyan, Economic Advisor; and Simon Bland, First Secretary, Head of Development Section, UK Embassy. Martin Harris and Kim Bradford-Smith from DFID also provided invaluable support and guidance to the team at earlier stages of the work.

Although the report is a World Bank product, it is based on a collaborative, programmatic approach under a joint World Bank, DFID, and Russian government project, which received invaluable financial support from the DFID trust fund for enhancing measurement, monitoring, and analysis of poverty in Russia. The World Bank team is indebted to its Russian counterparts, under the leadership of Valeriy Yanvaryev, First Deputy Minister of Labor and Social Development of the Russian Federation, and Alexander Sourinov, First Deputy Chairman of the State Committee of the Russian Federation on Statistics. The counterpart team included Vladimir Zinin, Head of the Department of Population Income and Welfare; Natalia Antonova, Deputy Head of the Department of Population Income and Welfare; Marat Baigereev, Head of the Division of the Department of Population Income and Welfare (Ministry of Labor and Social Development of the Russian Federation); Elena Frolova, Head of the Department of Living Standards and Population Surveys; Irina Kharlamova, Deputy Head of the Department of Living Standards and Population Surveys; Olga Mukhanova, Deputy Head of the Department of Living Standards and Population Surveys; Tatyana Velikanova, Head of the Division of the Department of Living Standards and Population Surveys; Zinaida Ryzhikova, Deputy Head of the Department of Labor Statistics (State Committee of the Russian Federation on Statistics); Vladimir Ponizov, Head of the Department of Social Policy; Elena Kitova, Deputy Head of the Department of Social Policy (Ministry of Economic Development and Trade); and Svetlana Panarina, Deputy Head of the Department of Social Sphere and Science (Ministry of Finance). The World Bank Stage I core team, led by Radwan Shaban, with ongoing coordination by Olga Shabalina (Project Coordinator), consisted of Tatyana Alexandrova, Bob Barnes, Tulia Beltran, Valery Ciancio, Irina Datsuk, Vladimir Drebentsov, Ekaterina Kuznetsova, Michael Lokshin, Helena Makarenko, Alison Panton, Mansoora Rashid, Zurab Sajaia, Natalia Shagalina, Emil Tesliuc, Ruslan Yemtsov, and Elena Zotova. The program also benefited from the World Bank Institute's training and workshops and from assistance by Jaesang Hwang, Shahidur Khandker, Nidhi Khattri, Anton Kolesnichenko, Tatyana Leonova, and Vera Wilhelm. The team received invaluable advice from team coaches John Adams (HRSLO) and Suzane Otis (HRSCE).

Executive Summary

This report analyzes the main facets and dynamics of poverty in the Russian Federation since 1997. The analysis was conducted between 2003 and 2004 by Russian and international experts. It reflects the framework of the first stage of the program on enhancing the measurement, monitoring, and analysis of poverty—a collaborative project by the World Bank, the United Kingdom Department for International Development, and the Russian government team from the Ministry of Labor and Social Development, the State Committee of the Russian Federation for Statistics (Goskomstat), the Ministry of Economic Development and Trade, and the Ministry of Finance.

This programmatic poverty assessment has two advantages over its predecessors. First, all previous attempts at analyzing poverty in Russia have had to rely on data from the Russia Longitudinal Monitoring Survey (UNC, various years) and a few other publicly available surveys conducted irregularly. This report uses the vast micro data of the Household Budget Survey, a regular Goskomstat survey of 49,000 Russian households that has been in existence since 1952. In addition, this report presents one of the first poverty-related analyses of the data collected under the National Survey of Household Welfare and Program Participation (NOBUS), Goskomstat's survey of households' access to social services, carried out in 2003. While Goskomstat generously provided the data for this report, the methodology and results remain the sole responsibility of the World Bank.

Second, the poverty assessment both analyzes poverty on the basis of the available data and sets the stage for enhancing monitoring by recommending ways of improving sampling, survey data collection, and processing. The final poverty assessment report, scheduled for 2007, will be adjusted and improved for better poverty monitoring.

Part I examines the nature of poverty, both at the national and regional levels, to identify the groups with a high poverty risk. Part II examines the linkages between growth and poverty through the labor market, the contribution of growth and inequality to recent poverty reduction, and the expected impact of accession to the World Trade Organization on overall growth and poverty. Part III examines the scope for improving social policy in ways that will have a direct impact on the poor: by strengthening the safety net, reforming the housing and utilites services, and reorganizing the education and health sectors. The last chapter of the report provides recommendations for monitoring of poverty outcomes on the basis of the Household Budget Survey.

The fact that this report is based on a much larger dataset than previously available studies makes its results invaluable for formulating poverty reduction policies. It is, however, not a Poverty Reduction Strategy. The report's recommendations, presented below, represent a roadmap of pillars of a poverty reduction strategy rather than a specific and detailed action plan.

Pillar 1: Growth is essential for poverty reduction

Following the 1998 financial crisis, consumption dropped precipitously across all income groups. The drop was particularly severe among the poor. As a result of the collapse in incomes and the rise in inequality, in 1999 poverty levels reached an all-time high for the transition period. Four out of every 10 people slipped into poverty, unable to meet nutritional and other basic needs.

Fortunately, the economic rebound after the crisis was both impressive and broad based—albeit uneven—across both sectors and regions. It increased the demand for labor and led to significant wage increases, reduced unemployment, and increased hours of work. In addition to higher earnings, households benefited from the improved fiscal position of the government that resulted from higher oil revenues. The government was able to achieve a substantial reduction in arrears in wages and social benefits, raise pensions and public sector wages, and increase public spending on social policies, which had been drastically cut in real terms in the aftermath of the 1998 crisis. Government social spending was procyclical, exacerbating the negative impact of the downturn but strengthening the positive impact of the recovery. Although the recovery was accompanied by an increase in consumption among all groups, the increase was greatest for the poorest groups, making growth in 1999–2002 pro-poor.

The result of this increase in growth was a dramatic reduction in poverty, the incidence of which fell from 41.5 percent in 1999 to 19.6 percent in 2002 (figure A). Yet one out of every five people was still poor in 2002, leaving no room for complacency by the authorities, who aim to halve the poverty incidence by 2007.

The goal of cutting poverty in half is potentially achievable but very difficult. It would require a uniform increase in per capita consumption of

Figure A. The incidence of poverty peaked in 1999

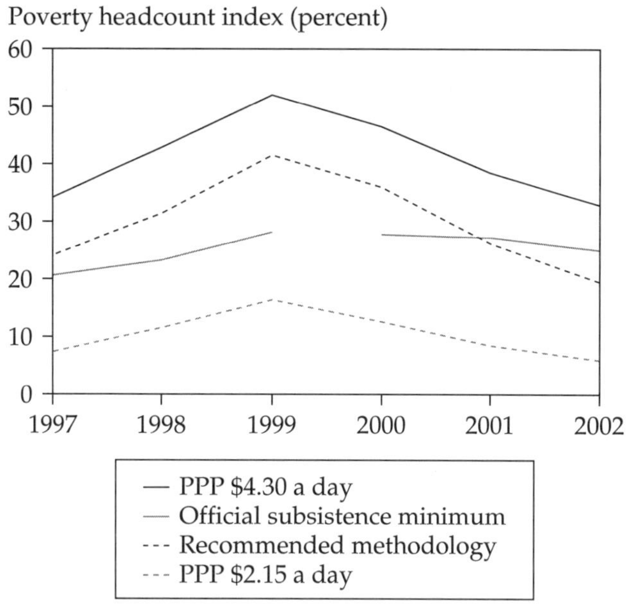

Source: Chapter 6, table 6.3.

at least 5 percent a year. Consumption growth of 3 percent a year would reduce poverty by only a third.

Increased inequality would substantially weaken the poverty reduction impact of a given rate of growth. While inequality may increase as returns to education increase and wages become increasingly decompressed—positive developments as market forces become entrenched—attention will need to be paid to the extent to which the poor are sharing in growth.

The transition has been accompanied by increasing inequality in asset ownership and returns to education, generating increasing levels of consumption and income inequality. The trend contributes to poverty and has been weakening the poverty-reducing impact of growth. Russia is already at the high end of inequality among the Commonwealth of Independent States (CIS), even if its inequality is still moderate by international standards.

To achieve a sustained annual growth rate of 5 percent in consumption, Russia will have to increase GDP by more than 5 percent a year. Further output increases will need to be attained by expanding the capital stock and devoting a larger share of output to investment rather than consumption. Consumption is likely to rise less than income in the future, as households start to increase their savings rate. While this will help sustain growth in the long run, it implies that GDP will have to grow faster than consumption to realize the poverty reduction goals.

Future growth will also be increasingly challenging, as the key drivers for growth and poverty reduction since 1999 may have run their course. Capacity utilization increased by about 20 percentage points between 1997 and 2003; future growth will require expanding the productive capacity of the economy. The real exchange rate depreciated by about 40 percent between July and October 1998, propelling recent growth, but it has since appreciated in real terms, approaching its pre-devaluation levels. High oil prices benefited the economy in the past three years. However, given price uncertainty, basing a development strategy on continued high oil prices is risky. An oil price drop would depress output and increase poverty.

Diversifying the economy is essential for achieving sustainable growth. Policies to do so constitute the first pillar of the poverty reduction strategy. They include improving the business environment and, in particular, leveling the playing field to expand job creation at small and medium-size enterprises; reducing the tax burden, which, in turn, requires much greater efficiency in public service provision; making sweeping changes in technical regulations and their enforcement, ensuring an independent judiciary and the rule of law; and completing accession to the WTO. Accession to the WTO is an important part of the growth and reform agenda, as it is likely to provide substantial benefits to Russia, increasing the Russian consumption level by 7 percent in the medium term and considerably more in the long term. Moreover, unskilled labor is expected to obtain a higher return from accession than capital, and the poor will gain slightly more than the average Russian household.

Pillar 2: Targeted interventions are needed to reach deep pockets of poverty

Identifying the most vulnerable groups is important for designing policies that reach deep pockets of poverty that may not be affected by general economic improvements. In 2002 the groups with the highest rates of poverty were people living in rural areas, small and remote towns, and certain depressed regions; children; the unemployed; and people living in households whose head had no more than a primary education:

- About 30.4 percent of the rural population lived in poverty, while only 15.7 percent of the urban population was poor. Living in small and remote towns also carried a higher risk of poverty than living in large urban areas.

- There are large regional differences in the incidence of poverty, which ranged from 3.1 percent to 55.6 percent.
- While the national incidence of poverty was 19.6 percent, the incidence of poverty among children under 16 was 26.7 percent. Child welfare projects are needed to address the problem, and social assistance needs to be targeted to families with children.
- One out of every three unemployed people was poor, compared to one out of every five persons in the population at large.
- People with primary education were 50 percent more likely to be poor than the general population.

Interventions properly targeted at each of these groups will reach those most severely affected by poverty, but they may not necessarily reach a majority of the poor. The composition of the poor is different from the above profile:

- The majority of the poor (88 percent) live in families in which at least one member works.
- About one-third of the poor live in households with no children, another third live in households with one child, and the remaining third live in households with two or more children. Poverty programs based solely on targeting households with many children will miss a large number of the poor.
- A majority of the poor (58.5 percent) live in urban areas, where 73.2 percent of the Russian population lives.

The majority of the poor are working urban families with children, in which bread earners earn low wages. Many workers with wages below the official poverty line are concentrated in education, culture, health, and other public services. For these people, growth with rising wages would most likely suffice to increase income and hence consumption to above the poverty line.

Pillar 3: The poverty impact of social policies needs to be enhanced

Government policy has a huge untapped potential to reduce poverty through redistributive social spending. Privileges that benefit the rich more than the poor account for about 4 percent of GDP. Phasing out these regressive subsidies and replacing them with targeted social assistance would constitute an important pillar of the government's poverty reduction strategy.

At the same time, the targeting of programs aimed at the poor needs to be dramatically improved. Currently, the two programs that have the largest share of the poor among their beneficiaries are the child allowance program and the decentralized social assistance programs. Yet only about 30 percent of child allowance beneficiaries and 28 percent of social assistance beneficiaries are from the poorest quintile, and about half come from the richest 60 percent of the population. Moreover, with the excep-

Figure B. Russia's social welfare programs are not as well targeted as programs in other countries

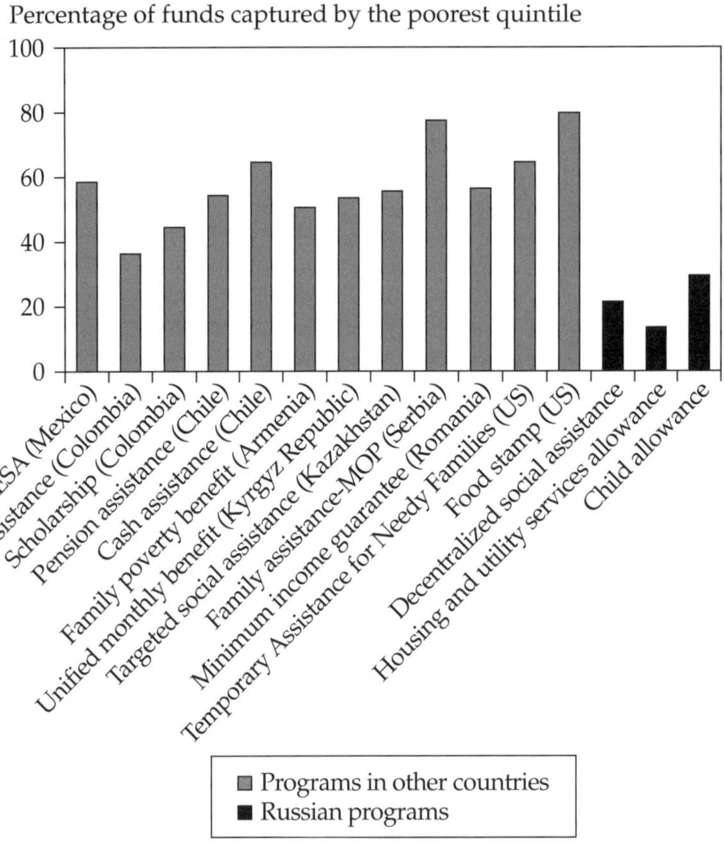

Sources: For Latin America and the United States, Castañeda and Lindert (2005); for Europe and Central Asia, various World Bank poverty assessments.
Note: Figure shows share of funds captured by poorest quintile.

tion of the child allowance, the average benefit received by the rich is larger than the average benefit received by the poor (figure B).

The system of decentralized social assistance programs needs to be strengthened through improved financing and better targeting instruments. The report recommends introducing proxy means testing to reduce the leakage of funds to the nonpoor. It also recommends transforming the unfunded mandate of the decentralized social assistance programs into a single core program that is federally funded and monitored but locally implemented. The targeting threshold should be made consistent with funding availability, so that it reaches the poorest households.

Social spending should also become more targeted, and it should increase in some areas, to address emerging deprivation in access to education and health care. If these issues are not tackled, a vicious cycle of reproducing the underclass may develop. Despite Russia's strong position in terms of compulsory education enrollment and completion, children from poor households have less access to preschool and postcompulsory education, which is increasingly determined by income and wealth. Children who begin behind their peers in basic learning skills tend to remain behind. The lowest-income adult population has two to three years less schooling than the highest-income population, diminishing its income potential. As returns to earnings have been decompressed, the children of the poor have a higher than average risk of becoming poor adults.

Deprivation of good-quality health care is a concern for the poor, who have worse health outcomes than better-off people. This situation reflects causality in both directions: poverty breeds ill health and ill health keeps poor people poor. Illness may have a substantial impact on income. The situation has recently been exacerbated by the development of private (even if informally) health care, which has placed an increasing burden on families to make informal out-of-pocket payments for care. Private expenditures are estimated to represent 30–55 percent of total spending on health, and out-of-pocket payments for health care constitute a disproportionately high share of consumption among the poor.

Conclusion

This report identifies broad directions for reform rather than an action plan for implementing a specific set of policies. That said, the sectoral recommendations are summarized below (table A).

Table A. Sectoral policy recommendations

Issue	*Policy priorities*
Access to quality education, particularly at the preschool and postcompulsory levels, is increasingly being determined by income.	Set modern standards and measure their achievement; improve the relevance of secondary vocational programs; earmark funding for remedial programs in areas where performance is lagging.
Funding for education is inequitably allocated.	Allocate funding on the basis of transparent per student formulas; establish universal fees for higher education; target noneducational subsidies at the poor.
Health outcomes are deteriorating.	Implement public health interventions to close health gaps and protect vulnerable subpopulations and to control risk factors for infectious and noncommunicable diseases.
Paying for health care increasingly requires out-of-pocket expenses, which place a disproportionate burden on the poor and vulnerable and affect treatment compliance and access to basic services.	Formalize informal payments through a standardized copayment system and develop explicit exclusions for the poor and vulnerable; make private supplementary insurance more accessible for emerging middle-income groups.
Health expenditure is allocated inequitably across regions.	Change the regional allocation formula for health expenditure to better reflect the population and its health needs; improve the pooling of resources at the federal and regional levels to reduce the fragmentation of funding sources, allowing for redistribution from healthy to sick and rich to poor.
Noncontributory social protection programs do a poor job of targeting the poor.	Reform the system of privileges to ensure equitable access to subsidized goods and services; reduce the scope for labor-based privileges; reallocate the freed-up resources to other poverty alleviation programs; improve the efficiency of targeted social assistance programs by using a proxy means test formula instead of the current formal income test.
Cost coverage of housing and utility tariffs needs to be improved, while protecting poor households.	Revise the formula used to calculate the housing allowance to improve targeting; consider using a proxy means test to determine program eligibility or improve targeting performance by including additional criteria for program eligibility, related to housing conditions or endowment with key durables or real estate.

Part I
The Nature of Poverty in the Russian Federation

To design a sound poverty reduction strategy, policymakers must understand the nature of poverty in Russia. Part I of this report examines poverty measurement, the basis for examining the specifics of poverty in Russia. It profiles poverty in order to capture features that can help policymakers design targeted interventions. A special feature of poverty—its spatial and regional dimension—is examined in detail.

Chapter 1 is methodological in nature but very important given the increased policy attention to the quantitative targets of poverty reduction. It briefly reviews the official methodology for measuring poverty, identifies specific areas where improvements can be made, and proposes an alternative methodology for measuring poverty. The recommended methodology is based on using survey-based estimates that rely on consumption as a welfare measure and adopt an objective and regionally consistent poverty line. The chapter examines the implications of adopting this methodology.

In order to examine the scope for targeted interventions, chapter 2 looks at the specifics of the poverty profile in Russia along three dimensions: who is at risk of poverty, who are the poor, and what are the causes of poverty. The chapter concludes that those with a higher than average risk of falling into poverty live in rural areas or small towns, have children, and are unemployed. Yet most poor people in Russia belong to working families with children, and they live in regions in which the incidence of poverty is average. By international standards, the chapter shows, inequality in Russia is moderate, although the level is at the high end for the Commonwealth of Independent States (CIS).

Chapter 3 examines the regional dimensions of inequality and poverty. It documents the large interregional differences in socioeconomic conditions but points out that most inequality is within regions. The incidence of poverty is greater in regions that have lower average output, higher unemployment, or lower wage rates. Though there are large differences in the incidence of poverty across regions, most of the poor live in regions in which the level of poverty is not substantially different from the national level. Thus a poverty reduction strategy should aim for broad-based growth in average regions, complemented by targeted interventions for a small subset of regions in which the incidence of poverty is very high. At the same time, federal policies should be adopted that encourage the regions to fight poverty within regions.

1
Improving the Methodology for Measuring Poverty in Russia

Poverty measures in Russia are used to formulate public policy, administer social protection programs, and conduct research at the national and regional levels. The government adopted its first official poverty methodology in 1992, relying on an absolute poverty line grounded in a nutritionally based food basket supplemented by an allowance for nonfood needs. The methodology was updated in 2000, when a normative basket for both food and nonfood goods was created and greater regional differentiation was introduced in the determination of poverty. Official poverty estimates are calculated by Goskomstat using the Household Budget Survey, which was improved substantially in 1997, and an "imitation" model that ensures conformity with macroeconomic aggregates.

Despite its achievements in improving poverty monitoring, the current methodology has several drawbacks. The welfare aggregate is income based, derived from expenditure data and subjected to various adjustments to conform to aggregates from the national accounts. The poverty line is regionally inconsistent and normative, with prescribed baskets for both food and nonfood goods.

This chapter briefly reviews the official methodology for poverty measurement; identifies areas for improvement; proposes an alternative methodology directly based on survey data, with a consumption-based welfare aggregate and an objective poverty line grounded in household behavior; and spells out the implications of adopting the recommended methodology. Serious consideration of the proposed methodology is important, given the Russian government's commitment to reducing poverty dramatically by 2007.

Russia was home to 31.8 million poor people in 2003—20.4 percent of the population, according to official estimates. A key policy objective of the second Putin presidency is to fight poverty.

Official poverty measurements are used to formulate broad public policy. Poverty measurement is also used in the administration of targeted social assistance and in policy research at the national and regional levels. The new Labor Code declares a goal of eventually raising the minimum wage to the minimum subsistence level, as the poverty line is called. The minimum subsistence level is also invoked in the policy debate on the minimum pension for retirees and used to determine stipends, allowances, and other social payments.

The Official Poverty Measurement Methodology

First introduced in 1952, the Household Budget Survey is the only source for monitoring poverty at the national and regional levels in Russia. Official poverty estimates are based on the survey. Since 1997, when it was revised in line with international practice, the survey has been a credible source for analyzing poverty and inequality nationally. The revision of the survey changed the unit of observation from the family to the household. Sampling, which had been based on quota sampling, was revised to include a random stratified sample representative of the whole population, as well as samples for every region and for rural and urban subgroups within those regions, on the basis of the 1994 microcensus. The questionnaire was also revised substantially.

The sample includes 49,000 households drawn from throughout the country, with data collected each quarter. The period under analysis in this report starts in 1997, which ensures the comparability of the analysis. This period is also important from a policy perspective, as it encompasses changes in welfare before, during, and after the financial crisis of 1998. Chapter 12 examines the use of the Household Budget Survey for poverty monitoring and the current plans for improving it.

Although the Household Budget Survey does not collect income data, the official methodology for poverty estimation requires use of an income measure, given that the law defines the minimum subsistence level on the basis of income. An estimate of the increment in financial assets is derived and added to cash expenditure to generate money income.

An "imitation model" is used to derive national and regional poverty estimates. Unlike elsewhere in the world, poverty headcount estimates in Russia are not directly based on survey data. Instead, an "imitation model" is used: the mean per capita money income estimated from macroeconomic data is combined with the money income inequality data from the Household Budget Survey. The model produces a single number, an estimate of the number of people with a per capita income below the subsistence minimum in a given region.[1]

The poverty profile is produced from the survey, but adjustments are made to the weights to ensure conformity with macroeconomic data on income. As richer households are believed to have a higher nonresponse rate, their responses are weighted more heavily than responses by poorer households.

The official poverty line was first adopted in 1992 and revised in 2000. The official poverty line was established under guidelines developed by the Ministry of Labor and Social Development. It is based on the cost of meeting certain food and nonfood requirements deemed necessary to maintain health and minimum activity levels, both personal and social, taking into account the geographic setting (notably the climate). The food portion of the subsistence minimum is calculated as the cost, at current prices, of an officially adopted food basket that satisfies nutritional requirements. The nonfood component of the poverty line during 1992–99 was calculated as a constant coefficient derived from the consumption structure of the lowest decile. Three changes were introduced in the poverty line methodology adopted in 2000. First, the components of the food basket were changed. Second, the calculation of the cost of the nonfood component of the minimum subsistence level was based on a normative basket of essential nonfood goods, services, and payments. Third, greater regional differentiation was introduced in the subsistence minimum, with more zones for food and nonfood baskets. The updated poverty line is more generous than the older poverty line, which leads to higher poverty estimates.

The food baskets are based on nutritional requirements for calories, proteins, fats, and carbohydrates for six different groups: infants, children 1–6, children 7–15, men 16–59, women 16–54, and elderly people (men 60 and older and women 55 and older). Baskets vary across the 16 geographical zones of Russia to account for caloric differences by climatic zones and regional differences in food consumption patterns. Nutritional requirements in the coldest Arctic regions are about 15 percent higher than in the more temperate southern regions.

Three zones for nonfood goods and three zones for services and utility baskets are defined, based on climatic conditions. The basket for nonfood goods provides detailed expert-specified quantities to be consumed by various groups of people. These groups are similar to the groups used in the construction of the food basket, except that separate baskets for nonfood goods are defined for elderly men and women. The service basket consists of consumption norms for seven utilities. While the food and nonfood baskets are defined at the individual level, the service baskets are defined on a per capita basis. Every item in the nonfood bundle has an approximate usage time that varies for different age and gender groups.

Local governments determine the composition of goods and services in the regional baskets. An interrministerial expert committee reviews the draft consumer baskets submitted by local governments and proposes recommendations to the federal government, which makes the final decision on the composition of the regional baskets. The expert committee evaluates the nutritional composition of every regional basket as well as the composition of the nonfood components.

The poverty line is calculated each quarter, using prices collected by the State Committee of the Russian Federation for Statistics (Goskomstat) from 200 cities. In the fourth quarter of 2000, 50 percent of the consumer basket represented food items, 25 percent other goods, 19 percent services, and 6 percent mandatory payments.

Drawbacks to the Official Measurement Methodology

There are three important elements to establishing a poverty estimate: setting a credible poverty line, determining what aggregate to use to measure welfare, and coming up with a statistically reliable population estimate. There are drawbacks to the Russian method on all three counts.

Problems Concerning the Official Poverty Line

The official food baskets are normative, selected by nutritional experts rather than based on household consumption patterns. The official methodology rightly adopts an absolute poverty line based on the cost of basic needs, in particular the need to satisfy nutritional requirements, and it allows for variation across demographic groups. Since actual nutritional intake is difficult to monitor to determine whether a household is poor or not, expenditure on food is usually taken as the measure of whether a household can satisfy the nutritional requirement. The cost of the calorie intake of the food basket is therefore calculated using local prices and food conversion factors. The calorie cost of the basket varies across regions and demographic groups. Thus the quality and hence the economic costs of baskets are not uniform. For example, children appear to have higher calorie costs than adults. When the underlying average calorie costs for each region and each individual are calculated using the estimated population share, the calorie costs of children are 20–30 percent higher than those of adults in the same region, because the normative food basket for children tends to reflect the wishes of experts rather than actual consumption patterns. Internationally, the preferred method is to derive the food basket from actual consumption habits of low-income people rather than having nutritional experts specify it.

The official nonfood baskets are also normative. Constructing the nonfood basket is more difficult than designing the food basket. The Ministry of Labor and Social Development constructs the official basket on a purely normative basis. The basket provides very detailed quantities of nonfood items that should be consumed by active men, active women, retired people, and children. Rather than base the basket on subjective value judgments, it should be based on consumption patterns observed in the Household Budget Survey.

The official food poverty lines are inconsistent across regions. Each region's determination of its subsistence minimum is subject to federal guidelines and approval. In order to make legitimate interregional comparisons of poverty, the poverty lines should be consistent across regions: two individuals with the same standard of living who live in different regions should be identified as either poor or nonpoor.

To assess the welfare level provided by two different baskets, local prices can be used in both regions. If the resulting total costs of both baskets in local prices are comparable, the baskets would be likely to yield the same level of welfare. Using this concept, Ravallion and Lokshin (2003) find that the official poverty lines are not consistent across regions. The lack of consistency is due partly to built-in assumptions in the law framework that guided the adaptation of regional poverty lines to take climatic differences into account. But the inconsistency of poverty lines within the same climatic zone indicates that it also reflects the manipulation of poverty methodology at the local level.

The nonfood component of the official poverty line does not capture the economies of scale that result from individuals living together. Nonfood goods and services are defined on a per capita basis and thus do not capture savings from living together in a household and sharing the consumption of goods such as housing or durable goods. International experience suggests that households can save up to a third of their income through such economies of scale (Kakwani and Sajaia 2003). This should lead to a per capita poverty line that declines with household size. Official estimates, which do not account for these economies, overstate poverty for larger households.

Problems Concerning the Welfare Aggregate Measure

Though official poverty estimates rely on income to measure poverty in order to achieve consistency with official guidelines on poverty lines, the derived income measure is not consistent with the official poverty line. The law defines the minimum subsistence level as the income needed to attain a certain standard of living. But income data are not collected directly in the Household Budget Survey and are likely to be underreported in a country with a large informal economy. Goskomstat calculates the "money income" of a household by adding net savings to the cash expenditures reported in the Household Budget Survey. An inconsistency arises in this calculation, as cash expenditures include the value of actual spending on durable goods, while the official guidelines for the subsistence minimum account for the use value of some of these goods. For example, the official annual subsistence minimum includes only one-eighth of the cost of a woman's winter coat, assuming that each woman needs a coat every eight years. But in reality a household does not spend one-eighth of the price of a coat every year; cash expenditures include either the full cost of a coat or zero.

The calculated income measure is biased because it underestimates net savings for richer households. Households participating in the Household Budget Survey maintain a diary for 2 weeks and a log book for 11 weeks per quarter. This way of measuring expenditure is rigorous and detailed. In contrast, the measurement of net savings, based on recalling aggregated transactions in financial assets, is very crude. Net savings data are subject to significant recall error and underreporting of savings, especially by richer households.

International evidence suggests that estimating savings as changes in financial assets is unreliable (Gibson and Poduzov 2003). A household survey in Pakistan permits derivation of money income by estimating consumption as well as net savings based on the change in assets in the same way as is done in the Russian Household Budget Survey. The results are very different from those obtained directly from income questions in the survey: the income of the rich is understated by 50 percent, and the income for all households is understated by 25 percent (figure 1.1).

Figure 1.1. Pakistan's household survey demonstrates the unreliability of estimating household net savings from changes in financial assets

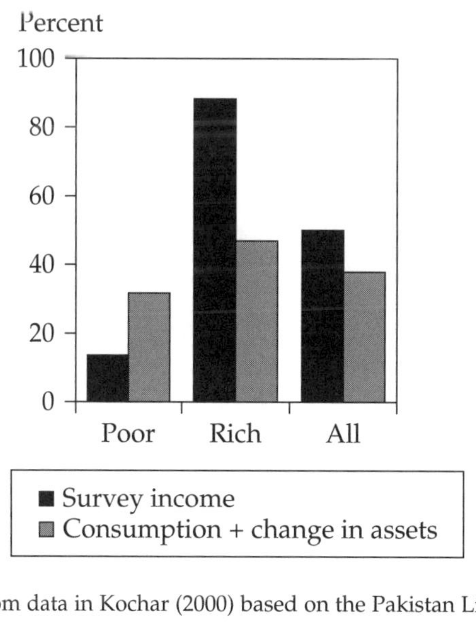

Source: Calculated from data in Kochar (2000) based on the Pakistan Living Standards Measurement Study.

Figure 1.2. Income and expenditure do not appear to deviate from each other in Russia, as they do in Vietnam

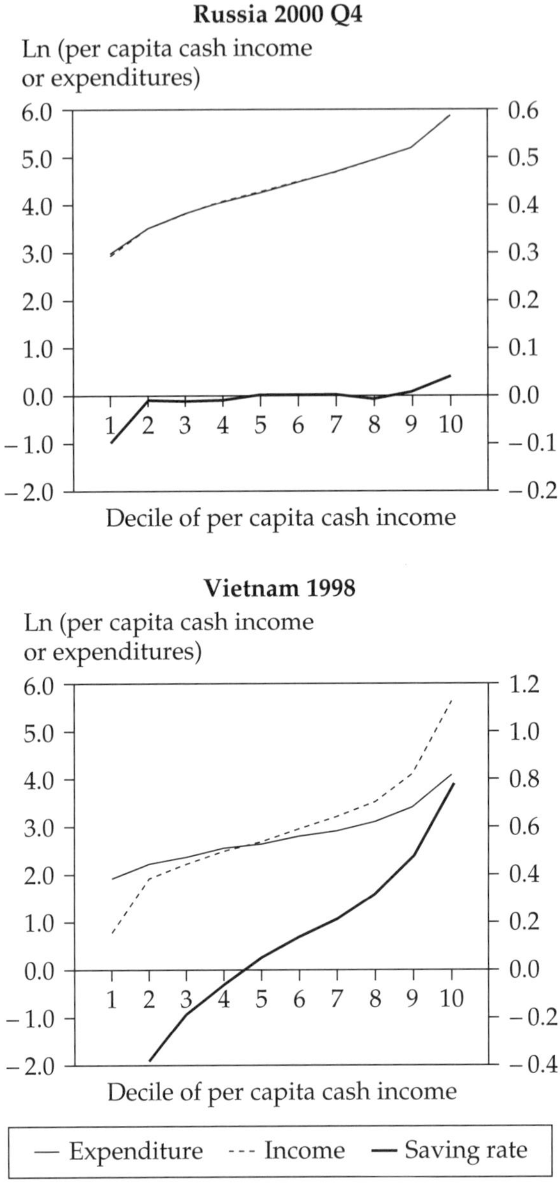

Source: Bank staff calculations based on data from the Household Budget Survey (Goskomstat, various years); Gibson and Poduzov (2003).

Note for Russia: Values are in 1997 rubles divided by 1,000; all log values have five subtracted to balance the two y-axes.

Comparison of the relation between expenditure and estimated income in Russia with that in China, New Zealand, and Vietnam reveals the bias in estimates of savings in Russia and the resulting understatement of incomes for richer households. The gap between income and expenditure increases after the third decile in other countries, while expenditure and income in Russia appear very close, except for the very richest and poorest deciles (figure 1.2). Moreover, the saving rate estimated from the Household Budget Survey appears stable for various quarters between 1997 and 2000, despite serious imbalances accompanying the Russian financial crisis in 1998, casting further doubt on the credibility of the estimate.

Problems Concerning the Population Estimate from the Household Budget Survey Sample

Adjustment of the income variable to ensure consistency with macroeconomic aggregates leads to extreme reweighting by increasing the weights for the rich and lowering them for the poor. The income aggregate derived from the survey is usually lower than a similar aggregate of household welfare derived from national accounts. In general, it is preferable not to modify household data for consistency with national accounts. But even if such an adjustment is made, the manner in which it is carried out creates extreme weights, leading to biases in various indicators. The micro-based estimate is lower than a similar estimate from the national accounts because of the higher nonresponse rate by richer households and the underestimation of net savings—and therefore estimated income—from the survey. Goskomstat considers only the nonresponse factor in its adjustment, by attaching heavier weights to richer households and lighter weights to poorer households. It applies the new weights to all Household Budget Survey indicators. This procedure creates extreme weights, which are not common in similar surveys in other countries. For example, in the fourth quarter of 2000, the five households with the heaviest sample weights had the same effect on calculated statistics as did the 5,400 households with the lightest (nonzero) weights. This extreme discrepancy between weights implies statistical and budgetary inefficiency. The heaviest weight is 200 times the lightest weight in Moscow but just 3 times as great in Jakarta for a comparable Indonesian survey (Gibson and Poduzov 2003). The understatement of savings leads to the understatement of the money income variable, which in turn causes a reliance on extreme weight adjustment in order to reconcile the survey estimates of income with the estimates from macroeconomic sources.

Recommended Poverty Measurement Methodology

In general, full transition to survey-based poverty monitoring is recommended. To conduct such monitoring, a consumption measure of welfare is recommended. It is also recommended that Russia establish an objective, regionally consistent, and absolute poverty line. The economies of scale in household size and the equivalent scales by age and gender should be applied to either the poverty line or the welfare aggregate. As the Russian practice incorporates equivalent scales and regional adjustments in the official poverty line, the recommended methodology also applies the adjustments for household composition, household size, and regional prices to the poverty line. It also monitors nonmonetary indicators of poverty in addition to monetary poverty.

Base the Measurement of Poverty Fully on Survey-Based Monitoring

The official poverty rate is currently produced for the federation and for each region using an imitation model that relies on a money income average obtained from macroeconomic accounts and an inequality estimate derived from the Household Budget Survey data and additional modeling assumptions. The Household Budget Survey data are first used to calculate the shares of each decile for the urban and rural populations and for the total population. The decile shares are then used to calculate an estimate of the variance, using a lognormal model for interval approximation. This inequality measure is then used by the imitation model, along with the money income from the national accounts, to produce the poverty rate. The official regional poverty rates are then computed by applying regional poverty lines using the imitation model. Similarly, the national poverty rate is calculated by applying the model at the national level. This imitation model approach is not used by other countries. One problem with the imitation model is that the number of officially counted poor in the country as a whole is not necessarily the same as the sum of officially counted poor in all regions. The resulting poverty estimates may ultimately be driven more by trends in the national accounts and modeling assumptions than by observed patterns in the Household Budget Survey.

Adopt Consumption as the Welfare Measure

No single indicator can capture all of the multidimensional aspects of poverty. The "capability" approach proposed by Sen (1985) is an attempt to recognize the fact that deprivation involves more than low levels of income and consumption. Despite their imperfections, however, income

Box 1.1. International practice is to measure poverty in terms of consumption

International practice is increasingly to rely on consumption or expenditure-based measures to analyze poverty. In a compilation of household surveys from 88 developing countries, constructed to establish world poverty counts in 2001, 52 surveys used expenditure as the welfare measure and 36 used income. Only Latin America relies heavily on income surveys, and even in that region there is increased use of expenditure surveys. In major developing countries, consumption-based measures dominate poverty analysis. Official poverty counts in India are based on the National Sample Survey, which collects information only on consumption expenditures. In Indonesia the SUSENAS survey collects information on both income and consumption, but poverty measurement is always based on the consumption estimates. In China the situation is a little more complex. Before 1998 poverty was measured using the household income data from the national rural sample survey, even though this survey also collected expenditure data. Since 1998 the State Statistical Bureau has been using both income and the expenditure data.

Sources: Ravallion (2001); Deaton (2001); Park and Wang (2001).

and consumption remain dominant welfare measures in poverty analysis today, because they can be easily interpreted and are often highly correlated with "capabilities." There is a widespread view among economists that household consumption is a better welfare indicator than income for measuring poverty. This belief underlies the strong international practice of relying on consumption-based welfare indicators rather than income (box 1.1).

In principle, the best measure of a household's long-term economic resources is wealth or permanent income. The present value of expected labor earnings, an important component of wealth, is unobservable. While current income is observable, it has both permanent and transitory components, and the transitory components obscure any ranking of households based on permanent income.[2] As a result of transitory income change, income-poor households could include those that have suffered temporary reductions in income. Because their permanent income remains high, such households will have high ratios of expenditures to current income. Similarly, high-income households will include those with temporary increases in income that result in low ratios of expenditures to income. If individuals know that a reduction in their income is transitory, they will not immediately adjust their consumption level. Moreover, a household could save or not save and use an informal support network to smooth consumption over time. Because it is less influenced by transitory income fluctuation and is therefore more stable, consumption is a better measure of permanent income.

Consumption is also easier to measure accurately than income, for several reasons. First, survey questions on income typically require a longer reference period to capture seasonal agricultural incomes, increasing the likelihood of recall errors. And high inflation affects estimates if respondents report values from the time of the transaction. Second, household income is hard to construct for self-employed households and for people working in the informal sector, because it is difficult to separate business costs and revenues. While consumption data are not immune to these problems, they are not as severe for consumption data. Third, questions about consumption are usually viewed as less sensitive than questions about income, especially if respondents are concerned that information on income will be used for tax purposes or if a substantial portion of their household income is generated by illegal activities. As a consequence, survey-based estimates of income are often substantially lower than those of consumption. While it is possible that consumption is exaggerated and income is accurate, studies suggest that it is more likely that income is underestimated (McKay 2000; Martini, Ivanova, and Novosyolova 1996).

It is recommended that the consumption measure for poverty analysis be calculated on the basis of recommendations made by Deaton and Zaidi (2002) and guidelines established by the International Labour Organization (ILO) (2003). Ideally, use values of durable goods and housing would be included, but the Household Budget Survey does not collect the information required to calculate these values. Durable goods can be dealt with in several ways in the welfare aggregate (box 1.2). The recommended consumption measure can be calculated from indicators such as cash expenditures plus in-kind receipts less intermediate consumption; taxes; other expenditures (alimony, gifts, advance payments); food gifts; and durables purchases.

Further improvements can be made to the consumption aggregate by improving the collection of Household Budget Survey data. There is a need to account for the imputed use value of durables, which requires collecting information on the purchase value, estimated resale value, and date of acquisition of durable goods. Estimation of in-kind consumption from gifts and self-produced food is currently made by applying a regional average unit value based on the reported ratios of purchase values to purchase quantities. This method could lead to biases that are difficult to estimate, since the necessary detailed information is held at the *oblast* level[3] and is therefore unavailable. Further improvements could be made by collecting data on the quality of self-produced goods and on the

Box 1.2. How should durable goods be treated when their use value cannot be estimated?

According to the International Labour Organization, "When the consumption expenditure aggregate is to be used in welfare analysis . . . the consumption approach is conceptually preferable" (2003, p. 33). This approach calculates the use value of durable goods and fixed assets such as housing instead of the actual spending on durables in the welfare aggregate. This approach contrasts with the acquisition approach, which adds the entire value of the durable good during the reference period while ignoring the use value of goods acquired before the reference period. Given the acceptance by Goskomstat of the ILO recommendations, redesigned versions of the Household Budget Survey should collect the needed information on durable goods to permit calculating their use value.

The Household Budget Survey data for 1997–2002 do not include the information required for calculating the use value of durable assets. Thus the welfare aggregate calculated in this report excludes the use value as well as the purchase value of durable goods. This is in line with the recommendations by Deaton and Zaidi (2002) and general practice of the World Bank and other welfare analysts. The key rationale for this convention is the need to generate a consistent poverty profile, so that households with large purchases of durable goods in the reference period do not appear richer than they really are. Using the Russia Longitudinal Monitoring Survey (RLMS) dataset (UNC, various years), Decoster and Verbina (2003) demonstrate the limited impact of omitting durable expenditures altogether relative to calculating the user cost of durable goods.

This study uses the NOBUS (Goskomstat 2003b) dataset, which includes the information required to calculate the use value of durable goods, for sensitivity analysis. Excluding the use value of durable goods, the NOBUS estimate of the poverty headcount index is 23.1 percent and the Gini index of inequality is 32 percent. The sensitivity analysis leads to the following conclusions:

- The use value of durable assets is about 10 percent of the consumption welfare aggregate, calculated in accordance with Deaton and Zaidi or ILO methodology, and the ratio is roughly the same for all deciles of the population. This reflects the endowment of the poor of durable goods, a special feature in Russia.
- The purchase of new assets is significant only for the rich. For the poorest three deciles, the average cost of purchased durable goods is less than 3 percent of total purchases. In contrast, those in the richest decile *spend half of their purchases* on durable goods.
- For the same poverty line, the addition of the use value of durable goods generates a poverty estimate of 18.3 percent. Reapplication of the poverty line recommendations made in this report yields a poverty headcount index of 24.6 percent.

(continued)

Box 1.2 *(continued)*

- The estimates of inequality are almost identical for the consumption aggregate with and without the use value of durable goods. However, when the full value of purchases is added, the Gini coefficient of expenditure is much higher (44 percent). Excluding the use value of durable goods is better than including the full purchase value of durable goods in predicting the appropriate welfare position or poverty status of the household. Excluding durable goods permits the proper identification of the poverty status in almost 97 percent of cases; including the full purchase value of durable goods leads to correct identification of the poverty status only 82 percent of the time. Moreover, if the purchase value of durables is added to the welfare measure for the Household Budget Survey dataset used in this report and the same poverty line is used, estimates of poverty for 1997–2002 decrease by about 1.1–1.6 percentage points. The Gini coefficient of inequality increases about 2–3 percentage points because of greater spending on durable goods by the rich, but the trends in poverty and inequality are similar to those established in the report.

Sources: Goskomstat (2003b); ILO (2003); Deaton and Zaidi (2002); Decoster and Verbina (2003); Goskomstat (various years); UNC (various years).

household's own estimate of the value of self-produced goods. The revised Household Budget Survey should also permit estimation of employer-provided and government-provided subsidies.

Adopt an Objective, Regionally Consistent, and Absolute Poverty Line

It is recommended that Russia continue to adopt an absolute poverty line that captures the absolute cost of basic needs and does not vary in the short run with changes in welfare. The recommend improvements mainly involve making the official poverty line objective in reflecting observed household behavior and calculating both the food and nonfood components of the poverty line. A desirable poverty line would be consistent across regions and account for individual needs by age and sex, equivalent adult scale, economies of scale, differences in regional cost of living, and consumption patterns. To meet this objective, a calorie-based food poverty line is constructed, and the nonfood poverty line is then derived from household consumption behavior. The proposed poverty thresholds are constructed at the regional level for 2002 and then adjusted for earlier years using the consumer price index.

Table 1.1. Calorie cost rises with consumption

Consumption quintile	*Cost per 1,000 calories in 2002 (rubles)*
1	8.2
2	10.1
3	11.5
4	13.1
5	17.0

Source: Bank staff calculations based on data from the Household Budget Survey 2002 (Goskomstat).

The official calorie requirements by age and gender are taken as a starting point in deriving the food poverty line. The official nutritional requirements are specified for active men 16–59, active women 16–54, retirees, infants less than 1 year old, children 1–6, and children 7–15. Climatic variations in nutritional requirements are also taken into account. Given the expert view of the nutritional requirements, the food basket that satisfies these requirements is assumed to be what households actually consume, as implicit in the behavior captured by the Household Budget Survey. The food poverty line is then taken as the cost of satisfying the calorie requirements, calculated as the calorie requirement multiplied by the calorie cost. The average per capita calorie requirements for each region and each type of individual are calculated using the population shares from the 2002 Household Budget Survey. The computed average per capita daily calorie requirement for the whole population is 2,283 calories.

The calorie cost increases with consumption. In 2002 it was equal to 8.2 rubles per 1,000 calories for the poorest quintile and 10.1 for the second poorest quintile. The actual calorie intake of each household is calculated by converting the household's consumed food bundle from the 2002 Household Budget Survey, using readily available food calorie conversion factors. The household-specific calorie cost is then the food expenditure divided by the calorie intake. The calorie cost rises monotonically with the standard of living, as richer households buy more expensive calories (table 1.1).

To determine the poverty line, it is necessary to select a reference group that includes the population generally regarded as poor. The calorie requirement multiplied by the reference calorie cost is the food poverty line. Thus, the food poverty line using the calorie cost of 8.2 rubles per 1,000 calories from the lowest quintile is defined as the food poverty line; the calorie cost of 10.1 rubles per 1,000 calories from the second quintile can be taken as a basis for a higher poverty line.

Based on the calculations described above, the recommended federal food poverty line in 2002 is 570 rubles per capita per month. The higher food poverty line is 703 rubles per capita per month. Regional food poverty lines are calculated using spatial price indexes to account for food price variation. To ensure the regional consistency of poverty lines, they should only vary according to price differences and not according to the region's standard of living. The real cost of calories is then taken as the same constant standard of living across different regions. Spatial price indexes measure the relative costs of living in different regions and communities.

Using the unit record data of the 2002 Household Budget Survey, the spatial price indexes for each of the 88 regions (all regions except Republic of Chechnya, for which the Household Budget Survey was not conducted) were computed, with the federal index set at 100. The *oblast*-specific food poverty line was then calculated as the federal food poverty line multiplied by the spatial price index (see appendix table A.1). The food poverty line is equal to the calorie requirement multiplied by the calorie cost, adjusted for spatial price variation and averaged across quarters (see appendix table A.2 for the food poverty line for each region).

Adjustments are made to take account of economies of scale in nonfood poverty lines. The mean nonfood poverty line involves seven components (table 1.2). Each component reflects a different degree of economies of scale, adjusted using a parameter that ranges from 0 (common or public good) to 1 (individual or private good). If the scale parameter is 1, every household will be allocated the same per capita expenditure of the mean nonfood poverty line. If the parameter is 0, each household is allocated the mean nonfood poverty line multiplied by the average household size. The assumed scale parameters are 1.0 for health, 0.9 for clothing and footwear, and 0 for housing, water, electricity, gas, furniture, and household equipment. The variable used for transportation and communication is the number of working adults divided by household size; the variable for education is the number of children divided by household size.

The regional cost of living adjustment is also made to the nonfood poverty line. The nonfood component of the poverty line is adjusted to take account of cost of living differences in nonfood items of consumption across *oblasts.* This adjustment is made using estimated spatial price indexes for nonfood consumption items (see appendix table A.1). The nonfood poverty line is multiplied by the nonfood spatial price index compared with the base index of 100 for the federation. The per capita total poverty line in each *oblast* is equal to the sum of the food and nonfood poverty lines (see appendix table A.2).

The nonfood poverty line is derived from standard consumer theory as the nonfood expenditure when the per capita food expenditure equals the per capita food poverty line. This method avoids making normative judg-

Table 1.2. Average nonfood poverty line, by component, 2002 (rubles per person per month)

	Poverty line		*Higher poverty line*	
	Monthly per capita expenditure	*Percent of total*	*Monthly per capita expenditure*	*Percent of total*
Food	570.3	54.0	702.5	56.2
Nonfood, of which:	485.5	46.0	548.5	43.8
Clothing and footwear	196.5	18.6	211.4	16.9
Housing, water, electricity, and gas	129.6	12.3	154.1	12.3
Furniture and household equipment	19.7	1.9	24.0	1.9
Health	26.1	2.5	33.4	2.7
Transport	66.3	6.3	71.4	5.7
Communications	23.2	2.2	27.8	2.2
Education	23.9	2.3	26.3	2.1
Total	1,056	100.0	1,251	100.0

Source: Bank staff calculations based on data from the Household Budget Survey 2002 (Goskomstat).

ments regarding the components of nonfood requirements. Applying this method yields a federal nonfood poverty line of 486 rubles per capita per month. The estimated monthly federal poverty line using this methodology is 1,056 rubles per capita in 2002, with a higher poverty line estimate of 1,251 rubles per capita per month. The implied food share in the poverty line is 54 percent.

Using the recommended welfare aggregate and the recommended poverty line of 1,056 rubles per capita a month, 19.6 percent of Russia's population was estimated to be poor in 2002. Using the higher poverty line (of 1,251 rubles per month), an estimated 29.0 percent of the population fell below the poverty line in 2002.

Include Nonmonetary Aspects of Poverty

Nonmonetary indicators can complement monetary welfare measures and offer a more comprehensive assessment of poverty. Deprivation and poor living conditions are important attributes of poverty. Thus the set of poverty indicators should cover such dimensions as health, education, employment, and assets. Use of such multicriteria poverty lines helps identify the poorest category of households, which should be regarded as the priority target for social welfare projects. This broader concept of poverty could be incorporated in a revised program for the Household Budget Survey. Nonmonetary forms of poverty and social exclusion also involve access to resources such as information, rights, the environment for human habitat, and the quality of housing (see chapter 12).

Implications of Using the Recommended Methodology

Adopting the recommended welfare aggregate and poverty lines will lead to different estimates of welfare and poverty. The recommended consumption aggregate is lower than the official money income, but the recommended poverty line is also lower than the official poverty line. The poverty estimates and estimates of inequality derived on the basis of the recommended methodology are currently lower than the official estimates, but the trend in poverty change is sharper.

The recommended consumption aggregate is lower than the money income measure used by Goskomstat to measure poverty (table 1.3). The significant difference is partly attributable to the fact that the income variable includes an estimate of net savings and expenditures on durable goods, but it is mostly due to adjustments made by an imitation model to ensure consistency with aggregates from the national accounts.

The recommended poverty line is also lower than the official subsistence minimum level. The difference is large, suggesting that the official level is quite generous when evaluated against the methodology advocated here and widely practiced in numerous countries (table 1.4).

The estimated headcount index of poverty based on the recommended methodology is of the same order of magnitude as the official poverty

Table 1.3. The recommended consumption aggregate is lower than the official money income measure currently used by Goskomstat

Year	*Money incomes (published)*	*Recommended consumption aggregate*
1997	942	518
1998	1,012	601
1999	1,659	925
2000	2,281	1,205
2001	3,060	1,700
2002	3,888	2,159

Source: Bank staff calculations based on data from the Household Budget Survey 1997–2002 (Goskomstat).

Note: For 1997, figures show monthly averages in thousands of rubles per capita.

Table 1.4. The recommended poverty line is significantly lower than the official subsistence minimum level

Year	*Subsistence minimum level*	*Recommended poverty line*
1997	411	273
1998	493	345
1999	908	655
2000	1,210	793
2001	1,500	940
2002	1,808	1,056

Source: Bank staff calculations based on data from the Household Budget Survey 1997–2002 (Goskomstat).

Note: For 1997, figures show monthly averages in thousands of rubles per capita. In 2000 the methodology used to calculate the subsistence minimum was changed.

estimate, but it increased more rapidly during the financial crisis and declined more rapidly during the economic recovery. Given that both the recommended welfare aggregate and the poverty line are lower than the official indicators, the headcount index of poverty generated by the recommended methodology could be higher or lower than that generated by the official methodology. For 2002 the official methodology estimates that one-fourth of Russia's population was poor, while the recommended methodology estimates that about one-fifth was poor (table 1.5). A key difference between the two methodologies is the greater sensitivity of the recommended methodology to economic trends. Since the official poverty estimates are intermediated by a complex imitation model, this could have a built-in force toward greater stability.

Table 1.5. The recommended methodology can yield a higher or lower headcount index than the official methodology

Year	*Headcount index using official measurement methodology (percent)*	*Headcount index using recommended methodology (percent)*
1997	20.7	24.1
1998	23.3	31.4
1999	28.3	41.5
2000	28.9	35.9
2001	27.3	26.2
2002	24.2	19.6

Source: Bank staff calculations based on data from the Household Budget Survey 1997–2002 (Goskomstat).

Figure 1.3. Cash expenditures and the recommended consumption aggregate measure yield different levels and trends in inequality

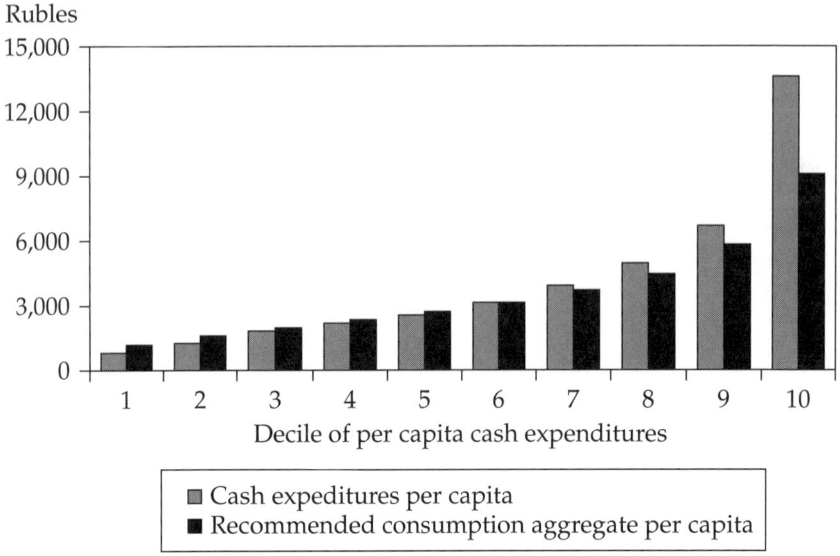

Source: Bank staff calculations based on data from the Household Budget Survey 2000–04 (Goskomstat).

The recommended methodology yields different levels and trends of inequality. The official methodology shows that the reported Gini coefficient of money income has been about 0.40 for several years. This figure is largely a result of modeling assumptions and does not fully reflect the underlying data, such as cash expenditure. The Gini coefficient of the cash expenditure indicator in the fourth quarter of 2000 was 0.45. The inequality of the recommended consumption aggregate is much lower, estimated at 0.36 for the fourth quarter of 2000. The difference between the two measures, reflected in expenditures on durables, gifts, intermediate consumption, and taxes, is greatest for the richest households (figure 1.3).

Implementing the improved poverty measurement methodology requires delinking the poverty measurement methodology from the criteria used to determine eligibility for targeted social assistance. The Russian Federation uses the same methodology for identifying and measuring poverty and for determining the eligibility of low-income families for targeted, income-tested federal benefits, such as child allowances (since 2000) or, to some extent, the allowance for housing and utility services (since 1994).[4] This close linkage between poverty measurement and

Box 1.3. Delinking poverty monitoring and eligibility criteria for social assistance in the United States

In most countries the function of poverty monitoring is delinked from the eligibility criteria for targeted social assistance. The United States provides an illustrative example. Like Russia, the United States has an official methodology for measuring poverty. A major concern for poverty monitoring in the United States is that the measurement be consistent across space and over time. Poverty analyses are an important ingredient in the development of federal and state-level welfare policy. However, for most welfare programs, eligibility is not linked to the federal poverty line but is determined by the availability of budgetary resources at the federal and state levels.

Cash assistance in the United States is provided under the program known as Temporary Assistance for Needy Families (TANF), which emphasizes helping needy families achieve economic independence. Three key features help promote self-sufficiency through an "active" welfare policy: work requirements, a five-year lifetime welfare time limit, and support for, and links to, other key complementary social and work services, such as child care, transport subsidies, and employment services. Many U.S. states also impose additional conditionalities geared toward encouraging behavioral change and long-run investments in human capital, such as requirements involving school attendance or achievement, immunizations, and health screening. The income test for TANF is linked to state-level income thresholds, which range from 25 to 200 percent of the federal poverty line, supplemented by asset-test and behavioral conditionalities.

Source: Moffitt (2002).

social policy is not common in other countries (box 1.3). Goskomstat aims to measure poverty according to the legal definition of the subsistence minimum level and the legal stipulation of those eligible to receive targeted social assistance. This explains the derivation of an income measure, despite the difficulty of measuring income and lack of income data in the Household Budget Survey.

The linkage of poverty measurement and targeted social assistance generates several tensions. First, it is not conceptually correct to provide poor households with transfers that are equal to the shortfall needed to bring them up above the poverty line. If this were to occur, it would create a disincentive to work for households just below the poverty line, who would effectively be facing a 100 percent marginal tax rate, as any increase in their income would be fully compensated by a reduction in social transfers. Second, there is an inherent tension between the adequacy of the program benefit and its budgetary cost. Russia's political choice was the adoption of a generous poverty line and the design of programs with extensive coverage but low benefit adequacy (see chapter 8 for the discussion of the social safety net). Generous poverty lines imply that programs need to cover a larger group of beneficiaries, siphoning resources away from the less-informed poorest groups of the population. Furthermore, when budgetary resources become scarcer, the typical response is to erode program benefits or payment arrears, which tends to affect the poorest more than other groups. A more conservative poverty line based on actual consumption patterns of the poor, as advocated here, would help focus more social assistance resources on the poorest group. It would also have a larger impact on poverty if it were accompanied by improvements in program implementation.

There is a need for an improved measurement methodology and improved targeting criteria for social programs. For national policymaking it is important to have a sound methodology of poverty measurement in order to assess the welfare of the population. However, government programs do not necessarily need to use the same definition of poverty at the household level in providing benefits, as is currently the case. Who receives benefits depends on the objective of the program and the resources available. Clearly, if the provision of household-level benefits remains tied to the official definition of poverty, revising the poverty methodology will be very difficult. Delinking them will improve poverty measurement and allow policymakers to more effectively program resources for poverty alleviation. The link between poverty status and social programs should be maintained at the aggregate level in designing the poverty programs and resource allocation among these programs. But the delinkage discussed here would allow the criteria for household-specific transfers to be tied more closely to the program goals, taking into account criteria other than the household-specific official poverty status. Since it is impossible for the government to survey the entire population and collect the information needed to determine individuals' poverty status, the government has to devise means to determine who should receive resources in an efficient and equitable manner. Poverty monitoring based on objective criteria would allow the government and citizens to see how well government programs are performing in this respect.

Notes

1. The national estimate of the poverty headcount index is obtained from a separate model. As a result, the sum of the poor populations in all regions is not necessarily the same as the estimate of national poverty. This inconsistency represents a serious challenge for the regional analysis and monitoring of poverty based on official data.

2. For example, the home ownership rate in the United States is 30 percent among people considered income-poor but only 15 percent for people considered consumption-poor.

3. In this report, the terms *oblast* and *region* are used interchangeably to denote any of the 89 administrative territorial divisions within the Russian Federation. Some of these divisions are called oblasts, while others are called republics, territories, or autonomous regions. To distinguish the generalized term *oblast* from references to specific oblasts, the former is italicized and begins with a lowercase letter. Specific oblasts, republics, territories, or autonomous regions are not italicized and begin with uppercase letters.

4. Other means-tested benefits, financed and implemented from regional or local funds, use different eligibility criteria, generally expressed as a fraction of the regional poverty line.

2
The Profile of the Poor

Reducing poverty is a priority of the Russian government. According to official data, the well-being of a large share of Russia's population is below the minimum standards of modern Russian society. But asking "how much poverty exists?" is only the first step. To develop policies to reduce poverty, policymakers must also ask "who are the poor?" and "why are people poor?" This chapter provides answers to these questions.

Understanding Poverty

If poverty is defined as "unacceptable human deprivation" (World Bank 2000b), measuring poverty requires a definition of what deprivation is and how much deprivation is unacceptable. Analysts in Russia and around the world define poverty differently. This report accepts the view of poverty as encompassing low levels of consumption and develops an objective absolute poverty line as a minimum living standard. Such a definition of poverty has a long tradition in the Russian literature (see Prokofieva 2003 for a recent review). As poverty is ultimately a measure of welfare in a given society, the fact that one of every five Russians is poor in an absolute sense is deeply disturbing. It provides motivation to study the dynamics of poverty, its relationship with economic development, and its characteristics in order to design better policies.

The Russian Federation is rich in information and analysis of poverty levels and trends during the transition period. Although different surveys use different methodologies and concepts, they all agree that the level of poverty is high (box 2.1).

The definition of poverty used in this report—material deprivation—has important limitations in terms of its content and coverage. In terms of coverage, poverty involves not only low consumption of commodities but also low levels of other individual capabilities, such as health, nutrition education, and empowerment. Someone who is poor in terms of consumption may not be poor in terms of education and vice versa. Given the difficulties of measuring individual capabilities, a reasonable solution is

Box 2.1. Rich data sources are available for measuring poverty in Russia

Many surveys capture one or more dimensions of poverty in Russia:

- The Household Budget Survey (Goskomstat, various years) is the main data source used in this report and a key data source for official poverty estimates in Russia (chapters 1 and 3 provide thorough descriptions of the survey). Goskomstat has been using Household Budget Survey data to estimate poverty since 1992. However, as explained in chapter 1, the official methodology uses models and imputations rather than the primary data themselves. This report represents the first application of internationally comparable poverty measurement to the Household Budget Survey primary data.
- The Russia Longitudinal Monitoring Survey (UNC, various years) has been the key source of information for monitoring poverty and inequality. The survey is a nationally representative, multitopic, integrated survey that includes a panel element which allows the movements of households in and out of poverty to be traced over time. Despite its advantages and accessibility, the survey has not been referred to or used in any official statistical document.
- The Russian Public Opinion Survey Center (VCIOM) survey is a smaller-scale opinion poll of about 2,400 randomly selected adults in a two-stage stratified sample. It collects some socioeconomic information about households (employment, sources of income, level of income) but focuses primarily on subjective perceptions. The survey was first conducted in 1989, allowing comparisons with the pretransition period to be made. No other nationally representative survey in Russia has this feature.
- Sociological and qualitative research relies on a number of smaller-scale local surveys (a panel survey of the Taganrog population, targeted surveys of certain groups, and so forth). Such research offers very interesting insights into coping strategies, inter- and intrafamily relations, and other issues, but it allows little comparability over time and only limited generalization to the population.
- The Survey of Household Welfare and Participation in Federal Programs (NOBUS, Goskomstat 2003b) is the newest integrated household survey carried out by Goskomstat and the Ministry of Labor and Social Development, with technical assistance and financing from the World Bank. The survey has a sample of about 44,500 households and is representative both nationally and for 46 larger subjects (regions) of the Federation. The survey captures various aspects of household welfare (material as well as nonmonetary) and government policies.

to monitor selected nonincome indicators alongside income ones. However, even selected nonincome data are limited. Experimental efforts to measure welfare in these dimensions suggest that poverty affects a significant fraction of the population (Prokofieva 2003). In addition, the homeless, people living in institutions (such as residents of elderly homes or orphanages), and internally displaced people are often excluded from household surveys (Rimashevskaya 1999). For these reasons, the measures of poverty presented in this report may undercount the poor in Russia. The measures nevertheless capture poverty as a mass phenomenon, as a plight of a typical household, and as an economic and social phenomenon that is subject to the set of policies developed at the national and regional levels.

Poverty in Russia is shallow. While it is quite widespread, it is not severe: most of the poor have levels of consumption that are close to the poverty line. The baseline poverty number used in this report is a poverty headcount of 19.6 percent of the population in 2002. Though the headcount is the headline figure for poverty measurement, it has a number of pitfalls. To address them, other measures, such as the depth and severity of poverty, are used to assess the average gap between consumption of the poor and the poverty line and to determine whether a significant number of households falls considerably below the poverty line (box 2.2). In 2002 poverty depth was 5.1 percent, meaning that an average poor person in Russia had a shortfall of consumption that was about 26 percent of the poverty line. Poverty severity was 2 percent. If the poor had been equally distributed below the poverty line, the severity of poverty in Russia would have been 3.5 percent. Thus the poor tend to group close to the poverty line rather than across the entire spectrum of low-consumption ranges. Both measures suggest that, on aggregate, poverty in Russia is neither deep nor very severe.

Shallow poverty does not mean that all poor are alike; there are some deep pockets of poverty, and there is a considerable concentration of population just above the poverty line. Based on the food poverty line, almost 4 percent of the population was poor in 2002. Using the higher poverty line developed as part of the recommended methodology adds another 9.3 percent of the population to the ranks of the poor. Although the higher poverty line is 18 percent above the baseline, poverty increases 48 percent. The group whose consumption falls between the baseline and the higher poverty line is called the near poor in this chapter.

Subjective estimates of poverty in Russia are both similar to and different from objective assessments. The VCIOM data described in box 2.1 report the subsistence minimum and poverty line as they are perceived by Russia's population. The data show that the subjective subsistence minimum (2,600 rubles per capita per month in 2002) is perceived as a more reasonable standard than a welfare minimum. A welfare minimum is given

Box 2.2. How should poverty be measured?

This report relies on three aggregate measures of poverty: incidence, depth, and severity, captured by three standard Foster-Greer-Thorbecke (1984) aggregate poverty measures. The incidence of poverty is measured by the headcount index or ratio (*P0*). It estimates the percentage of the population that is poor. The headcount ratio is easy to interpret, but it says nothing about the depth or severity of poverty.

The depth of poverty is measured by the poverty gap ratio *(P1)*, defined by the mean distance below the poverty line as a proportion of that line, where the mean is formed over the entire population, counting the nonpoor as having zero poverty gap. Thus the sum of poverty gaps aggregated across all individuals reflects the minimum amount of consumption that needs to be transferred to pull all the poor up to the poverty line.

The severity of poverty index *(P2)* represents the mean of the squared proportionate poverty gaps. Unlike the headcount ratio and the poverty gap ratio, it takes into account inequality among the poor. The severity of poverty index is sensitive to the distribution of consumption among the poor, in that heavier weights are given to those whose consumption falls far below the poverty line. This index is thus more sensitive to changes in welfare of the ultra poor (those with extremely low consumption below the poverty line) than it is to those just below the poverty line.

The poverty measures are defined as follows:

$$P0 = \frac{q}{n}$$

$$P1 = \frac{1}{n}\sum_{i \in Q} \frac{(z - y_i)}{z}$$

$$P2 = \frac{1}{n}\sum_{i \in Q} \frac{(z - y_i)^2}{z^2}$$

where n represents the total population and q represents the number of individuals with consumption y_i less than the poverty line z.

Source: Foster, Greer, and Thorbecke (1984).

by a subjective poverty line that averaged about 1,600 rubles per capita per month in 2002. The large difference between the two subjective indicators reveals that the population distinguishes different degrees of poverty.

Subjective assessment data over an extended period provide useful supplementary information on living standards. According to VCIOM surveys, in 2002, 40 percent of the population considered their income below their subjective subsistence minimum, while only 10 percent were poor according to the average subjective poverty line (the figures for 1999 were 49 percent and 19 percent, respectively). The subjective assessment of poverty line is tightly linked to household living standards. VCIOM estimates that for each ruble increase in household income, the reported subjective poverty line increases by 0.20 ruble. The poor and the rich have different standards of what they call poverty. Poverty looks different to different people; subjective indicators cannot substitute for an objectively defined measure.

Poverty Profile

The poverty profile is a description of poverty focused on two related yet different questions: who is at risk of poverty and who are the poor. Examining which population groups face higher risks of poverty provides insights into the factors associated with poverty and helps identify groups with high incidences of poverty. But as some of these risk factors affect only a small share of the population, a group with a high poverty risk does not necessarily account for a large fraction of the poor. The second part of the poverty profile examines the composition of the poor and shows which groups are overrepresented. Both parts of the poverty profile have important policy implications. The first—who is at risk—helps reveal causal factors of poverty and allows policymakers to design interventions that are most likely to help targeted groups. The second—who are the poor—helps identify factors and policies that will likely affect the majority of the poor.

Who Is at Risk of Poverty?

The major characteristics associated with poverty are location, the demographic composition of the household (especially the number of children), and unemployment.

Rural households are much more likely to be poor. The risk of being poor is 30 percent in rural areas and 17 percent in urban settlements (excluding Moscow, a positive outlier) (table 2.1). Rural poverty is also slightly more severe than urban poverty. On average the consumption of the rural poor is 28 percent below the poverty line, while that of urban dwellers is 25 percent below the poverty line. While the rural population represents about 25 percent of Russia's population, rural inhabitants account for more than 40 percent of the poor.

The incidence of poverty is also high in small towns. The number of towns in Russia with fewer than 20,000 inhabitants is much larger than in most other countries (World Bank 2004a). The Household Budget Survey data available for this analysis do not allow identification of the urban community below the *oblast* level. The NOBUS data, however, clearly show that

Table 2.1. Poverty in Russia has a rural face (percent)

Location	*Incidence of poverty*	*Depth of poverty*	*Severity of poverty*	*Incidence of near poverty*	*Share of poor*	*Share of near poor*	*Share of population*
Urban	15.7	3.9	1.5	8.5	58.5	67.0	73.2
Moscow	6.6	1.1	0.3	7.4	3.1	7.3	9.2
Other urban	17.0	4.2	1.6	8.7	55.4	59.7	64.0
Rural	30.4	8.6	3.5	11.5	41.5	33.0	26.8
Total	19.6	5.1	2.0	9.3	100.0	100.0	100.0

Source: Bank staff calculations based on data from Household Budget Survey 2002 (Goskomstat).

the smaller the urban community, the higher the incidence of poverty (table 2.2).[1] The incidence of poverty in urban communities with fewer than 20,000 inhabitants is twice that in cities with more than 1 million people.

The incidence of poverty varies markedly across Russia's regions. The incidence of poverty exceeded 40 percent in 2002 in the Dagestan, Ingushetiya, and Kabardino-Balkariya Republics in the South; the Tuva, Ust-Ordynskiy Buriatksiy, and Aginskiy Buriatksiy Autonomous Regions in Siberia; and the Komi-Permyatskiy Autonomous Region in the Volga (figure 2.1). At the other end of the spectrum, the regions with a poverty incidence of less than 10 percent are Moscow City and the Tula and Belgorod Oblasts in the Center, St. Petersburg City in the North West, and the Khanty-Mansiyskiy and Yamalo-Nenetskiy Autonomous Regions in the Urals.

Table 2.2. Poverty is pervasive in small urban communities as well

Population	*Poverty headcount*	*Contribution to poverty*
1 million people and more	12	8
500,000–999,900 people	13	5
250,000–499,900 people	16	7
100,000–249,900 people	16	7
50,000–99,900 people	21	7
20,000–49,900 people	21	8
Less than 20,000 people	25	12
Rural	39	45
Total	23	100

Source: Bank staff calculations based on data from NOBUS (Goskomstat 2003b).

Figure 2.1. Poverty map of the Russian Federation, 2002: Regional headcount index of poverty

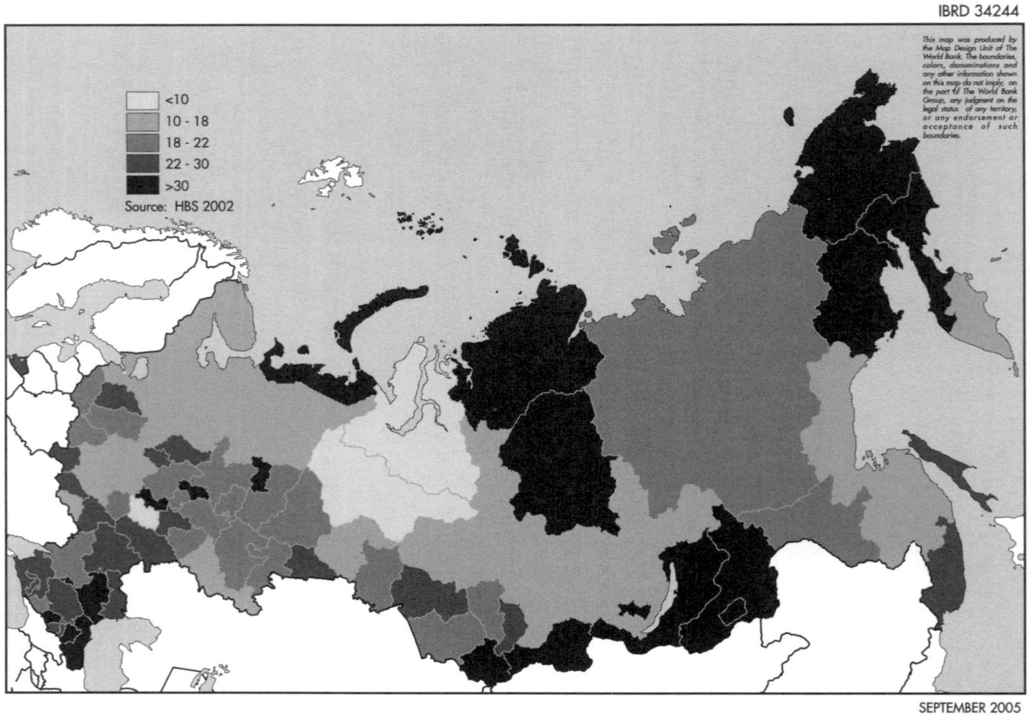

Source: Bank staff calculations based on data from Household Budget Survey 2002 (Goskomstat).

Note: Legend refers to the incidence of poverty: the lighter shade represents a lower fraction of the poor in a region's population.

A peculiarity of Russia's poverty is its spatial heterogeneity: in contrast to other countries, most of which have contiguous pockets of poverty, poverty in Russia is not concentrated in any particular part of the country. As many of the poorest regions are sparsely populated, they account for only a minority of the poor (figure 2.2). The highest concentration of the poor is in the center of European Russia and the North Caucasus, while many regions in Siberia and the Far East, which have sparse populations, have fewer poor people.

Children, especially young children, face a higher risk of poverty than adults or elderly people. While demographic factors are a mere symptom of the true causes of poverty, they are useful in identifying vulnerable segments of the population. Children in Russia face a risk of poverty that is 36 percent higher than average (table 2.3). While this evidence justifies child-focused poverty interventions, it puts in question the efficiency of public programs targeting children, such as the child allowance.[2]

The risk of poverty changes over the life cycle, peaking during childhood (figure 2.3). Among working-age people, the highest incidence is among people 35–40. Among the elderly, the highest incidence is among people over 70. As a group, the elderly have the lowest risk of poverty, one-quarter lower than the national average, suggesting that the income protection offered by pensions is effective in helping the poor avoid poverty.

The unemployed are at highest risk and working pensioners at lowest risk of poverty. One of the persistent poverty pockets in the Russian Federation is the unemployed. In 2002 the risk of poverty among the unemployed was 65 percent higher than the national average (table 2.4). At the other extreme, the working elderly face the lowest risk of poverty—about one-third the national average.

Table 2.3. Children are at greatest risk of poverty (percent)

Age group	*Incidence of poverty*	*Depth of poverty*	*Severity of poverty*	*Incidence of near poverty*	*Share of poor*	*Share of near poor*	*Share of population*
Children (under 16)	26.7	7.4	3.0	10.4	24.9	20.4	18.3
Working-age adults	18.8	4.9	1.9	8.9	62.0	62.1	64.8
Elderly	15.1	3.5	1.2	9.7	13.0	17.5	16.9
Total	19.6	5.1	2.0	9.3	100.0	100.0	100.0

Source: Bank staff calculations based on data from Household Budget Survey 2002 (Goskomstat).

Figure 2.2. Poverty map of the Russian Federation, 2002: Distribution of the poor

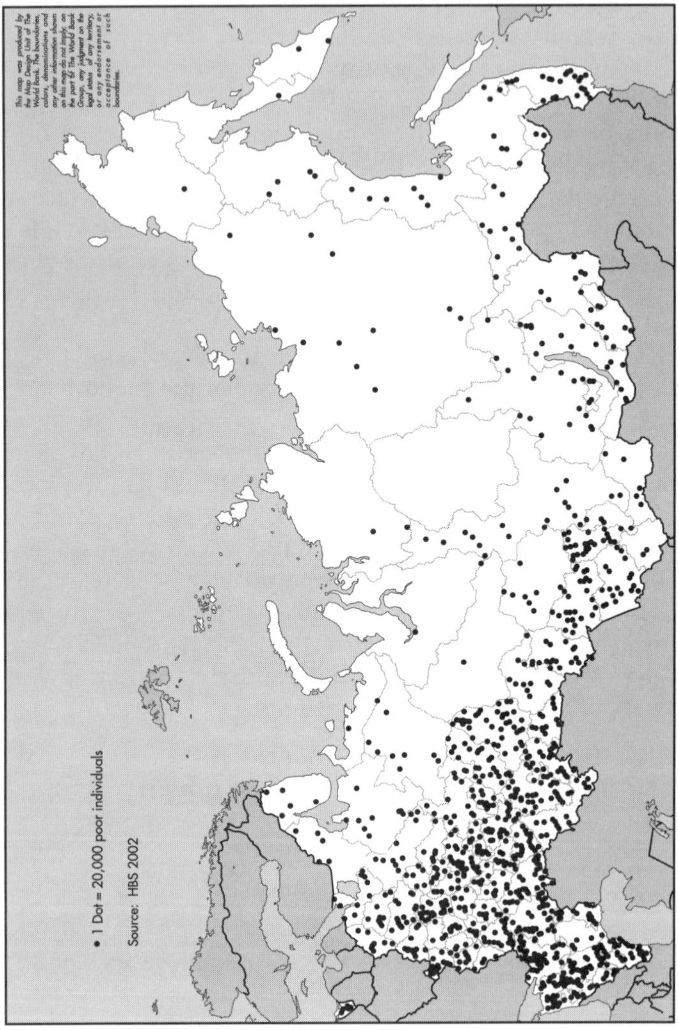

Source: Bank staff calculations based on data from Household Budget Survey 2002 (Goskomstat).

Figure 2.3. The risk of poverty changes over the life cycle

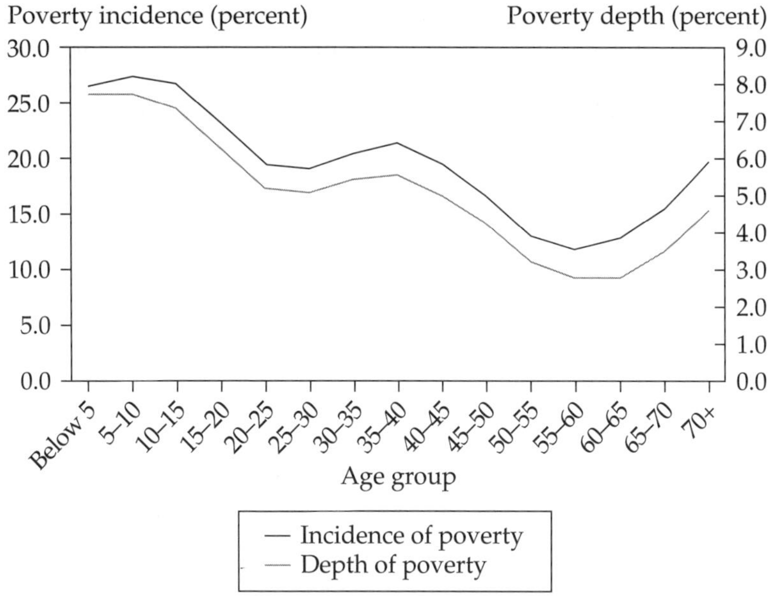

Source: Bank staff calculations based on data from Household Budget Survey 2002 (Goskomstat).

Table 2.4. Poverty by employment status (percent)

Employment status	*Incidence of poverty*	*Depth of poverty*	*Severity of poverty*	*Incidence of near poverty*	*Share of poor*	*Share of near poor*	*Share of population*
Wage employed	16.6	4.1	1.6	8.6	39.8	43.4	47.1
Self-employed	17.7	4.5	1.7	7.8	1.6	1.4	1.7
Working elderly	6.1	1.3	0.4	5.5	1.0	2.0	3.3
Unemployed	32.4	9.7	4.2	10.9	12.0	8.5	7.3
Children	26.7	7.4	3.0	10.4	24.9	20.4	18.3
Students	19.5	5.0	2.0	9.4	8.6	8.8	8.7
Other	17.4	4.0	1.4	10.7	12.0	15.5	13.6
Total	19.6	5.1	2.0	9.3	100.0	100.0	100.0

Source: Bank staff calculations based on data from Household Budget Survey 2002 (Goskomstat).

Households affected by a combination of risk factors face the highest risk of poverty. For example, while rural poverty is higher than urban poverty for all demographic and employment groups, it is particularly high among the rural unemployed (44 percent poverty incidence) and rural children (40 percent poverty incidence) (table 2.5).

Poverty is both more widespread and deeper among vulnerable groups. All groups with higher poverty risk experience deeper and more severe poverty. Moreover, the differences between groups are sharper on the basis of the poverty gap or poverty severity.

Table 2.5. Households facing cumulative vulnerabilities face the highest risk of poverty (percent)

	Urban		*Rural*	
	Poor	*Near poor*	*Poor*	*Near poor*
Age				
Children (under 16)	21.0	9.4	40.1	12.7
Working-age adults	14.9	8.1	30.4	11.5
Elderly	13.3	9.4	19.6	10.1
Total	15.7	8.5	30.4	11.5
Gender				
Male	15.9	8.6	31.7	11.8
Female	15.5	8.5	29.3	11.3
Total	15.7	8.5	30.4	11.5
Education				
Primary or less	15.5	9.0	19.8	11.3
Secondary	13.0	7.9	26.0	11.2
Vocational	9.9	7.0	19.1	10.0
Higher	4.8	3.8	13.1	7.6
Total	10.4	8.5	23.4	11.5
Employment				
Wage employed	13.5	7.8	26.9	11.2
Self-employed	9.5	5.0	30.4	12.0
Working elderly	5.4	5.2	10.0	7.1
Unemployed	25.7	9.8	43.8	12.6
Children (under 16)	21.0	9.4	40.1	12.7
Students	15.6	8.8	31.2	11.4
Other	15.8	10.8	20.5	10.4
Total	15.7	8.5	30.4	11.5

Source: Bank staff calculations based on data from Household Budget Survey 2002 or fourth quarter 2002 (for education) (Goskomstat).

Who Are the Poor?

The majority of the poor are found in working families, have secondary and vocational education, and have children. Working families account for the largest share of the poor, even though they have a lower incidence of poverty than the national average. The overwhelming majority of the poor—87 percent—live in households in which at least one member works (table 2.6).

Larger households with children are at high risk of poverty. The risk of poverty is particularly high among households with three or more children: half of these households were poor in 2002. These households represent only 3.3 percent of the total population, however, and hence contribute only 8.2 percentage points to the total poverty headcount (table 2.7). While the risk of poverty rises sharply with the number of children, 59 percent of the poor come from households with one or two children, and one-third of the poor have no children. Thus a national policy focused primarily on protecting children against the risk of poverty would bypass one poor person out of three.

Education is a powerful shield against poverty. In the Russian Federation, as in most countries, there is a monotonic negative correlation between the risk of poverty and the level of education of the household

Table 2.6. The majority of the poor live in working households (percent)

Household employment status	*Incidence of poverty*	*Depth of poverty*	*Severity of poverty*	*Incidence of near poverty*	*Share of poor*	*Share of near poor*	*Share of population*
One member working	22.3	6.2	2.5	9.3	27.6	24.3	24.3
Two or more members working	18.0	4.5	1.7	9.1	59.7	63.3	65.0
Jobless households[a]	47.3	15.3	7.0	12.7	6.8	3.9	2.8
Nonworking-age households[b]	14.7	3.2	1.1	10.2	5.9	8.6	7.9
Total	19.6	5.1	2.0	9.3	100.0	100.0	100.0

Source: Bank staff calculations based on data from Household Budget Survey 2002 (Goskomstat).

a. Households in which at least one member is economically active but no adult is working.

b. Households in which all members fall into one of the following categories: children under 16, young adults 16–23 who are in school, women 55 and over, and men 60 and over.

Table 2.7. The incidence and depth of poverty are greatest among households with three or more children (percent)

Number of children in household	*Incidence of poverty*	*Depth of poverty*	*Severity of poverty*	*Incidence of near poverty*	*Share of poor*	*Share of near poor*	*Share of population*
No children	13.6	3.2	1.2	8.4	33.1	42.7	47.7
One child	20.3	5.2	2.0	9.5	34.9	34.3	33.8
Two children	30.8	8.5	3.4	11.8	23.8	19.2	15.2
Three or more children	48.9	16.1	7.3	10.7	8.2	3.8	3.3
Total	19.6	5.1	2.0	9.3	100.0	100.0	100.0

Source: Bank staff calculations based on data from Household Budget Survey 2002 (Goskomstat).

head (table 2.8). The important impact that human capital accumulation has on individual earnings and on shielding households from poverty is suggested by the fact that 24 percent of households in which the head lacks primary education but just 6 percent of households in which the head is a university graduate are poor. However, as a result of the policy of free access to public education, the majority of the population has similar skills level. Hence the majority of poor adults (83 percent) have secondary or vocational education.

Why Are Poor People Poor?

Russia's GDP per capita was $6 a day in 2002, well above the official poverty line of about $3 or the recommended poverty line of about $2 proposed in chapter 1. If GDP were split equally among all residents, poverty would have been zero in Russia. In fact, one in five Russians lived in poverty.

Poverty exists in Russia because not all of GDP can be consumed and because income is not distributed equally. The aggregate data suggest that wages constitute about 40 percent of GDP in Russia (even including the imputed hidden components). Social transfers account for about 10 percent of GDP and entrepreneurial incomes and property incomes for another 10 percent. A discrepancy between GDP and money incomes is normal and may represent both "healthy" factors (such as investment) and "unhealthy" factors (such as capital flight). The discrepancy is quite large in Russia, however, where wages and transfers represent only a half of GDP. This gap

Table 2.8. Education and poverty status are negatively correlated (percent)

Level of education	*Incidence of poverty*	*Depth of poverty*	*Severity of poverty*	*Incidence of near poverty*	*Share of poor*	*Share of near poor*	*Share of population*
All adults							
Primary or less	17.8	4.0	1.5	10.2	5.5	5.3	3.9
Secondary	17.4	4.4	1.7	9.0	45.4	39.9	32.8
Vocational	12.2	2.9	1.1	7.8	37.4	40.3	38.4
Higher	5.9	1.3	0.4	4.3	11.7	14.5	24.9
Total	13.9	3.4	1.3	7.7	100.0	100.0	100.0
Household head							
Primary or less	24.1	6.0	2.3	12.0	4.7	4.2	2.7
Secondary	21.1	5.5	2.1	9.5	37.9	30.6	24.8
Vocational	14.3	3.5	1.3	8.5	44.6	47.6	43.1
Higher	6.0	1.4	0.5	4.6	12.8	17.6	29.4
Total	13.9	3.4	1.3	7.7	100.0	100.0	100.0

Source: Bank staff calculations based on data from Household Budget Survey, fourth quarter 2002 (Goskomstat).

between macro data and the household-level welfare of the poor grows once inequality between households is taken into consideration.

Real per capita incomes are low

For the economically active population, a prime cause of poverty is low wages, particularly in certain sectors in which wages are below the subsistence minimum. The average monthly wage was about 4,108 rubles in 2002—equivalent to $140. Below-average wages are widespread in agriculture (where they affect 75 percent of the employees) and in public services (culture, geology, education, and health) (table 2.9).

Inequality has increased

The large increase in inequality during the transition is another cause of poverty. The transition has been accompanied by growing inequality in asset ownership, returns to education, and access to publicly financed health and education, which have increased inequality in consumption and income and contributed to poverty. The increase in inequality has been extremely large: the Gini index of nominal per capita income rose from 0.26 in 1992 to 0.40 in 2002 (official data) (figure 2.4). The average change in the Gini index of income inequality in any country is 3 percentage points per decade (Deininger and Squire 1996). An increase of

Table 2.9. Many workers earn less than the official subsistence minimum, especially in agriculture and public services

Sector	*1995*	*1999*	*2000*	*2001*	*2002*
Industry	32.5	26.5	25.7	23.9	18.9
Agriculture	80.2	82.0	84.6	81.3	75.0
Construction	27.8	29.3	29.0	24.5	18.7
Transportation	15.5	19.2	20.6	16.2	11.5
Communication	30.5	37.4	37.1	29.1	24.2
Information services	26.1	31.1	33.3	29.3	18.1
Geology	65.4	58.0	58.8	51.7	43.4
Housing	35.7	38.9	39.2	36.3	29.3
Health care	63.7	67.2	65.7	61.0	38.8
Education	64.6	70.5	67.5	61.3	41.4
Culture	70.8	72.2	70.7	68.4	51.2
Science	53.7	49.6	39.6	29.1	21.6
Finance	28.5	23.4	20.8	12.3	8.9

Source: Goskomstat (2003a).
Note: Figures are percentages of workers in each sector earning wages below the official subsistence minimum.

11 percentage points over a decade, as found in Russia, is close to a record.

Consumption inequality in Russia is high compared with countries in the CIS or Central and Eastern Europe, though moderate by broader international standards. Adjusting consumption data to reflect the large spatial variation in prices and using the methodology adopted by other middle-income countries reduces the Gini index for Russia to about 34 percent. This level is in line with that of other transition economies and Turkey (table 2.10). Inequality in income, expenditure, and assets is much higher in Russia than consumption inequality; nominal income inequality was 42 percent in 2002.

The relatively moderate level of consumption inequality suggested in this report contrasts with the common perception that inequality is extremely high in Russia. The estimates reported in this poverty assessment are consistently below previously published estimates, whether official or derived from the Russia Longitudinal Monitoring Survey (UNC, various years). Such differences stem primarily from different methodologies.

Official estimates capture inequality in per capita income, which is more volatile and less precise than per capita consumption. Moreover, income data are often incomplete and less reliable than data on consumption. In most countries, income inequality is higher than consumption inequality (table 2.11).

Figure 2.4. Estimates of inequality differ from survey to survey, primarily due to methodological differences

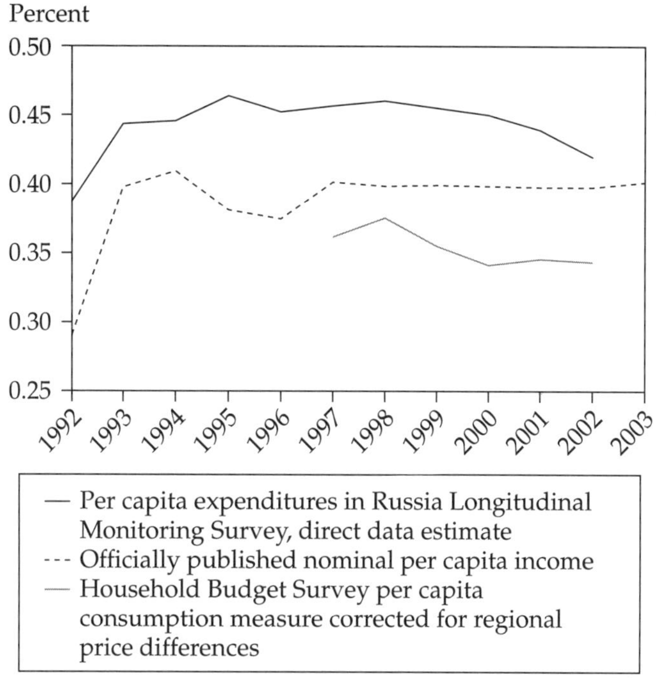

Source: Russian Statistical Yearbook 1992–2002 (Goskomstat), Russia Longitudinal Monitoring Survey 1992–2003 (UNC), and Bank staff calculations based on data from the Household Budget Survey 1997–2002 (Goskomstat).

Inequality estimates based on nominal per capita consumption or income tend to be higher than estimates based on real data, because the cost of living is higher in richer areas. Official estimates of inequality are not corrected for regional price variation and thus are higher than the estimates presented here. The use of nominal rather than real values generates a 1–4 percentage point difference between Gini indexes computed using the same data and methodology.

The income indicator used to estimate official inequality includes the purchase value of durables acquired during the reference period of the survey (the quarter). These highly volatile elements of consumption are excluded from the consumption indicator used in this report, in conformity with international practice.

The level of inequality found in the Russia Longitudinal Monitoring Survey is higher than that reported in the Household Budget Survey because

Table 2.10. Gini coefficients and annual income and consumption in selected countries

Country (year)	*Annual income or consumption per capita ($)*	*Gini coefficient (percent)*
Income (with imputed rents where possible)		
Albania (2002)	—	58
Bosnia and Herzegovina (2001)	1,445	39
Bulgaria (1999)	820	33
Croatia (1998)	3,200	35
Estonia (2001)	1,600	38
Hungary (1999)	1,800	26
Macedonia (2000)	1,205	34
Serbia (2002)	1,480	33
Slovenia (1998)	4,900	26
Turkey (2002)	1,290	47
Consumption		
Albania (2002)	668	28
Bosnia and Herzegovina (2001)	1,912	26
Bulgaria (2001)	1,159	28
Croatia (1998)	3,854	27
Macedonia (2000)	1,049	31
Serbia (2002)	1,910	28
Turkey (2002)[a]	1,057	38

Sources: Milanović (2003), State Institute of Statistics-Turkey and World Bank (2005), and Bank staff calculations based on data from various Living Standards Measurement Surveys.

— Not available.

a. Data for Turkey are from the 2002 Household Income and Consumption Expenditure Survey (State Institute of Statistics-Turkey 2002).

of the smaller sample size of that survey, which makes it less robust to the presence of outliers and measurement error. Given its larger sample, the Household Budget Survey is better suited to monitoring the evolution of inequality over time.

Inequality in other dimensions of living standards—such as access to running water, hot water, sewerage system, gas, telephone, and bathrooms—is significant. A major dimension of inequality in the endowment of modern housing amenities is between urban (well endowed) and rural (poorly endowed) households (figure 2.5). With the exception of access to gas in urban areas, richer households have better amenities than poorer households.

Do the Household Budget Survey data fully capture the extent of inequality at the top of the distribution? The problem of covering the rich

Table 2.11. Estimated inequality is lower for consumption-based indexes than income-based ones and for real versus nominal consumption

Measure	*1997*	*1998*	*1999*	*2000*	*2001*	*2002*
Household Budget Survey						
Money income, nominal	0.47	0.46	0.46	0.45	0.46	0.45
Cash expenditures, nominal	0.45	0.46	0.45	0.44	0.45	0.45
Cash expenditures, real (deflated using subsistence minimum)	0.43	0.42	0.41	0.41	0.41	0.41
Disposable resources, nominal	0.44	0.43	0.42	0.43	0.42	0.42
Disposable resources, real (deflated using subsistence minimum)	0.41	0.39	0.39	0.39	0.39	0.39
Consumption, nominal	0.37	0.39	0.37	0.36	0.37	0.37
Consumption, real (using poverty line)	0.35	0.36	0.34	0.33	0.33	0.33
Russia Longitudinal Monitoring Survey						
Existing expenditure variable, nominal	—	0.48	—	0.46	0.45	0.44
Existing expenditure variable, real	—	0.47	—	0.45	0.44	0.42
Consumption, nominal	—	0.42		0.40	0.39	0.39
Consumption, real	—	0.41	—	0.39	0.38	0.37
Existing income variable, nominal	—	0.47	—	0.43	0.42	0.42
Existing income variable, real	—	0.45	—	0.41	0.40	0.40

Source: Bank staff calculations based on data from Household Budget Survey 1997–2002 (Goskomstat) and Russia Longitudinal Monitoring Surveys 1998 and 2000–02 (UNC, various years).
— Not available.
Note: Figures are Gini coefficients.

with household surveys is pervasive in all countries. Russia is no exception to that rule, so the international comparison of inequality should not be affected by this problem. Not only the rich but also the upper-middle class is practically missed by the Household Budget Survey (box 2.3). In the context of poverty analysis, that in itself may not be a problem as far

Figure 2.5. Rural households have less access to modern housing amenities than urban households

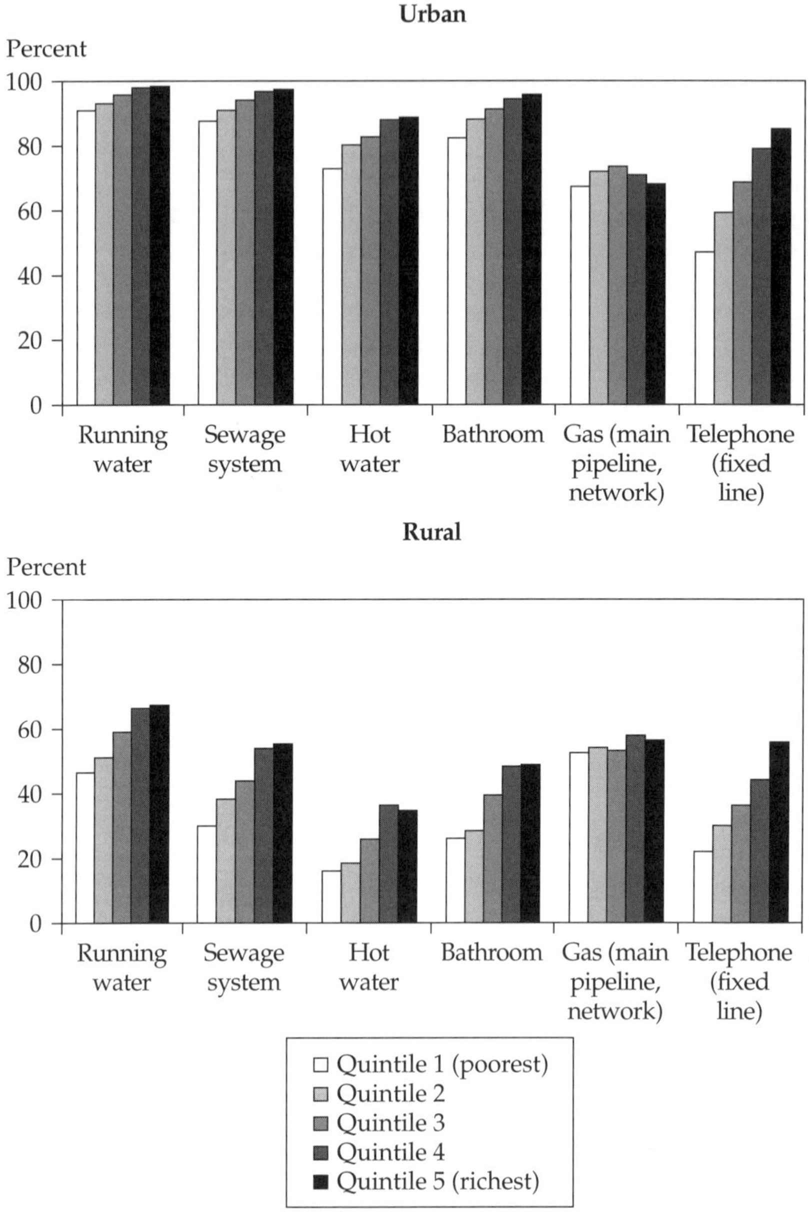

Source: Bank staff calculations based on data from Household Budget Survey 2002 (Goskomstat).

Box 2.3. Are Household Budget Survey data accurate enough to fully capture the extent of inequality?

Survey field work may miss a significant fraction of the population. According to the Household Budget Survey, only 3 percent of the "rich" live in Moscow, a finding that is at odds with common perceptions. Moreover, the consumption level of the rich indicated by the survey seems low relative to the upper-middle class. For example, according to the 2002 Household Budget Survey, the median monthly consumption among the 100 richest households was about $1,000 per household, or about $525 per capita. In contrast, the World Bank's job market survey of private companies in Moscow revealed salaries that were more than twice as high, even for basic professional levels (unpublished data). These discrepancies suggest that the Household Budget Survey is missing not only the rich but the upper-middle class who work for competitive Russian and foreign firms.

Box figure. Monthly salary at top Russian and international firms operating in Russia and monthly consumption of richest 100 households in Household Budget Survey, 2002

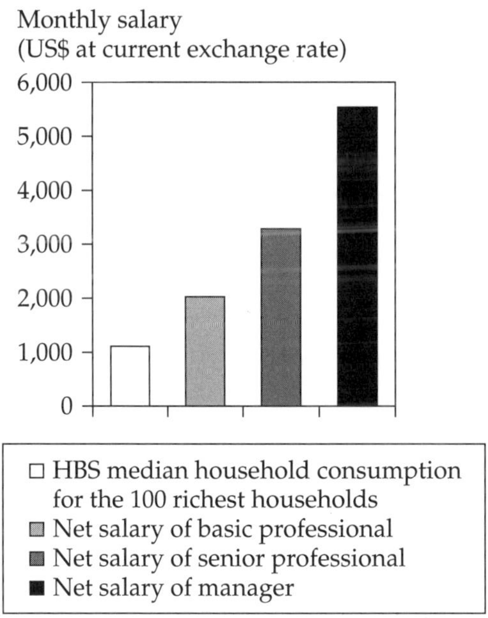

Source: Bank staff calculations based on data from the Household Budget Survey (2002) and World Bank (unpublished data).

as inequality is concerned, however (Mistiaen and Ravallion 2003). A more serious problem is the use of Household Budget Survey data to assess the full extent of inequality in Russia. The ongoing work on improving the sample, interviewer training, and organization of the survey may significantly reduce this bias and produce more reliable data on inequality (see chapter 12 for more details).

Throughout the world, inequality is an important determinant of poverty and a significant factor influencing the dynamics of poverty and its responsiveness to growth. For this reason, monitoring inequality and obtaining a more accurate measure of its level is an important component of poverty monitoring. In the Russian Federation, inequality is monitored using inappropriate indexes (such as the ratio of average income of the top to the bottom decile) and deficient indicators of living standards. The decile ratio misses changes in inequality over the entire distribution of income or consumption. Looking at decile measures can be very informative, but it should not be the sole measure of inequality. This report argues that the use of the Gini index or other indexes of inequality, the use of proper welfare measures, and improvements in the quality of the data would produce a more accurate assessment of inequality.

Conclusions

The poverty profile analysis reveals the following:

- Poverty in Russia is shallow, with a large number of people located just above and just below the poverty line. Shallowness of poverty, which is closely linked with the moderate levels of inequality, has both positive and negative implications. On the positive side, any upturn in economic activity brings significant numbers of the poor out of poverty, and the poor in Russia have not developed into a large underclass that is excluded from mainstream society. On the downside, any crisis moves large numbers of people into poverty, and poverty affects (directly or indirectly) a large share of the population.
- The major risk factors associated with poverty are location, the demographic composition of the household (especially the number of children), and employment status. Based on these characteristics, the poor can be identified for targeted interventions with reasonable precision. This has important implications for the design of poverty reduction policies (see part III).
- The majority of the poor are working families with children. Labor market and family policies (such as child allowances) must therefore be at the forefront of measures aimed at reducing poverty.

Notes

1. The NOBUS-based poverty estimates are based on a different survey instrument and questionnaire and therefore differ from those based on the Household Budget Survey.

2. The low adequacy of the program, which has been eroded continuously since 1998, prevents it from providing an effective shield against poverty for this vulnerable group. See chapter 8 for more details.

3
The Regional Dimension of Poverty

There are large socioeconomic differences across Russia's regions, but interregional inequality in living standards has declined somewhat since 1999. While inequality across regions is an important concern, inequality within regions dominates. Although there are large differences in the incidence of poverty between the extremes of rich and poor regions, most of the population and the poor live in regions in which poverty levels are close to the national average. Labor market outcomes are important correlates of regional differences in poverty: regions with higher unemployment and lower wage levels have a higher incidence of poverty. Thus a poverty reduction strategy should both encourage the growth of regions with average levels of poverty, where most of the poor live, and include targeted interventions for regions with extremely high levels of poverty. It is recommended that federal policy induce regions to adopt policies that fight poverty.

The Russian Federation consists of 89 politically equal members (subjects), including 21 national territorial entities (Republics), 55 administrative territorial entities (Territories and Oblasts), two federal cities (Moscow and St. Petersburg), and 11 smaller national territorial entities (Autonomous Regions and Oblasts).[1] (Appendix table C.1 gives population figures for each of these entities.)

The regions (or subjects of the Russian Federation) vary dramatically in size—from 18,000 to 10.4 million residents—but they represent valid units of socioeconomic analysis because of their role in the political structure. This chapter takes these regions as the unit of observation. The approach is justified by the fact that broadly similar geographic, historic, and social conditions prevail within each region and the regions are the agents of fiscal, structural, and social policy in the Russian Federation. They have the right to levy local taxes, invest in local infrastructure, provide subsidies to enterprises, influence the business climate, legislate local social transfers, supplement federally mandated transfers, and provide housing and utility subsidies to households.

The chapter is based on survey data from the Household Budget Survey and the Labour Force Survey and on economic data available at the regional level.[2] The Household Budget Survey is considered to be representative for each member of the Federation and therefore offers a wealth of data for understanding poverty dynamics. These data offer striking insights into the regional dimension of living standards. This chapter uses the methodology presented in chapter 1 alongside standard official approaches.[3]

Regional Differences in Living Standards

Interregional differences in living standards are large in terms of socioeconomic conditions and gross regional products. Differences in consumption per capita and other measures based on household surveys are smaller. Real interregional differences in output and consumption—that take account of large interregional price variations—are much smaller than nominal differences.

Socioeconomic development varies widely across Russia's regions. An internationally comparable indicator that combines several dimensions of living standards was produced for Russian regions by the United Nations Development Programme for the 2002/2003 *Human Development Report for the Russian Federation.* The Human Development Index varied from 0.633 in Tuva Republic to 0.864 in Moscow. If the Russian regions were treated as countries, the wealthiest would rank 32nd and the poorest 119th among the 173 countries for which the Human Development Index has been computed. Moscow is on a par with Argentina and Portugal, while Tuva compares with Indonesia and Nicaragua. The median Russian region (Kursk Oblast) is well below the Russian average and is comparable to Albania, Azerbaijan, or Sri Lanka. A key component influencing these differences is the variation in output.

Regional differences in output are huge, although they narrow when price differences are taken into account. The per capita Gross Regional Product (GRP) of the richest region was 67 times that of the poorest region in 2002 (appendix table C.1). Much of the variation reflects large regional price differences, however. For example, in December 2000 the same fixed basket of 19 food items was worth 603 rubles in Ulianovsk Oblast (the region with the lowest prices) and 2,300 rubles in Chukotka Autonomous Region (the region with the highest prices), with a national average of 750 rubles. Nonfood prices also vary. Using the GRP deflator, real GRP in the richest region was 33 times GRP in the poorest region in 2002, half the nominal difference.

Interregional inequality in Russia is large, but it is not severe by international standards. Comparison of real per capita GRP in the richest and poorest regions provides a quick, easy to comprehend, and politically powerful measure of regional inequality. If this measure is small (close to 1), different regions have relatively equal GRP. If this measure is large, the interpretation is more problematic, as it does not tell us whether the high

Figure 3.1. Regional inequality in Russia is comparable to that in other large low- and middle-income countries

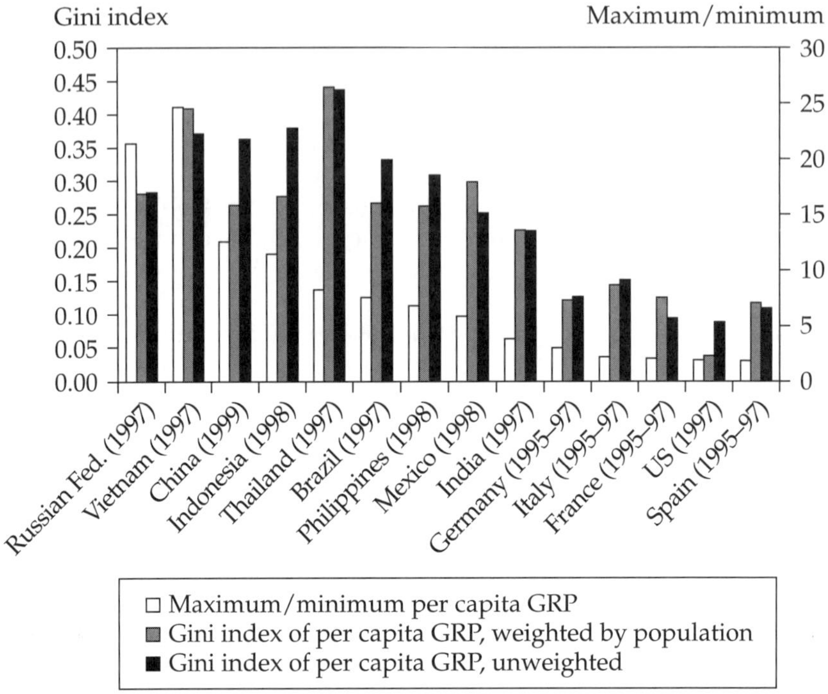

Source: Shankar and Shah (2001).
Note: All data are corrected for regional price differences using GRP deflators, where available.

ratio is due to substantial variation in per capita GRP or the presence of outliers—small regions with extremely peculiar economic conditions. Inequality measures take into account the whole distribution rather than only the extremes. The Gini index (see appendix C) shows that regional inequality in Russia is comparable to that observed in other large low- and middle-income countries. The Gini index for Russia of about 0.28 for both weighted and unweighted distributions of GRP is below the value in Thailand and Vietnam; similar to that in Brazil, China, Indonesia, and Mexico; and higher than that in India and most OECD countries (figure 3.1). Regional inequality in Russia thus partly reflects the presence of outliers.

Household surveys reveal less regional inequality than GRP data. Household nominal disposable resources in the richest region were nine times those in the poorest region, and nominal consumption per capita was six times as high in 2002 (appendix table C.1). Correcting for regional price differences further reduces the spread, indicating that inequality in Russia is not dramatically different from that in other large countries with complex regional structures. Using poverty lines as spatial price deflators, the richest and poorest regions differed by a factor of four in terms of real disposable resources and three in terms of real consumption in 2002. The Gini indexes (weighted by population shares of regions) were 0.117 for regional per capita disposable resources and 0.096 for consumption.

The GRP and survey-based consumption data are remarkably consistent at the regional level, despite differences in levels and dynamics (figure 3.2). Higher production leads to higher consumption, but the increase is smaller than the increase in production. This relationship explains why regions that are very diverse in terms of production are much closer in terms of consumption. GRP computations are based on production data and depend crucially on the formal location (registration) of the reporting units. Several resource-rich regions are characterized by very high reported value added, which is distributed and used elsewhere in the economy. Inequality in household consumption or income is a more accurate measure of regional variation in living standards in Russia.

Figure 3.2. As expected, regional production and consumption in Russia exhibited a logarithmic relationship in 2002

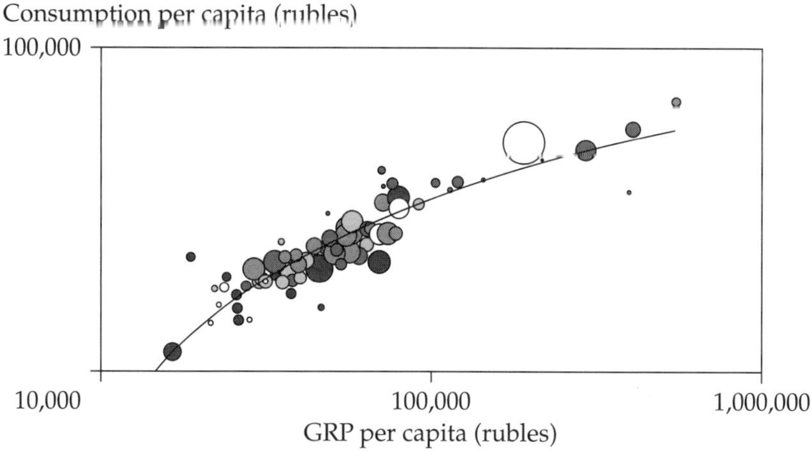

Sources: Regions of Russia 2002 (Goskomstat), and Bank staff calculations based on data from Household Budget Survey 2002 (Goskomstat).
Note: Size of bubbles reflects regions' population.

Table 3.1. Most measures of inequality between regions declined in Russia between 1997 and 2002

Variable/year	*Maximum/ minimum*	*Gini index (unweighted)*	*Gini index (weighted by population)*
Per capita GRP (in 2002 prices)			
1997	25.5	0.319	0.336
1999	33.2	0.307	0.335
2002	35.7	0.316	0.350
Per capita real GRP[a]			
1997	21.4	0.283	0.280
1999	13.9	0.231	0.237
2002	11.6	0.233	0.227
Per capita nominal money income			
1997	12.1	0.232	0.307
1999	12.6	0.247	0.324
2002	16.4	0.259	0.351
Per capita real money income[b]			
1997	8.1	0.147	0.208
1999	12.4	0.184	0.247
2002	11.6	0.203	0.259
Per capita nominal average wage			
1997	10.0	0.294	0.212
1999	11.6	0.293	0.220
2002	8.7	0.287	0.227
Per capita real average wage[b]			
1997	4.7	0.147	0.122
1999	5.0	0.172	0.143
2002	4.9	0.153	0.135
Per capita nominal disposable resources			
1997	9.2	0.197	0.272
1999	5.2	0.181	0.210
2002	6.5	0.179	0.200
Per capita real disposable resources[c]			
1997	4.0	0.127	0.139
1999	3.6	0.117	0.118
2002	4.0	0.119	0.117
Per capita nominal consumption			
1997	6.0	0.148	0.203
1999	3.7	0.136	0.165
2002	4.4	0.147	0.170

Table 3.1. Most measures of inequality declined in Russia between 1997 and 2002 (continued)

Variable/year	*Maximum/ minimum*	*Gini index (unweighted)*	*Gini index (weighted by population)*
Per capita real consumption[d]			
1997	3.9	0.092	0.126
1999	2.5	0.085	0.102
2002	2.8	0.088	0.096

Sources: Goskomstat, Ministry of Economy and Trade, and Bank staff calculations based on data from Household Budget Survey 1997–2002 (Goskomstat).

Note: For consistency over time, this table reports summaries based on regional data for 77 regions, with larger regions including the smaller constituent parts (formed after 2000).

a. Regional GRP deflators used to correct for spatial price variation.

b. Official regional poverty lines of the current year used as deflators.

c. Official regional poverty lines for 2002, adjusted with regional CPI for 1997 and 1999, used as deflators.

d. Regionally consistent poverty lines developed by Kakwani and Sajaia (2004) used as deflators (see chapter 1).

Inequality across regions has remained largely stable. Survey data indicate that inequality has not increased since 1997. Differences across regions increased during the early transition period (Hanson and Bradshaw 2000), but opinions differ as to whether such differences increased or remained stable between 1997 and 2002. For all series except per capita nominal and real money incomes, inequality across regions either was stable or declined (table 3.1).

The postcrisis recovery (1999–2002) was broad based and benefited both the richest and the poorest regions. All regions except Kamchatka Oblast increased their real GRP between 1999 and 2002 (appendix table C.1). The absolute gain in real per capita GRP was similar across regions (figure 3.3), leading to some reductions in regional inequalities. Given the presence of outliers, which influence some statistics on regional differences, and the somewhat mixed evidence presented in table 3.1, it is important to use a robust set of measures to assess whether there is a tendency toward convergence or divergence across Russian regions.

Interregional inequality did not increase after the 1998 crisis. The intuitive presentation of convergence hypothesis is given in figure 3.4, which shows GRP and consumption per capita from national accounts data in 1999 on the horizontal axis and the average annual growth rate between 1999 and 2002 on the y-axis. A clustering of regions along a downward sloping trend line means that the lower is initial GRP per

Figure 3.3. Per capita GRP rose in all but one region between 1999 and 2002

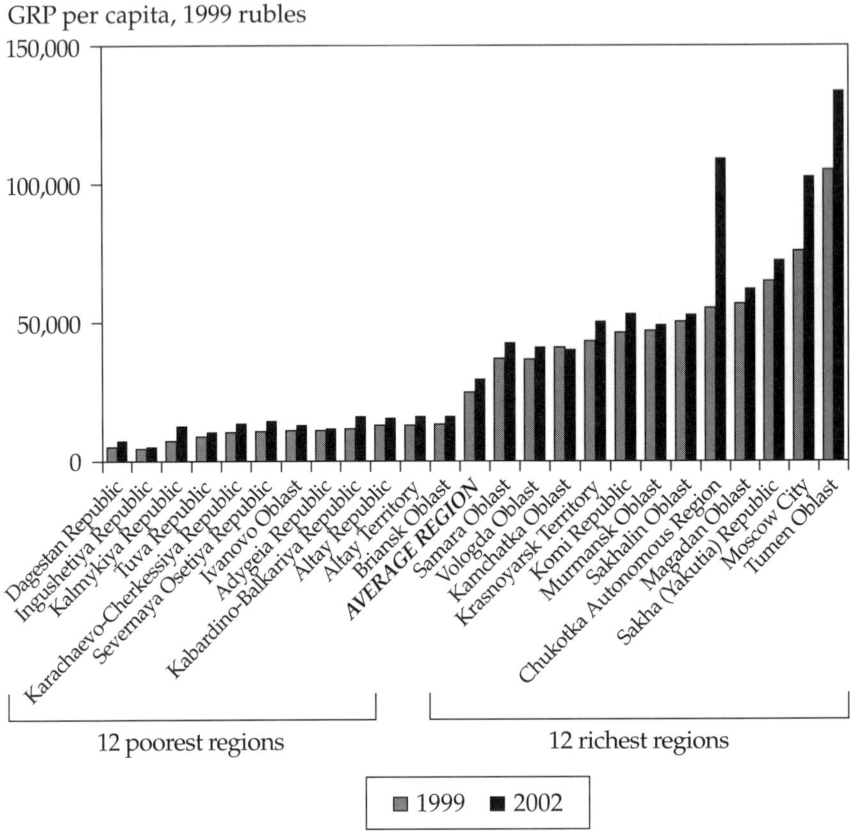

Source: Regions of Russia 1999 and 2002 (Goskomstat).
Note: GRP deflators used.

capita or consumption per capita, the higher is the subsequent growth rate. This trend would imply convergence, while an upward sloping trend line would indicate divergence. The trend lines shown in figure 3.4 suggest convergence. Although the results are not statistically significant, they at least indicate that interregional per capita GRP and consumption did not diverge between 1999 and 2002.

Convergence operates through a variety of channels, including the movement of people in response to differences in labor market conditions and incomes. Mobility should reduce poverty if not inequality (box 3.1).

Figure 3.4. Interregional differences in per capita GRP and consumption declined between 1999 and 2002

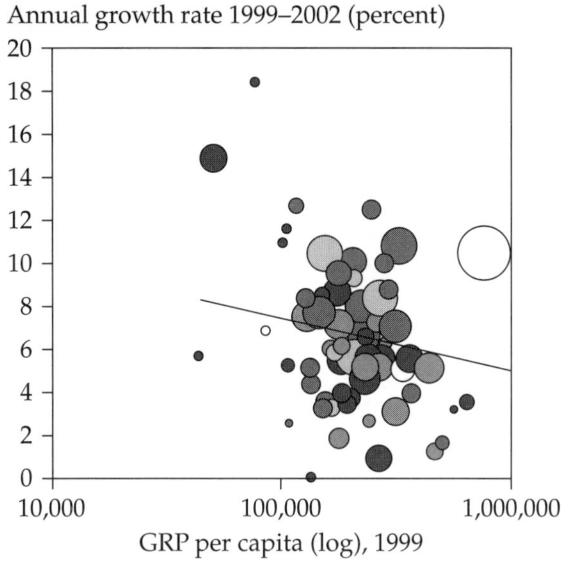

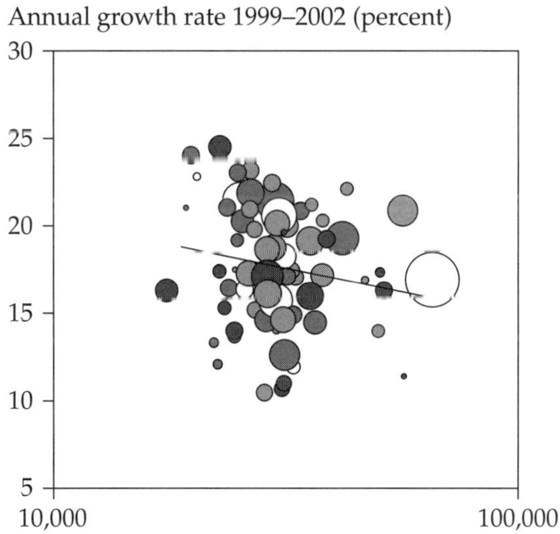

Sources: Regions of Russia 1999–2002 (Goskomstat), and Bank staff calculations based on data from Household Budget Survey 1999–2002 (Goskomstat) reported in appendix table C.1.
Note: Size of bubbles reflects regions' population.

Box 3.1. A significant number of Russia's villages have been abandoned

The 2002 census sheds light on the demographic aspect of regional differences. In addition to revealing important trends in the distribution of the population across regions and significant cross-regional mobility, it reveals an astonishing trend in the distribution of population within regions. The most striking result is the identification of an increasing number of abandoned villages (ghost towns), listed in the census as "settlements without population." When census takers arrived, they found villages that had been abandoned entirely or in which no permanent residents lived. These 13,032 abandoned villages constituted 8.4 percent of all villages in Russia. Another 34,803 rural settlements had fewer than 10 residents each. Thus nearly one-third of all Russian villages are either "dead" or near extinction. The bulk are located in the central part of the country, in the Central, North West, and Volga districts—areas containing some of the highest shares of elderly people in the country. These villages are losing population, as the last elderly people living in them die and young people migrate to nearby urban areas.

Elsewhere in Russia, the ghost town phenomenon reflects other causes. Not surprisingly, the regions with the largest share of ghost towns are the two regions with the largest percentages of population decline, Magadan Oblast and Chukotka Autonomous Region, which experienced a reduction in population of about 50 percent between 1989 and 2002. One-third of all settlements in these regions have been abandoned. Many of these empty towns and villages continue to be supplied with electricity, gas, and other services, a costly drain on the state budget.

Source: Heleniak (2003).

Correcting for regional price differences shows an even stronger trend toward the reduction of inequality across regions between 1999 and 2002. National inequality can be broken down into two components: inequality between regions and the contribution to national inequality of inequality within each region (table 3.2). The procedure involves decomposing the value of inequality for the whole population into the inequality observed within each region and the inequality due to variation in average incomes between regions, using the Theil index of inequality (see appendix B for details). Both per capita real disposable resources and per capita real consumption show that interregional inequality fell between 1997 and 1999 and was stable between 1999 and 2002.[4]

Intraregional differences are more important than interregional differences as a driver of national-level inequality. By 2002 only 9 percent of consumption inequality came from differences in average living standards across regions, while 91 percent came from inequality within

Table 3.2. Decomposition of inequality by regions for survey-based indexes, 1997–2002

Measure	*1997*	*1998*	*1999*	*2000*	*2001*	*2002*
Per capita real disposable resources						
Gini	0.412	0.392	0.386	0.392	0.389	0.388
Theil inequality, of which:	0.291	0.264	0.256	0.263	0.258	0.256
Between regions	0.032	0.028	0.023	0.027	0.026	0.023
Share of total (percent)	11	11	9	10	10	9
Within regions	0.260	0.235	0.233	0.236	0.232	0.233
Share of total (percent)	89	89	91	90	90	91
Per capita real consumption						
Gini	0.346	0.361	0.340	0.330	0.331	0.330
Theil inequality, of which:	0.205	0.221	0.199	0.185	0.186	0.183
Between regions	0.029	0.030	0.017	0.014	0.018	0.016
Share of total (percent)	14	14	8	8	10	9
Within regions	0.176	0.191	0.182	0.171	0.168	0.167
Share of total (percent)	86	86	92	92	90	91

Source: Bank staff calculations based on data from Household Budget Survey 1997–2002 (Goskomstat).

Note: Official poverty lines are used as deflators for real disposable resources; recommended poverty lines are used as deflators for consumption.

regions (see table 3.2). Most regions in Russia are characterized by substantial inequality in the distribution of welfare (appendix table C.3).

Regional differences nevertheless represent an important policy concern. The fact that the intraregional component of inequality dominates the interregional component does not mean that differences between regions should be neglected. Shorrocks and Wan (2004) use income data from 13 countries to decompose national inequality into interregional and intraregional components. They conclude that interregional differences in Russia are among the largest in the world. Once a broader view of living standards is taken into consideration (see Ravallion 2004 and Kanbur 2003), even a small share of regional differences in overall inequality may have far-reaching consequences for policies and welfare (through the provision of region-specific public goods, for example). When there are constraints on mobility across regions, such differences can also be regarded as unjust. They can also persist (Commander and Yemtsov 1995), leading to increased polarization between extremes despite some convergence, on average (see Fedorov 2002 and Dolinskaya 2002). Finally, in Russia even controlling for other factors, such as education, employment, type of settlement, and demography, the region remains the largest contributor to inequality (IISP 2003). Inequality between regions in income or consumption is often related to the full spectrum of differences in some vital parameters of social and political life, feeding social exclusion and potentially weakening the tendency for convergence (see appendix C). Regional differences should therefore be closely monitored and addressed.

The existence of sizable but manageable differences in living standards across regions means that regional policies in Russia could play an active role, as they do in other countries. As the level of regional differences in living standards across Russian regions is similar to that observed in many large OECD economies, their experience in setting policy objectives based on regional outcomes would be very informative for Russian policymakers.

Between 1999 and 2002, economic reform efforts in the Russian Federation focused more on the creation of a level playing field than on following paternalistic protectionist policies that favored the poorest regions. This experience is in line with that of other countries and suggests that the most efficient policies for addressing regional inequality are promoting a common economic union through the removal of barriers to factor mobility and ensuring minimum standards of basic services across the country. At the same time, the role and importance of intraregional inequalities suggest that regional policies should look beyond a region as a single unit and address the problem of poor areas within regions as well.

Regional Differences in Poverty

Though regional differences in socioeconomic conditions are reflected in sizable differences in the incidence of poverty across regions, most poor people live in regions in which the incidence of poverty mirrors the national average. Regions with a higher incidence of poverty are those that have low output levels, low real wages, and high unemployment rates.

The incidence of poverty varies significantly across regions. In the region with the lowest incidence of poverty, just 3.1 percent of the population is poor. In the region with the highest incidence of poverty, the incidence of poverty is 18 times as high, affecting 55.6 percent of the population (appendix table C.2). Using the official poverty counts based on aggregate money incomes, the incidence of poverty ranges from 7 to 87 percent, more than a 12-fold difference.

Differences in poverty levels closely reflect variations in labor market conditions across regions. Poor regions have lower real wages and higher unemployment rates. The main transmission channel between the economic structure of a region and its poverty outcomes is the labor market. Both the rate of unemployment and the wage rate are correlated with poverty.

Interregional differences in unemployment in Russia are large and closely linked with poverty. Regions with higher unemployment, measured according to ILO methodology based on Labor Force Survey 2002 (Goskomstat) data, have higher poverty rates (figure 3.5). Unemployment rates in 2002 ranged from just 1 percent to more than 30 percent. This large variation in labor market outcomes is a significant factor driving regional differences in poverty rates.

Differences in real wages are significant and negatively associated with poverty incidence. The real wage rate, measured by the number of minimum subsistence baskets a net average wage can buy (recommended poverty line used), ranged from 2 to 11 baskets in 2002 (figure 3.6). The wage rate was closely and negatively linked to regional poverty incidence. As there is a link between regional unemployment and regional real wages (Commander and Yemtsov 1995), these effects on poverty reinforce each other.

Most of the Russian population resides in regions in which unemployment rates and real wages fluctuate around the national median.

Figure 3.5. The incidence of poverty is higher where unemployment is high

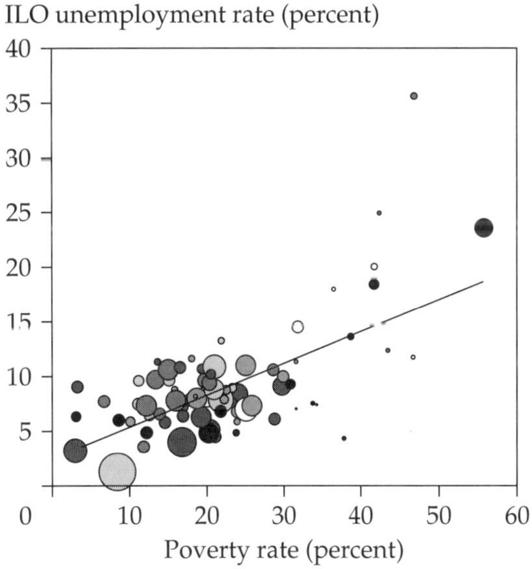

Source: Bank staff calculations based on data from Household Budget Survey 2002 (Goskomstat), Labor Force Survey 2002 (Goskomstat), and published unemployment rates based on Labor Force Survey.

Note: The recommended poverty line methodology is used. Size of bubbles reflects regions' population. The trend line is based on simple (unweighted) regression.

Figure 3.6. The incidence of poverty is lower where wages are high

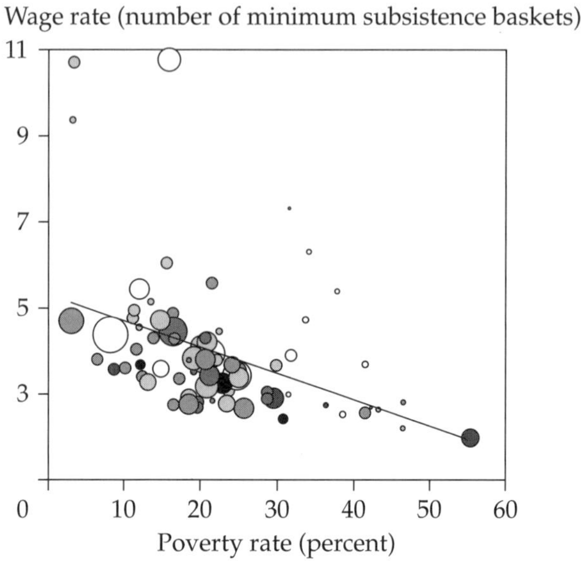

Source: Bank staff calculations based on data from Household Budget Survey 2002 (Goskomstat) and Goskomstat (2003a) wage data.
Note: The recommended poverty line methodology is used. Size of bubbles reflects regions' population. The trend line is based on simple (unweighted) regression.

Thus, despite the existence of extremes, the extent of regional inequality among a majority of Russian regions ("inequality in the middle") in any socioeconomic indicator is not large.

Despite large regional differences, most of the poor live in regions in which socioeconomic development is average. While there are substantial variations in unemployment and real wages, which lead to disproportionately high or low levels of poverty across regions, in most regions the unemployment rate and the regional real wage—and therefore the poverty rate—are close to the national average. This can be seen in figure 3.7, which plots the cumulative density curves for poverty. On the horizontal axis, the regions are ranked according to their level of poverty, from richest on the left to poorest on the right. The figure shows the evolution of the regional concentration of poverty between 1999 and 2002. The density function is very steep, forming almost a vertical line at the average poverty rate, particularly in 2002. This indicates that many of the poor live in regions in which the poverty incidence is close to the national

Figure 3.7. Many of the poor live in regions with average poverty incidence, particularly in 2002

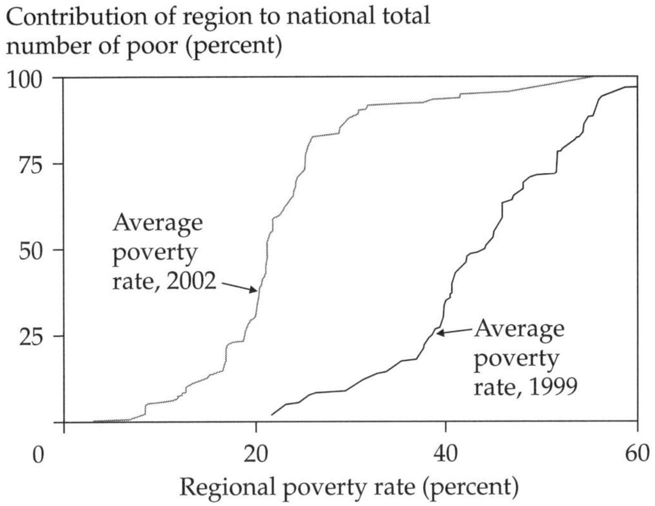

Source: Bank staff calculations based on data from Household Budget Survey 1999 and 2002 (Goskomstat).
Note: The recommended poverty methodology is used.

average. There is a significant top tail, with the poorest regions having more than twice the national poverty rate, but these regions account for only a minority of the poor, and there is no sign that this group is increasing. In most regions the 2002 poverty rate was half the 1999 level. The recovery has shifted the entire distribution almost exactly parallel to its precrisis level (not shown here), and the shape has become steeper, reflecting a greater concentration of poverty in the middle group of regions.

Despite a host of intervening factors, the regional incidence of poverty closely mirrors differences in output levels (figure 3.8). The relationship between poverty and output is negative, although for a given level of GRP, the poverty rate may vary significantly across regions.

Regional inequality plays a less important role as a correlate of poverty. Inequality and poverty are positively correlated: higher regional inequality is associated with higher poverty (figure 3.9). But, as appendix table C.3 shows, the dispersion of regional inequality indexes (as measured by Gini indexes for consumption, which ranges between 0.24 and 0.40) is significantly narrower than the regional variation of other socioeconomic indicators due to the nature of Gini indexes.. However, the val-

Figure 3.8. The relationship between regional output per capita and poverty is negative

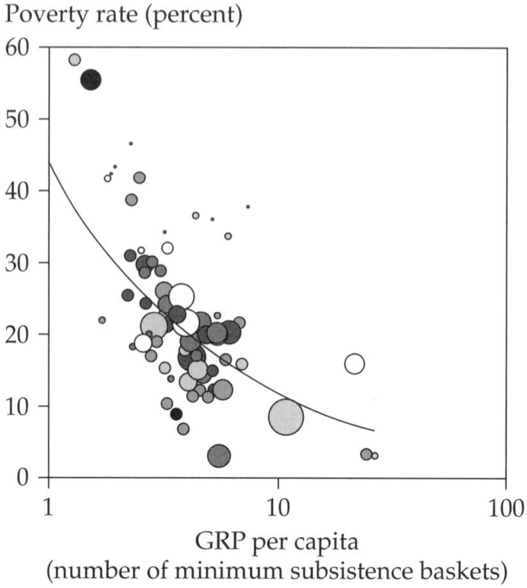

Sources: Regions of Russia 2002 (Goskomstat) and Bank staff calculations based on data from Household Budget Survey 2002 (Goskomstat data reported in tables C.1 and C.2).
Note: The recommended poverty methodology is used. Size of bubbles reflects regions' population. The trend line is based on simple linear (unweighted) regression. Consumption per capita is used to measure inequality.

ues observed in some Russian regions put them close to the least unequal societies in the world, while the upper limits of the Gini index are similar to significantly unequal developing countries. Nevertheless, there is no clear-cut relationship between inequality and poverty at the regional level based on household consumption data. An analysis of the matter using income data (Kolenikov and Shorrocks 2003a, 2003b) suggests that differences in inequality are at least as important as variations in regional income levels in explaining poverty and that both are closely linked to a set of geographic, economic, and political factors.

Ultimately, poverty in each region is completely determined by the level of consumption and the distribution of income among the region's people. Changes in poverty over time represent changes in real incomes and inequality, and both are sides of a single growth process. Thus a better understanding of the linkages between growth inequality and poverty at the regional level is required to guide policies aimed at poverty reduction through pro-poor growth.

Figure 3.9. Higher regional inequality is correlated with higher poverty

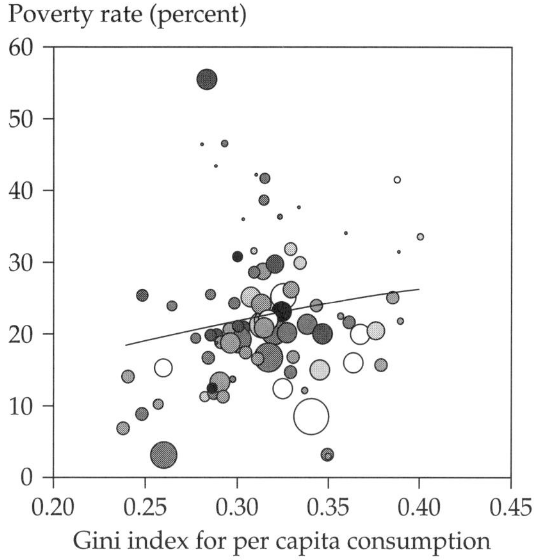

Source: Bank staff calculations based on data from Household Budget Survey 2002 (Goskomstat data reported in tables C.2 and C.3).
Note: The recommended poverty methodology is used. Size of bubbles reflects regions' population. The trend line is based on simple linear (unweighted) regression. Consumption per capita is used to measure inequality.

Regional Poverty Profile

The poverty profiles of Russia's 88 regions share similarities and differences.[5] Economic factors (such as the degree of urbanization and labor market status) show significant variation across regions, while demographic correlates of poverty are common across regions.

Differences in the level of urbanization, education, employment, and family size account for much of the regional differences in poverty rates in Russia. The average poverty rate in Moscow City and Tumen Oblast, two large regions, was 10 percent, while the average poverty rate in Dagestan and Tuva Republics was 45 percent. Rich and poor regions have very different demographic structures, employment rates, age profiles, and levels of urbanization.

Individuals with similar characteristics face different risks of poverty, depending on the region they live in. The simplest way to control for differences is to take observationally identical individuals in the survey from poor and rich regions and compare their poverty risks. If poverty is a function only of education, employment, demographics, and similar factors, differences in poverty across regions for similar people should be minimal. In fact, they are significant: residents of Tuva and Dagestan Republics are three times as likely to be poor as their counterparts in Moscow City or Tumen Oblast, suggesting that regional effects (differences in economic returns) are an important determinant of differences in poverty rates across regions.

Region-specific rates of return to various assets vary significantly. Explaining such differences would help unveil the causes of poverty. This section investigates these questions, focusing on rural residence, education, labor market status, and number of children.

The risk of poverty is systematically higher in rural areas in both wealthy and poor regions. However, wealthier regions have fewer rural residents. As a result, poverty is predominantly urban in wealthier regions, and rural in poorer regions. Figure 3.10 is composed of two panels. On the top panel, lines represent poverty risks by groups: the upper line shows the poverty incidence of the rural population in each region. In the region with the lowest poverty incidence (on the left), even the rural poor have almost no risk of poverty, while in the poorest regions, the rural population has a very high poverty risk (about 55 percent). Even though rural residents in better off-regions generally face a higher risk of poverty than urban residents, rural residents in these better-off regions still face a much lower risk of poverty than rural residents in poor regions.

The panel on the bottom divides the poor into urban and rural subgroups. It shows that as the regional poverty rate increases, the rural poor as a share of the total poor in each region increases. While rural residents of wealthier regions still face a higher risk of poverty than urban residents, wealthier regions tend to be much more urbanized. As a result, the poor in those regions are mostly urban residents. Poorer regions have a lower degree of urbanization and therefore a higher percentage of the poor live in rural areas.

The majority of the poor (80 percent) everywhere are working families, but in regions with a higher poverty incidence, fewer families have multiple earners. Poorer regions also have more unemployed among the poor. To analyze the link between labor market and poverty, a household-level definition of labor attachment is used.[6] Jobless households face a systematically higher poverty risk than other households across regions (figure 3.11, top panel). However, they represent a relatively small share of the population in each region, so that working families constitute a majority of the poor (figure 3.11, bottom panel). The poverty risks of nonworking-age families, who represent the smallest group among the poor, differ very little across regions.

Figure 3.10. Poverty is higher in rural areas, and poor regions have more rural residents

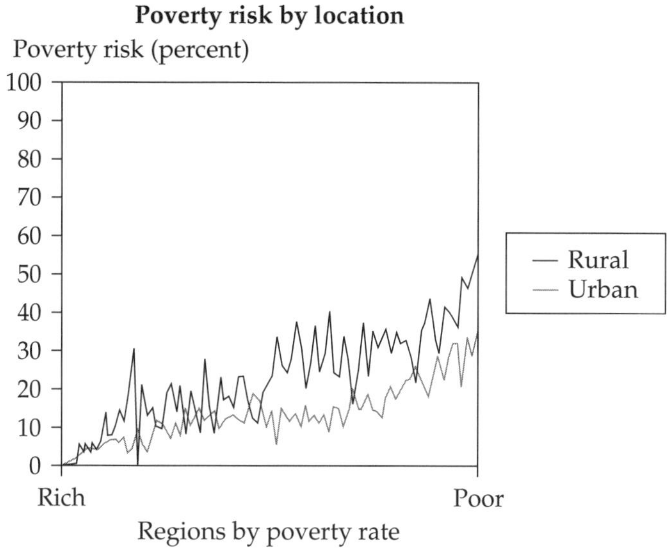

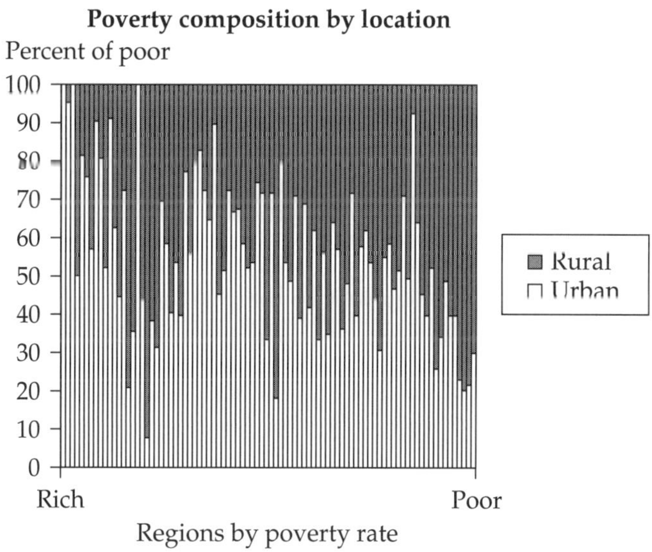

Sources: Bank staff calculations based on data from Household Budget Survey 2002 (Goskomstat); population from *Regions of Russia* (Goskomstat).
Note: The recommended poverty methodology is used.

Figure 3.11. Although the majority of the poor everywhere are working families, in poor regions fewer households have multiple earners

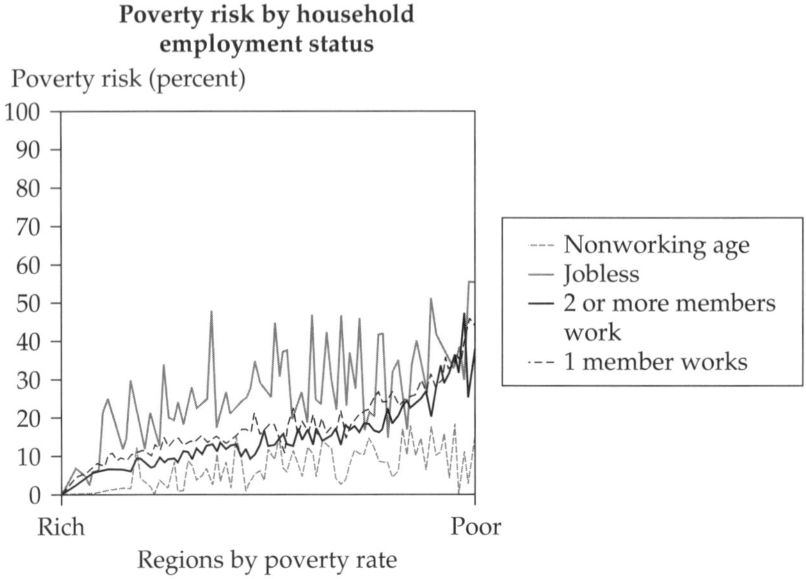

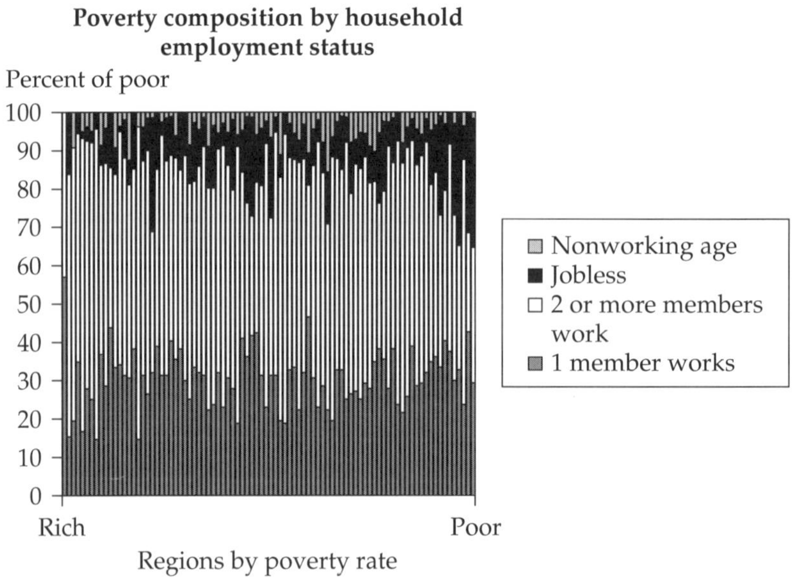

Sources: Bank staff calculations based on data from Household Budget Survey 2002 (Goskomstat); population from *Regions of Russia* (Goskomstat).
Note: The recommended poverty methodology is used.

Poverty profiles across regions do not differ much by education levels, with the risks of poverty moving in parallel with the regional incidence of poverty for all education groups. Russia's poor are relatively well educated; households whose head has only a primary education represent a minority of the poor and are sizable only in the wealthiest regions. Two people with a similar education level residing in different regions will have the same relationship with respect to the average poverty risk in their regions, but the magnitude of the poverty risk will depend on the extent of poverty in their region. Education does not guarantee against poverty in any region, however. In both rich and poor regions, the poor include people with higher education.

Families with children make up the majority of the poor in all regions. Children have the highest risk of poverty and pensioners the lowest risk across all regions. The poverty risk of a child ranges from 0.5 percent in the richest region to 60 percent in the poorest. Families with three or more children represent a very small share of the poor, and their high poverty risk has little link to the overall poverty incidence.

Policy Recommendations

The policy implications of this analysis are twofold. On the one hand, similarities in the poverty profile mean that policies, such as child allowances, that target people with certain common characteristics—especially labor market attachment and demographic risk factors—would reach the poor across the spectrum of regions. On the other hand, region-specific policies are needed to reach certain groups of the poor. Housing allowances that target the urban poor, for example, will have limited impact on reducing the overall number of poor in the poorest regions, where the majority of the poor live in rural areas. A proper balance between national and region-specific policies is required.

Specific policy recommendations include the following:

- Policymakers in Russia should not be discouraged by excessively large regional differences that seem to be beyond the scope of policies. The scale of differences in living standards across the regions is amenable to a set of well-designed policies that combine universal principles with region-specific instruments.
- Since pockets of poverty are found in virtually all regions, strategies need to focus less on singling out a small subset of poor regions and more on reducing the incidence of the pockets of poverty found in virtually all regions of the country.
- As most of the poor live in regions in which poverty levels are close to the national average, strategies emphasizing broad growth are likely to

have a large impact on poverty reduction. Such policies would reach the majority of Russia's poor.

- For regions with the highest incidence of poverty, targeted policies and interventions are needed that take into account the profile of the poor. Strategies to promote rural growth, develop backward areas, and increase the incomes of the rural population in the poorest regions would be the most appropriate way to target the poorest.

Notes

1. This distribution is not set in stone, as the recent referendum on the merger of one small autonomous region (Komi-Permyatskiy) with the largest region suggests.

2. For statistical purposes, since 1999 Autonomous Regions and Oblasts have been treated on a par with other members of the Federation. Before 1999 the autonomous regions and oblasts were considered parts of the respective territories or *oblasts*. Chechen Republic is excluded from statistical data collection.

3. The analysis benefited from joint work with Goskomstat on regional aspects of poverty and inequality.

4. The Russia Longitudinal Monitoring Survey data (UNC, various years) confirm the fact that falling interregional inequality has contributed to the decline in overall inequality. The calculations of the Independent Institute for Social Policy (Burdiak and others 2005) show a reduction of the interregional component between 1998 and 2002. In contrast, Yemtsov (2003) and Commander, Tolstopiatenko, and Yemtsov (1999) find that regional differences increased. This inconsistency points to the need to review the methodology for compiling the money income indicator, a task that goes beyond the scope of this chapter.

5. Chechen Republic is excluded from the poverty profile analysis, as statistical data were not collected there.

6. European Commission definitions are used here. Working families are split into two groups: those with one earner and those with two and more earners. Jobless households are those in which at least one member is economically active but no adult is working. Nonworking-age households are those in which all members are either under 18, 18–24 and in school, or 65 and over.

Part II
Economic Recovery and Poverty Reduction

During the first seven years of transition (1992–98), Russia experienced a prolonged recession, with GDP collapsing by almost 40 percent. Double-digit inflation, labor shedding, and mounting wage arrears dramatically increased poverty levels during this period.

Russia's economic rebound since the 1998 financial crisis has been impressive. With average annual GDP growth of 7.4 percent in 1999–2003, Russia not only quickly eliminated the negative effects of the crisis, it also overcame the losses incurred during the early years of transition. Employment increased, real wages soared, and household consumption surpassed the pretransition level by 2002.

This part of the report takes a closer look at how the strong rebound in growth in the postcrisis period translated into favorable poverty outcomes. Chapter 4 analyzes the mechanisms of the recovery and its main driving forces. It concludes that although achieved growth rates are impressive, the sustainability of growth remains in question. Growth to date has been due primarily to a favorable combination of temporary postcrisis effects (very low capacity utilization in the aftermath of the crisis and a dramatic reduction in the relative cost of production), which are not sustainable, and to positive external factors. The main concern is the dependence of growth on favorable external factors, particularly high (and rising) oil prices. This dependence continues to increase, with exports of a few commodities becoming ever more important in generating domestic demand and keeping macroeconomic balances in surplus. This vulnerability to external shocks brings diversification of the economy to the top of the government agenda. Sustainable broad-based growth—and hence a stable reduction in poverty and improvement in standards of living—can be generated only by increased investment in noncommodity sectors and nonpetroleum start-ups, particularly small and medium-size enterprises.

Chapter 5 presents an analysis of how growth has affected developments in the labor market. A significant increase in job creation and the utilization of the employed labor force has been reported since the 1998 crisis. Employment and working hours have increased, wage arrears have been dramatically cut, and real wages have been growing faster than output since 1999. The increase in household earnings has had a positive impact on poverty reduction.

Chapter 6 investigates three questions: has growth reduced poverty, how has the inequality that has accompanied economic growth affected poverty reduction, and has economic growth been pro-poor or anti-poor in Russia. It finds that all poverty measures increased between 1997 and 1999 and then decreased between 1999 and 2002. It also shows that growth has been broad based and has benefited the ultra-poor and people living in poor regions more than the poor with incomes close to the poverty line and those in more prosperous regions. Since 1999 growth has also been pro-poor in the sense that it has increased the consumption share of the bottom quintile.

The chapter concludes that during the four postcrisis years for which data are available (1999–2002), the poverty headcount ratio declined by 18.7 percentage points. Of this, growth was responsible for a reduction in the headcount ratio of 11.7 percentage points and lower inequality for 7.0 percentage points. Future growth may be less pro-poor. Making economic growth and social policies more pro-poor is therefore recommended to achieve further progress in poverty alleviation. Three additional challenges make this task increasingly important. First, the government has set a goal of halving the poverty headcount by 2007. Second, the social protection system will have to cushion the impact of some envisaged structural reforms, such as those in housing and communal services. Third, the social protection system will have to play a similar role in moderating the impact of Russia's accession to the World Trade Organization (WTO). These issues are reviewed in part III.

4
The Post-1998 Economic Recovery

The postfinancial crisis recovery has been impressive, but the sustainability of growth remains in question. Growth to date has been due primarily to very low capacity utilization in the aftermath of the crisis, to a dramatic reduction in the relative cost of production, and to positive external factors. The continued dependence of growth on favorable external factors, such as high oil prices, is of concern. This dependence increased during the postcrisis period, with exports of a few commodities becoming ever more important in generating domestic demand and keeping macroeconomic balances in surplus. This vulnerability to external shocks brings diversification of the economy to the top of the government agenda. Sustainable broad-based growth, and hence a stable reduction in poverty and improvement in standards of living, can be generated only by increased investment in noncommodity sectors and nonpetroleum start-ups, particularly small and medium-size enterprises.

Impressive Macroeconomic Performance in 1999–2003

Russia's macroeconomic performance in the five years following the 1998 crisis was impressive on all counts. The Russian economy grew 37.5 percent between 1999 and 2003, and output rose an estimated 4–5 percent in 2004. This rapid growth places Russia among the fastest growing countries in the world during this period (figure 4.1). Inflation gradually declined, from 84 percent in 1998 to about 12 percent in 2003. Between 1999 and 2003, Russia enjoyed a surplus in both the budget and the current accounts. The federal budget's surplus was 1.6 percent of GDP in 2003 and is estimated at 0.5 percent for 2004. The current account—which, unlike the budget, was in surplus throughout the entire transition period—reached 8.3 percent of GDP in 2003. Mirroring these surpluses, and in an attempt to sterilize the inflow of foreign exchange and contain the resulting appreciation of the national currency, the gold and foreign exchange reserves of the central bank increased to a record level of $77 billion by the end of 2003, from just $12 billion in the aftermath of the 1998 crisis (Central Bank of Russia, various years).

Figure 4.1. Real GDP in Russia grew rapidly between 1998 and 2003

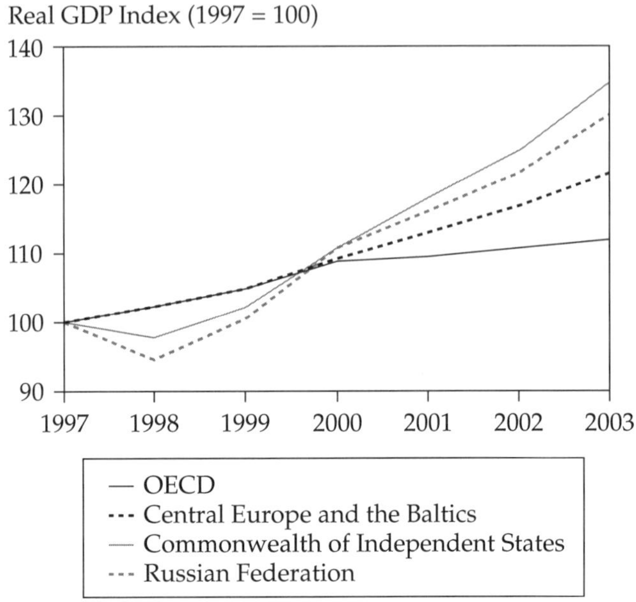

Source: Bank staff calculations based on data from Interstate Statistical Committee of the CIS (various years).

The postcrisis recovery looks particularly remarkable against the background of the preceding seven-year recession, which led to a massive 39.5 percent cumulative decline in GDP by 1998. While all major sectors contracted during the recession, two sectors were particularly hard hit: construction activities declined by 70 percent, and industrial output contracted by 49 percent (figure 4.2).

The postcrisis rebound affected all sectors, albeit at very different rates. The precrisis "losers"—agriculture, industry, and construction—were the growth leaders in the recovery (figure 4.3). Agriculture benefited from record crops several years in a row. But import substitution, triggered by the devaluation of the ruble in 1998, was an even more important factor behind the growth in the domestic production of agricultural products.

Construction has been driven largely by demand from the nonresidential sector. In 2001 (the latest year for which data are available), housing construction was still below the level achieved in 1997. With an abundance of underutilized capacity in the industrial and agricultural sectors until very recently, incumbent firms did not need to invest in new

Figure 4.2. All sectors declined during the recession, with construction and industrial output particularly hard hit

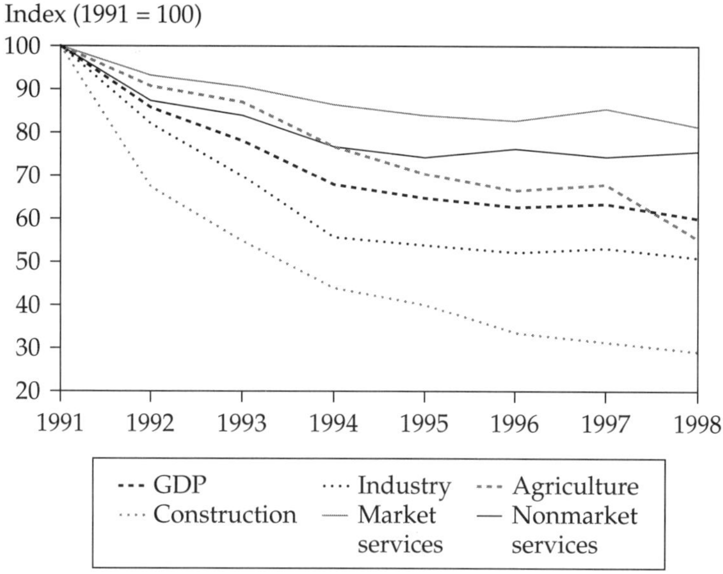

Source: Russian Statistical Yearbook 1991–98 (Goskomstat).

construction, and few start-ups were formed. The construction boom has been driven mainly by demand for new retail and wholesale facilities and office space.

Growth rates have varied within sectors, with industries that target the export market outperforming those targeting the domestic market in two recent years. The natural resource sectors started to outperform domestic manufacturing in 2002 for the first time since the beginning of the transition (figure 4.4).[1] Although the manufacturing sectors have since started to catch up, natural resource industries still grow faster. Unless this trend is reversed, the natural resource and export-oriented industries will increase their share in total industrial output and hence in the economy as a whole.

Official numbers underestimate the contribution of oil and gas production to Russia's economy. National accounts data do not reflect the peculiar Russian phenomenon of using transfer pricing to avoid (and often evade) taxes. This practice leads to a transfer of value added of the industrial sectors—primarily oil and gas—to the trade sector through grossly inflated trade margins. As a result, output in the trade sector—and hence in services as a whole—is overstated by about 12 percent of GDP.[2]

Figure 4.3. Sectors that were precrisis "losers" led the recovery

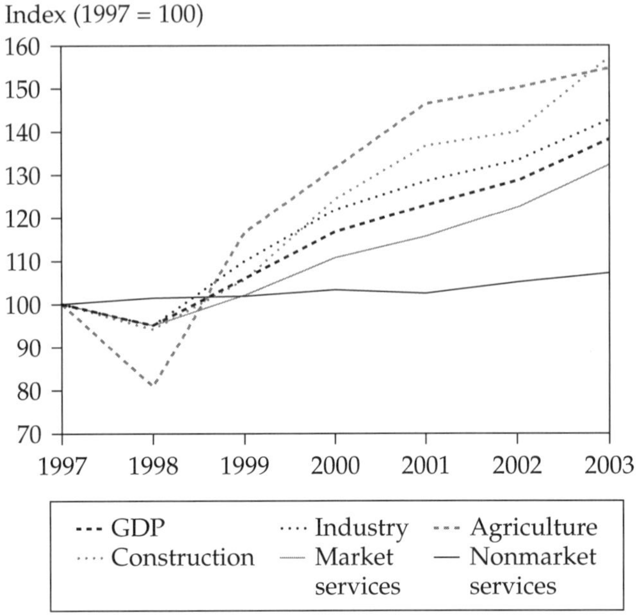

Source: Russian Statistical Yearbook 1997–2003 (Goskomstat).

Figure 4.4. Growth rates in manufacturing and natural resource industries (percent)

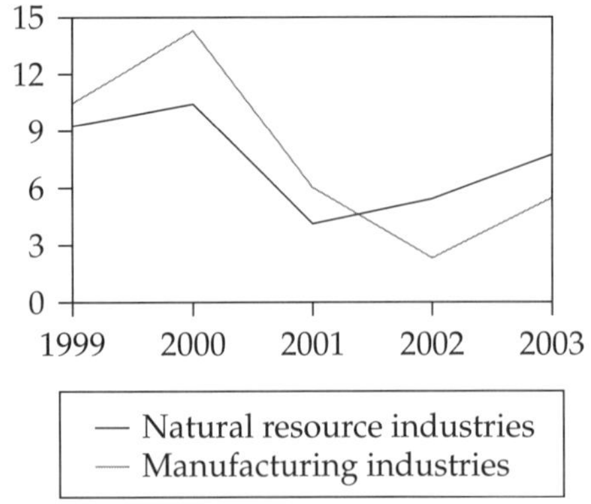

Source: Russian Statistical Yearbook 1999–2003 (Goskomstat).

Figure 4.5. Most regions contracted in 1998

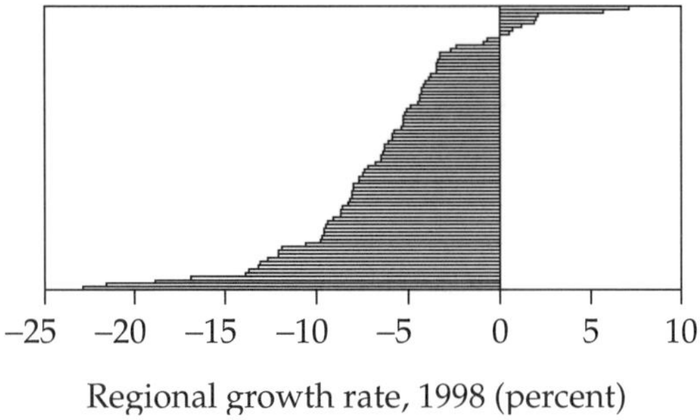

Source: Russian Statistical Yearbook 1998–2001 (Goskomstat).

Figure 4.6. All but one region grew between 1999 and 2001

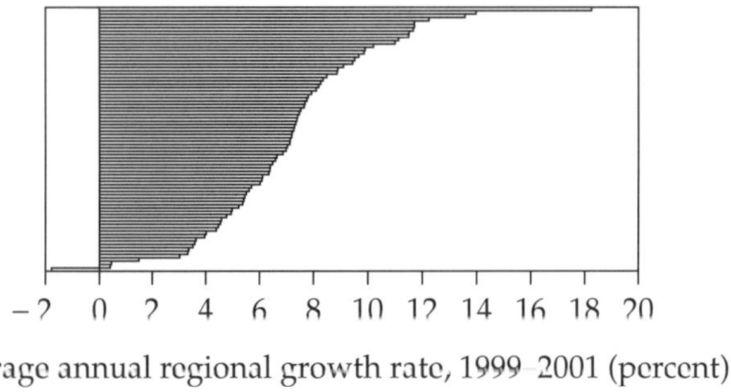

Source: Russian Statistical Yearbook 1998–2001 (Goskomstat).

Corrected figures increase the contribution of oil and gas to GDP to 20 percent—a huge contribution for a sector that employs just 1 percent of Russia's labor force.

The 1998 crisis affected regions unevenly. A handful of regions were able to maintain growth even in 1998, while the rest contracted 0.7–23.0 percent in a single year (figure 4.5).

Recovery was equally impressive but also uneven across regions. All but one region grew during the postcrisis period. Average growth between 1999 and 2001 was 7.4 percent a year, but regional growth rates deviated from the mean by as much as 10 percentage points in both directions (figure 4.6). There was little overlap between the regions that were the best or worst performers in 1998 and 1999–2001 (table 4.1). Only one region (Magadan Oblast) was among the 10 worst performers in both 1998 and 1999–2001. Another region (Ingushetiya Republic) was among the worst

Table 4.1. Best- and worst-performing regions in 1998 and 1999–2001 (percent)

Ten worst-performing regions in 1998	*Ten worst-performing regions in 1999–2001, annual average*	*Ten best-performing regions in 1998*	*Ten best-performing regions in 1999–2001, annual average*
Chukotka Autonomous Region (–23.0)	Kamchatka Oblast (–2.0)	Orlov Oblast (7.1)	Kalmykiya Republic (18.0)
Ingushetiya Republic (–22.0)	Magadan Oblast (0.4)	Novgorod Oblast (5.7)	Kabardino-Balkariya Republic (14.0)
Magadan Oblast (–19.0)	Mariy El Republic (0.5)	Severnaya Osetiya Republic (2.1)	Ingushetiya Republic (14.0)
Chelyabinsk Oblast –17.0)	Primorie Territory (1.5)	Tver Oblast (2.0)	Rostov Oblast (12.0)
Ivanovo Oblast (–14.0)	Irkutsk Oblast (3.0)	Kursk Oblast (1.9)	Severnaya Osetiya Republic (12.0)
Orenburg Oblast (–14.0)	Kursk Oblast (3.3)	Astrakhan Oblast (1.2)	Dagestan Republic (12.0)
Chita Oblast (–13.0)	Ulianovsk Oblast (3.4)	Briansk Oblast (0.7)	Leningrad Oblast (12.0)
Evreiskaya Autonomous Oblast (–13.0)	Khakassiya Republic (3.5)	Kabardino-Balkariya Republic (0.5)	Astrakhan Oblast (12.0)
Omsk Oblast (–13.0)	Kirov Oblast (3.6)	Karachaevo-Cherkessiya Republic (0.0)	Smolensk Oblast (12.0)
Volgograd Oblast (–12.0)	Kurgan Oblast (3.6)	Komi Republic (–0.7)	Arkhangelsk Oblast (11.0)

Source: Regions of Russia 1999 and 2003 (Goskomstat).

performers in 1998 and among the best performers in 1999–2001. Yet another region (Kursk Oblast), which fared during the 1998 crisis much better than most others, was among the worst performers in 1999–2001. At first glance the list of best performers seems to be more stable: three regions (Severnaya Osetiya Republic, Kabardino-Balkariya Republic, and Astrakhan Oblast) were on the list in both 1998 and 1999–2001. All three regions are in the Southern Okrug and have an advanced agricultural sector that benefited from import substitution in the consumption of foodstuffs.

Engines of the Postcrisis Recovery

In contrast to the international record—in which financial crises and national defaults traditionally led to a significant contraction in GDP growth rates in subsequent years—Russia rebounded quickly. The impact of the crisis on the real side of the economy appeared to be less adverse than many observers had expected. The recovery was also more rapid than in most other countries that experienced crises (figure 4.7).

Figure 4.7. Postcrisis recovery was stronger in Russia than in many other postcrisis countries

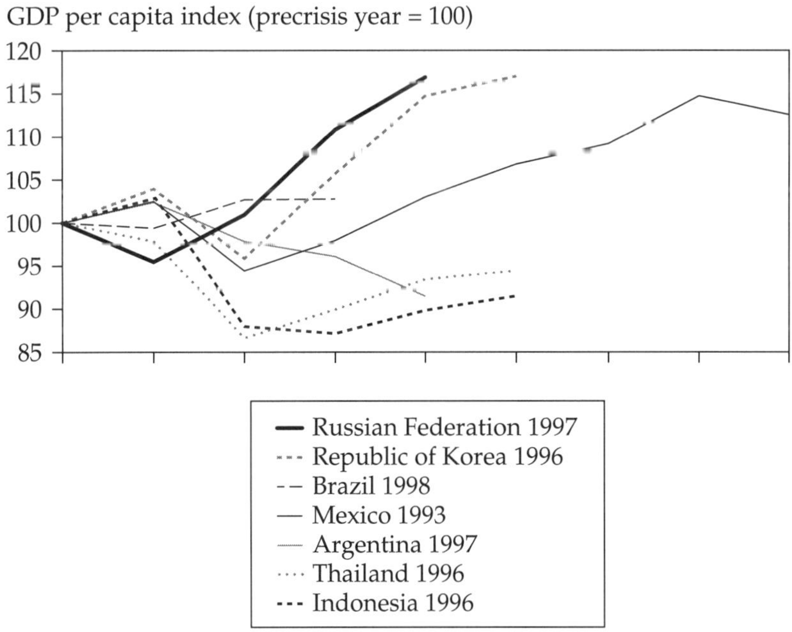

Source: World Bank (2003a).
Note: GDP per capita was measured in constant local currency units.

A broad range of complementary factors allowed for the impressive postcrisis recovery:

- Widescale import substitution was triggered by the fourfold devaluation of the ruble in the aftermath of the crisis. The cost of domestic production has fallen, as a result of positive changes in relative prices of domestic inputs (particularly real wages and electricity and natural gas tariffs).
- The bulk of capacity had gone unutilized in the main producing sectors by the time of the crisis, as a result of a prolonged precrisis contraction in output. The excess facilitated a rapid increase in output as soon as devaluation took place and high oil price-driven demand surged.
- Higher oil prices (from early 1999 on) increased export values, ensuring a constant inflow of foreign exchange and higher government revenues (the oil and gas sector contributes up to 40 percent to federal budget revenues).
- Hard budget constraints were imposed on the government by the inability to borrow either on the domestic government bond market or internationally. This meant that postcrisis governments had to balance their budgets or face hyperinflation.

This environment necessitated both prudent macroeconomics management (including introducing hard budget constraints for the private sector) and structural reforms. Structural reforms sought to increase efficiency in public service delivery and create a more favorable business climate.

Devaluation gave the first push to the postcrisis resumption of growth in Russia, but a shift in other relative prices controlled by the government was also significant. The real exchange rate collapsed by almost 40 percent in real terms between July and October 1998 (figure 4.8). Between July 1998 and December 1999, electricity and natural gas tariffs contracted by about 50 percent in real terms. By the end of 2003, both tariffs were still set by the government at a level below the one in force on the eve of the crisis. In October 2003 the electricity tariff was about 25 percent lower and the natural gas tariff was about 20 percent lower than in July 1998. Lower tariffs have had a beneficial impact on the cost of production for Russian companies.

The ability to utilize industrial capacity that had stood idle before the crisis enabled production to increase quickly. The government-run Center for Economic Analysis reports an increase in industrial capacity utilization of about 15 percentage points, while the independent Russian Economic Barometer reports an increase of about 20 percentage points between July 1998 and the end of 2003 (figure 4.9).

The rise in the price of oil has had a major impact on Russia's recovery. The largest increases in oil prices occurred in 1999 and 2000 (table 4.2)

Figure 4.8. Devaluation and lower utility tariffs contributed to postcrisis recovery in the Russian Federation

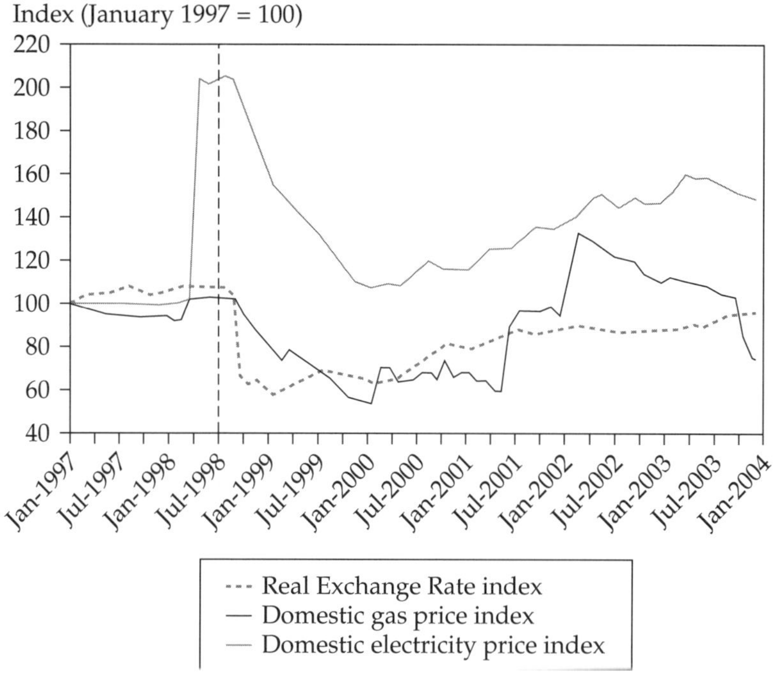

Source: World Bank (2004c).

—the years in which Russia experienced the highest growth rates. The price of Russia's main Brent (Urals) oil went from $10.3 per barrel in 1998 to $24.0 in 2003. Growth rates of 5 percent or higher were achieved in Russia only when oil prices rose substantially.

This comes as no surprise, given that commodity price dynamics strongly influence Russia's major economic indicators. Commodity exports contributed 78 percent to Russia's total exports in 2002, including 57 percent from oil and natural gas. More than 60 percent of Russia's fixed capital investment either goes into the hydrocarbon industries or is financed from the public purse, which in turn is overdependent on the petroleum sector. Thirty-seven percent of federal budget revenues come from the petroleum and gas sector (World Bank 2003b, 2004c). According to calculations by Bank staff, an increase in the price of Urals of $1 a barrel raises federal budget revenues by 0.35 percent of GDP and consolidated budget revenues by 0.45 percent of GDP.

Figure 4.9. Utilization of spare industrial capacity catalyzed the postcrisis increase in production

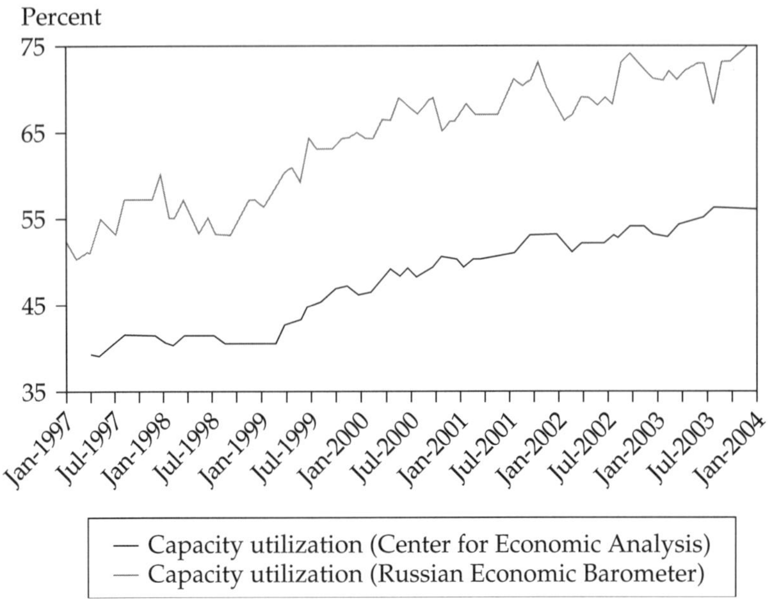

Sources: Center for Economic Analysis of the Government of Russia (various years); IMEMO (various years).

Table 4.2. The boom in oil prices spurred growth

Year	*Average annual price ($ per barrel)*	*Rate of increase (percent)*
1998	10.3	n.a.
1999	15.2	48
2000	24.0	58
2001	20.9	–13
2002	21.0	0
2003	24.0	14

n.a. Not applicable.
Source: World Bank (2004c).

Government policy is also an important driver of Russia's postcrisis recovery. The government's success in balancing its books, moderating inflation, and increasing the monetization of the economy by virtually eliminating noncash settlements and tax offsets has had a beneficial impact on the efficiency of the corporate sector. Hard budget constraints imposed by the government on all economic agents have streamlined business incentives and improved resource allocation, spurring growth. Structural reforms implemented by the government during the postcrisis period have contributed to the improvement of the business environment. Tax reform and debureaucratization efforts have perhaps been most important in this respect (box 4.1).

The reform program contributed to the perception of an improved business environment between 1999 and 2002. According to the Business

Box 4.1. The government's reform strategy has helped spur growth

Several hundred important pieces of economic legislation were enacted between 2000 and 2003. These included reforms in the following areas:

- *Tax code:* Imposed a flat income tax of 13 percent, reduced the profit tax from 35 to 24 percent, substituted a unified social tax of 35.6 percent for the previous dues to various extrabudgetary social funds, abolished the 5 percent sales tax, and introduced other measures.
- *Budget code:* Streamlined the administration of public expenditures and the division of responsibilities between levels of government.
- *Customs code:* Limited the discretion of customs officers in the implementation of customs regulations.
- *Land code:* Granted citizens the right to sell agricultural land (enacted in the summer of 2003, much later than the main body of the code).
- *Labor code:* Eased the procedures for hiring and laying off employees.
- *Law on Public Social Assistance:* Introduced the principles of targeting.
- *Pension reform package:* Gradually changed from a pay-as-you-go to a two-pillar system.
- *Deregulation package:* Reduced the burden of administrative regulations on businesses by introducing new laws on registration, licensing, inspections, and certification.
- *Law on the Principles of Technical Regulations:* Gradually abolished obsolete standardization and certification requirements.
- *Strategy for reforming RAO UES, the national electricity monopoly:* Separated potentially competitive electricity generation and distribution from the natural monopoly component of trunk transmission.
- *Housing and Communal Services Reform Plan:* Increased cost recovery.

Source: Bank staff assessment.

Environment and Enterprise Performance Survey (BEEPS), conducted by the European Bank for Reconstruction and Development and the World Bank in 1999 and 2002, businesses perceive progress in all dimensions of the business environment surveyed: access to financing, the quality of infrastructure, taxation, problems with crime and corruption, the judiciary, and regulations (figure 4.10). Discriminatory practices that favored old enterprises over small start-ups have begun to diminish. Corruption is now perceived as less of an obstacle, the rule of law is perceived to have become stronger, and perceptions of state capture—of parliaments, commercial courts, governments, and political parties—have fallen sharply.

The government used the revenues from higher oil prices to significantly increase social spending on health, education, and social protection, providing broad-based benefits. Spending on social sectors appears to be sensitive to the overall fiscal position, and there seems to be a large discretionary element in such spending. Both the absolute level of social spending and its share in the budget or GDP appear subject to large cyclical changes over a short time period that mirror oil price dynamics. As a proportion of GDP, spending on the social sectors declined between 1997 and 2000, from 24.1 percent to 14.5 percent, before rising to almost 20 percent in 2002 (table 4.3). In 2002 spending on these three sectors was significant, at one-fifth of GDP and about 57 percent of noninterest expenditures of the enlarged (federal and subnational) budget.

Social sector spending has been procyclical. Although higher oil prices have also enabled the government to provide broad-based benefits, it ap-

Figure 4.10. Perceptions of Russia's business climate improved between 1999 and 2002

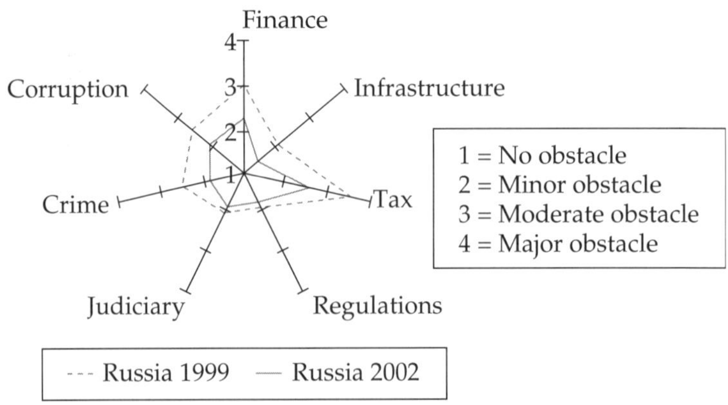

Source: EBRD and World Bank (1999, 2002).

Table 4.3. Social spending has risen since the crisis

Sector	*1997*	*1998*	*1999*	*2000*	*2001*	*2002*
Education	4.6	3.6	3.0	2.8	3.1	3.9
Health	3.5	3.4	2.9	2.8	2.9	3.2
Social protection	16.0	13.3	9.7	8.9	10.9	12.6
Total	24.1	20.3	15.6	14.5	16.9	19.7

Source: Bank staff calculations.
Note: Figures are percentages of GDP.

pears that social sector spending does not provide the built-in stabilization that such spending typically offers.

Implementation of key reforms set the stage for further growth and allowed the authorities to set more ambitious targets, among which the most challenging goals are doubling GDP per capita and halving the poverty headcount by 2007. The key goals for further reform were set in the Updated Medium-Term Program for 2004–07, approved by the government in the summer of 2003. Key targets include the following:

- Reduce poverty levels and income inequality by providing incentives for wage and employment growth and by strengthening the targeting of social assistance.
- Modernize the economy and increase enterprise efficiency by eliminating the subsidization embedded in low tariffs and by increasing the efficiency of infrastructure monopolies and housing and communal services.
- Increase the economy's innovative and technological potential.
- Create an institutional environment favorable to investment in the real sector and develop financial intermediation.
- Introduce effective protection of property rights; develop competitive markets for goods, services, and capital (including land); and increase the role of small and medium-size businesses.
- Improve fiscal efficiency by focusing budget expenditures on the priority targets of social and economic policy by improving control over the assets and liabilities of the state, streamlining the budgeting process, and creating an effective tax system.
- Reduce regional differences in social and economic development and strengthen the economic foundations of the Russian Federation by ensuring the conformity of subnational legislation with federal legislation by introducing clear functional divisions of authority and financial resources between the federal and subnational levels.

To achieve these targets, the government is working on several other reforms, the most crucial of which are in the civil service, the financial sector, and the judicial system.

The Challenges of Sustainable Growth

How much of the impressive postcrisis rebound in Russia was due to reforms, prudent macroeconomic management, and structural changes in the economy, and how much reflected the sheer good fortune of high prices in key commodity exports? The structural changes induced by the government's reform efforts have not yet become the main sources of growth. With the economy still heavily skewed toward the commodity sector, Russia's growth prospects are risky. Dependence on just a few exported goods means that growth is hostage to prices determined outside Russia. The sustainability of such growth depends on price shocks that Russia's government has little ability to mitigate. The chances that oil prices will continue to grow from record levels—and that such growth in prices will be prolonged—are slim. Given its dependence on oil prices, the likelihood of Russia's catching up with OECD countries, which would require growth rates in the range of 7–8 percent per year, is low.

This means that the challenge of diversifying Russia's economy—and thus making growth more sustainable—must move to the top of the government's agenda. Russia's economy needs to diversify both by type of business and by sector. These tasks are intertwined, as small and medium-size enterprises—whose contributions to output and job creation are much smaller in Russia than in most transition economies—are likely to emerge in noncommodity sectors. For this to happen, barriers to market entry must be dramatically reduced and the cost of doing business must decline. Competition and a level playing field need to be ensured by the continuation of the government's deregulation effort (cutting unnecessary interference and ensuring the openness of the economy) while enforcing antitrust rules (preventing privately erected barriers from replacing state barriers). Specific actions include the following:

- Reduce the tax burden on businesses, particularly by lowering the single social tax and value-added tax. Making these tax cuts bearable for the budget will require much greater efficiency in public service provision, especially in education, health care, housing and communal services, and social protection.
- Make sweeping changes in technical regulations and their enforcement, particularly in standardization and certification.
- Ensure the rule of law, particularly by reducing the authorities' discretion for interventions in business activities, ensuring an independent

judiciary, and setting transparent boundaries for administrative interference.

- Complete WTO accession (targeted for 2005) to facilitate the integration of Russian businesses with global value chains.

Significant improvement in the system of social protection will also be required to cushion the impact of many of these reforms. Chapters 9–11 assess the likely impact of the most socially sensitive reforms—housing and communal service, education, health care—and make recommendations on how to orient these public services toward the provision of equal opportunity and better target the social protection system to ensure social justice.

Notes

1. The export-oriented natural resource sectors are ferrous and nonferrous metals, fuel and energy, and wood processing. Domestic manufacturing includes electricity, chemical industry, machine building, construction materials, light industry, and food sectors.

2. Official statistics show that the trade sector accounts for an extraordinary 25 percent of Russia's GDP, while the oil and gas sector accounts for only 9 percent.

5
The Effect of Economic Recovery on Labor Earnings

Job creation grew significantly after 1998, especially in sectors that benefited from devaluation. Combined with a decrease in job destruction, the increase has led to growth in employment. Labor market institutions, while rigid in theory, appear to be flexible enough in practice to support job creation and destruction.

Economic growth was also accompanied by an increase in capacity utilization, in terms of both working hours and the number of people employed. The increase in employment was greatest in the market services sector and among smaller establishments.

Better use of labor resources is also revealed by an increase in productivity. This increase was highest in industry, construction, and agriculture. Most of the productivity increase resulted from within-sector improvements. As a result of higher productivity, the average real wage began to increase in 1999. The improved fiscal position helped increase public sector wages, although they continue to be very low in comparison with the private sector. Reduced unemployment, higher wages, and greater earnings contributed significantly to raising household incomes and reducing poverty in the economic recovery period. With higher wages and the increased share of private sector employment, there is evidence of increased returns to education and therefore of wage inequality.

This chapter reviews the utilization of labor resources and the changes in labor productivity and wages between 1997 and 2002. It also addresses the role of public policy and labor market institutions in determining labor outcomes in this period.

Economic Recovery Increased the Utilization of Labor Resources

In 1999 labor utilization grew for the first time since the transition. The fourfold devaluation in 1998 and the subsequent economic growth resulted in increased aggregate demand for domestic goods, which gave firms the opportunity to restructure and increase capacity utilization of both physical assets and labor. The growing demand for labor was

Table 5.1. Employment rose for the first time in 1999, following a decade of decline (million workers)

Measure	*1992*	*1997*	*1998*	*1999*	*2000*	*2001*	*2002*
Employment	71.1	60.0	58.4	63.1	64.5	64.7	65.8
Men	37.1	31.6	30.6	32.8	33.4	33.4	33.6
Women	33.9	28.5	27.9	30.2	31.1	31.2	32.2
Unemployment	3.9	8.1	8.9	9.1	7.0	6.3	6.2
Men	2.0	4.4	4.8	4.8	3.8	3.4	3.3
Women	1.9	3.7	4.1	4.3	3.2	2.9	2.8

Source: Goskomstat (2003c).
Note: Figures cover people 15–72. Beginning in 1999, figures include people self-employed on subsistence land plots.

accommodated by increased labor effort that resulted from declining unemployment and increased hours of work for the employed. By 1999 working hours and employment numbers began to increase after a decade of declining employment. A methodological change that added the self-employed on subsistence land plots to the employment figures as of 1999 accounts for most of the 4.6 million increase in jobs between 1998 and 1999. Under the same new methodology, the economic recovery created 2.7 million jobs, a 4.2 percent increase, between 1999 and 2002 (table 5.1).

Unemployment decreased steadily during the recovery period. The unemployment rate (based on the ILO definition) increased in the aftermath of the 1998 crisis to 13.2 percent. By 2002 it had fallen to 8.6 percent (table 5.2).

In 1999 increased labor demand accelerated job creation and contributed to a net employment increase in establishments with more

Table 5.2. Unemployment peaked in 1998 (percent)

Unemployment rate	*1992*	*1997*	*1998*	*1999*	*2000*	*2001*	*2002*
Total unemployment rate	5.2	11.8	13.2	12.6	9.8	8.9	8.6
Unemployment rate among men	5.2	12.2	13.5	12.8	10.2	9.3	9.0
Unemployment rate among women	5.2	11.5	12.9	12.4	9.4	8.5	8.1

Source: Goskomstat (2003c).
Note: Figures cover people 15–72. Beginning in 1999, figures include those self-employed on subsistence land plots.

Table 5.3. Net employment in manufacturing grew for the first time since transition in 1999

Period	*Job creation*	*Job destruction*	*Job reallocation*	*Net growth in employment*
1985–92	0.87	3.94	4.81	–3.06
1992–96	2.09	11.23	13.32	–9.15
1997–98	2.28	9.37	11.65	–7.10
1998–99	4.07	7.28	11.35	–3.21
1999–2000	6.07	4.66	10.73	1.41

Source: Brown and Earle (2002).
Note: All figures are percentage changes with respect to the previous period.

than 100 workers for the first time since 1992 (table 5.3). At the same time, the reallocation of labor (both within and across sectors) to higher productivity jobs continued, contributing further to labor productivity.

Employment growth was particularly strong in smaller firms and in the market services sector. Employment in smaller firms increased more rapidly than that in establishments with more than 100 workers. The highest net employment growth between 2001 and 2002 occurred in establishments with 31–100 workers. The share of large and medium-size enterprises in total employment diminished from 67.5 percent in 1998 to 62.9 percent in 2002, with the decline especially pronounced in the market services sector (where it fell from 44.7 percent to 37.3 percent) and in industry and construction (where it fell from 74.2 percent to 66.8 percent). While large establishments continue to dominate the employment scene, these figures point to the fact that new private sector firms start as small establishments and are more dynamic in creating jobs.

Employment in market services was particularly strong. The increase of 5.2 percent in nonagricultural employment can be broken down as follows: a 3.4 percent increase in industry and construction; a 3.4 percent increase in the nonmarket services (communal services, science, health care, culture, and education); and a 10.2 percent increase in employment in market services (trade, communications, transport, and finance) (Poletaev 2003).

The shift from public to private sector employment continues. Most of this shift occurred during the large-scale privatization at the beginning of the 1990s. Yet the shift in employment from the public to the private sector was also noticeable in recent years (table 5.4). This movement has been accompanied by a shift from larger to smaller firms, including a shift from the formal sector to the informal one and to self-employment. At the same time, it is widely believed that excessive employment in the public sector still exists (Poletaev 2003; World Bank 2004a).

Table 5.4. The private sector employs a growing share of Russia's workforce

Type of ownership	*1992*	*1997*	*1998*	*1999*	*2000*	*2001*	*2002*
State and municipal	68.9	40.0	38.1	38.2	37.9	37.4	36.9
Private	19.5	39.9	43.2	44.3	46.1	47.6	49.1
Nonprofit	0.8	0.6	0.7	0.8	0.8	0.8	0.8
Mixed Russian	10.5	18.3	16.4	14.9	12.5	11.6	10.7
Foreign, joint Russian and foreign	0.3	1.2	1.6	1.8	2.7	2.6	2.5

Source: Goskomstat (2003c).
Note: All figures are percentages.

The average number of hours worked increased. After a reduction of almost 20 percent between 1988 and 1996, average annual working time per worker increased from 1,690 hours in 1997 to 1,736 hours in 2002 (figure 5.1). The increase was even more dramatic in the industrial sector, where the number of hours rose from 1,548 in 1999 to 1,672 in 2002. The main reason for this increase was a significant decrease in involuntary leaves and in reduced hours of work (about 80 percent of the change), with the remaining reduction (20 percent) attributed to an increase in the length of the regular working day (Poletaev 2003).

Figure 5.1. Average working time has increased since 1997

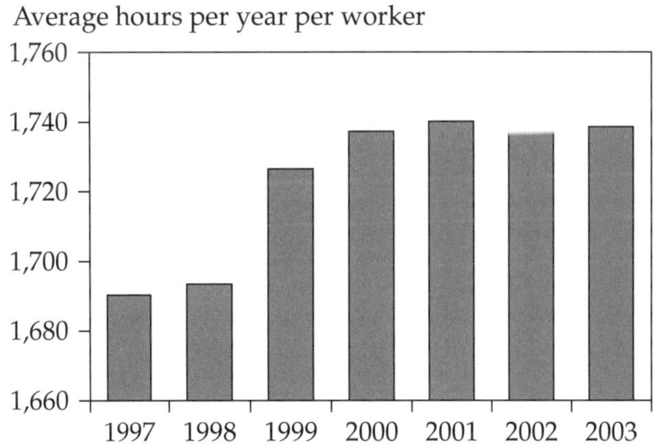

Source: Bank staff calculations based on data from *Labor Force in Russia* 1997–2003 (Goskomstat).
Note: Data are for medium-size and large enterprises.

One indication of the increased labor demand is the growing number of citizens from the CIS recruited to work in Russia. Between 1995 and 1999, the number of CIS citizens officially recruited to work in Russia declined from 134,000 to 95,000. The economic recovery led to a reversal of this trend, and the number of such workers more than doubled, to 193,000, by 2002. According to the Ministry of Interior, the number of illegal labor immigrants (mostly from the CIS) has also increased, reaching 4 million in recent years.

A Significant Increase in Labor Productivity Accompanied the Economic Recovery after 1999

The economic recovery was accompanied by a significant increase in labor productivity, with aggregate nonagricultural productivity growing at an average annual rate of 4.1 percent between 1999 and 2002. This sector includes industry, construction, and market services (such as trade, communications, transport, finance) as well as nonmarket services (such as education, health care, culture, and science). Between 1999 and 2002, the average annual growth rate of the nonagricultural sectors was 6.2 percent a year, about 2 percent of which is attributed to increased working time and about 4.1 percent of which is attributed to increased labor productivity (table 5.5). In other words, two-thirds of the increase in nonagricultural output was due to increased productivity, while one-third resulted from increased working time. Cumulatively, productivity increased 17 percent during the period.

Labor productivity increased significantly with the economic recovery. The largest increase in labor productivity was in industry and construction, followed by agriculture and market services. While overall

Table 5.5. Two-thirds of the increase in nonagricultural output between 1999 and 2002 was due to increased productivity

Period	*Employment*	*Annual hours*	*Working time*	*Output*	*Labor productivity*
1999	0.7	2.2	2.9	5.8	2.8
2000	0.9	0.7	1.6	9.9	8.1
2001	1.4	0.2	1.6	4.7	3.0
2002	2.1	–0.2	2.0	4.5	2.5
1999–2002	1.3	0.7	2.0	6.2	4.1

Source: Poletaev (2003).
Note: Figures represent annual percentage rate growth. Figures may not add up due to rounding errors.

Figure 5.2. Labor productivity began to increase in 1999, after declining during the transitional recession

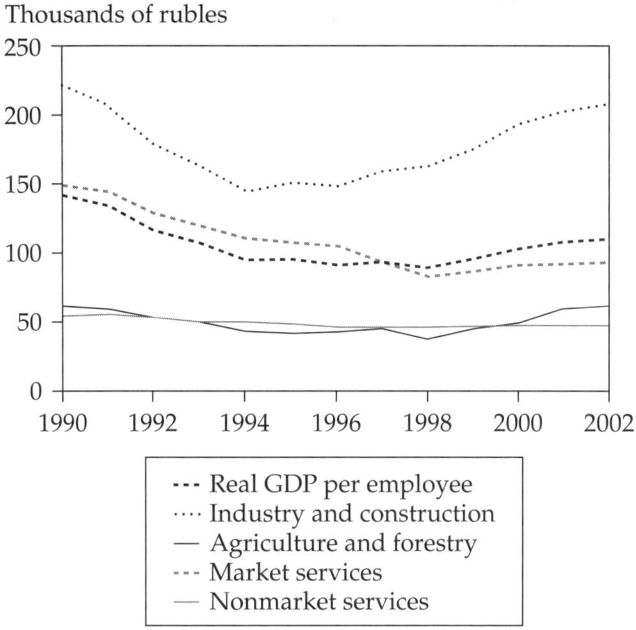

Source: World Bank (2004a).
Note: Figures are in adjusted rubles in 2000 prices.

productivity experienced a dramatic decline during the transitional recession, labor productivity has risen significantly since 1998 (figure 5.2). Between 1998 and 2002, labor productivity rose 67.2 percent in agriculture, 24.7 percent in industry and construction, 12.8 percent in market services, and 4.2 percent in nonmarket services. Productivity is highest in industry and construction and lowest in nonmarket (essentially public) services, where labor productivity is even lower than in agriculture.

Labor Earnings Have Risen

Real wages increased significantly in recent years, exceeding the pre-crisis level. The average real wage rate has been on the rise since 1999 (table 5.6). During the 1990s, the real wage rate declined, reaching its lowest point in 1999. Between 1999 and 2002, the real wage rate rose by almost two-thirds, exceeding its pre–financial crisis level. These trends are confirmed by the Russia Longitudinal Monitoring Survey (UNC, various

Table 5.6. Average real monthly wages began to rise in 1999

Year	*Average real monthly wage (1991 rubles)*
1997	291
1998	253
1999	197
2000	238
2001	286
2002	320

Source: Goskomstat (2003c).

years), which indicates that the real hourly wage rate increased by about two-thirds between 1998 and 2001.

As a result of growing employment and rising wages, real household disposable income grew faster than GDP. This was possible only at the expense of corporate profits, which started to fall as a share of GDP in 2000 (figure 5.3). To understand how this came about, it is helpful to look at the relative dynamics of the main labor-related indexes in Russia's industry.

Figure 5.3. GDP, wage, profit, and household income dynamics, 1996–2002

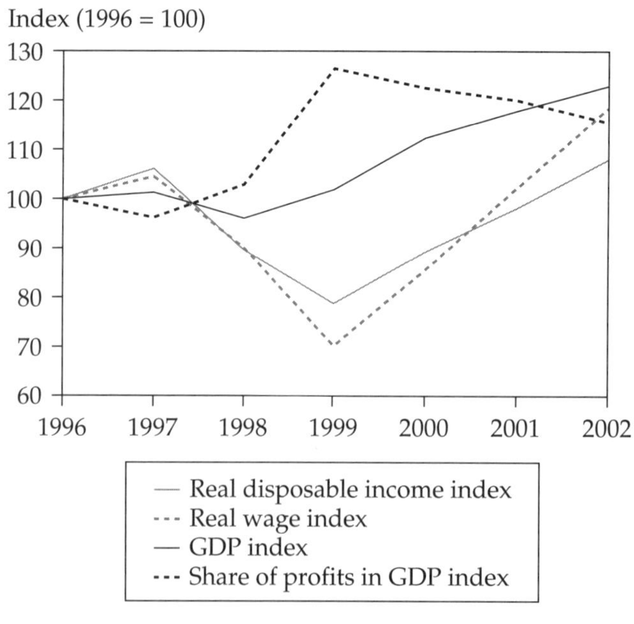

Source: Russian Statistical Yearbook 1997–2003 (Goskomstat).

Labor productivity rose markedly after the crisis, allowing industrial output to grow even faster than aggregate employment. In the aftermath of the 1998 crisis, the decline in real wages proved more important in helping enterprises survive (and hence keeping their workforces) than did the productivity boost that resulted from enterprises' adjusting employment to contracting output. Industrial salaries had fallen far more than either output or employment (figure 5.4), increasing the profitability of an hour worked in industry. The record low utilization rates of both labor and fixed assets in the precrisis period (capacity utilization was a mere 39 percent in 1998) made it possible to dramatically increase industrial output without major investment or restructuring.

Wage adjustment served as a substitute for restructuring. Only by the end of 2002 did the cumulative growth in industrial wages level off to the level of cumulative growth in industrial labor productivity. In addition to demonstrating the extraordinary tolerance of Russia's labor, this

Figure 5.4. After the 1998 crisis, a sharp decline in real wages allowed industrial enterprises to survive and retain more of their employees

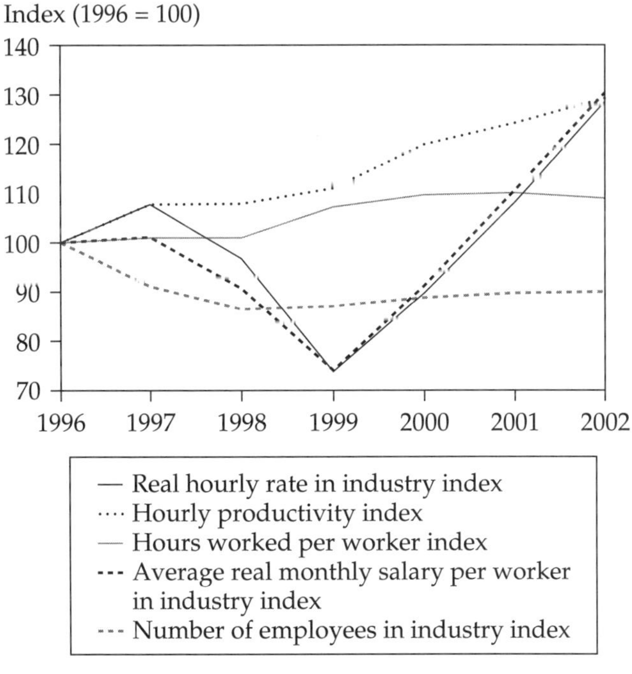

Source: Russian Statistical Yearbook 1996–2002 (Goskomstat).

phenomenon explains why real wages in Russia grew faster than either labor productivity or GDP over the past few years: wages had fallen so much after the crisis that there was a long way to go in order to "catch up." It follows that the period in which wages and real income growth could easily exceed GDP and productivity growth is over. In other words, from now on a given rate of GDP growth will result in fewer tangible benefits for wage-earning households than it did in 2000–2002.

There is significant variation in wage dynamics across sectors. Although the trend is similar for all sectors, some sectors (credit and finance, geology and geodesy, communications) have been leading in terms of real wage increase, while others (agriculture) have been lagging. Sectors such as fuel, nonferrous metallurgy, and credit and finance pay the highest wages and have enjoyed the most rapid wage increases (figure A5.1).

Figure 5.5. Wage arrears have plummeted since 1999

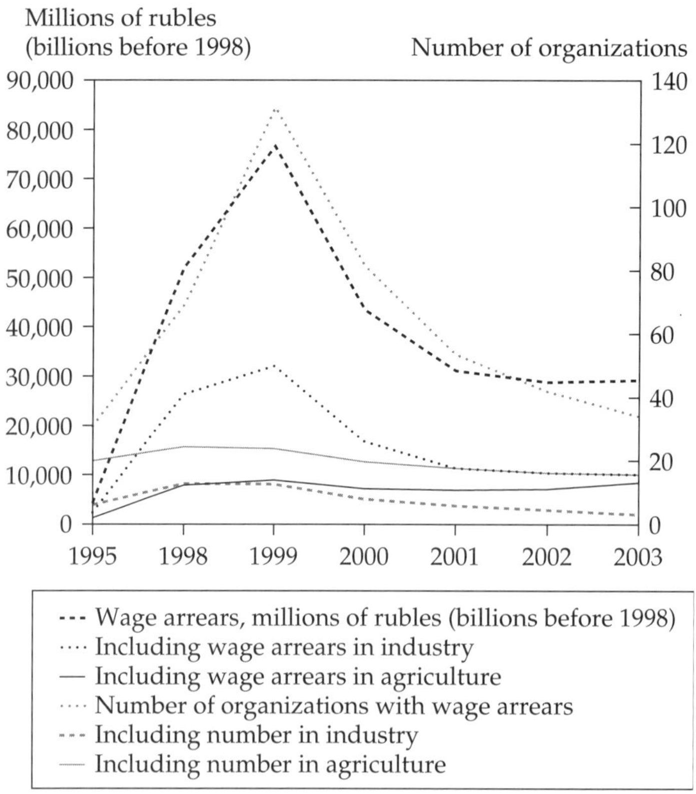

Source: Goskomstat (2003a).

The negative impact of wage arrears on household welfare diminished dramatically with the economic recovery. Since 1999 there has been a significant decline in both the volume of wage arrears and the number of organizations with arrears (figure 5.5). Wage arrears are now observed only in some regions and among some groups (rural areas, military people, agriculture).

The gap between skilled and unskilled labor, which had been decreasing before 1998, increased in 2000 and 2001 (figure 5.6). The wage differential (or premium) between nonmanual and manual workers seems to have stabilized at 65 percent since 1999, however (Sabirianova 2003).

Wages became decompressed in the 1990s. The returns to one year of schooling increased from 8 percent in 1996 to 11 percent in 2000. As a result, inequality in labor earnings increased. The estimated return to one year of higher education was 12.5 percent in 2000, up from 6 percent in 1994 (Sabirianova 2003). The Gini coefficient for various definitions of wages (based on the Russia Longitudinal Monitoring Survey) increased 0.2–0.3 percentage point between 1998 and 2000, stabilizing in 2001 (Lukyanova 2003). The rise is believed to reflect increased returns to skills in the era of the knowledge-based economy. However, inequality in household incomes in the same surveys has not increased, possibly because

Figure 5.6. The gap between skilled and unskilled labor increased in 2000 and 2001

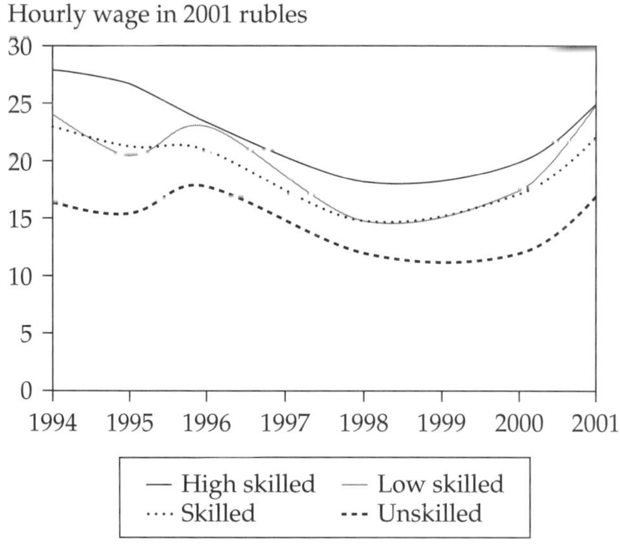

Source: Grishina (2003).

wage income, as reported by the survey, contributed only about half of total household income in 1998, 2000, and 2001. Indeed, the growth in real income between 2000 and 2001 for various percentiles of households did not increase income inequality (UNC, various years; see also the discussion of inequality in chapter 2). Wages are also subject to a gender gap (box 5.1).

Box 5.1. A growing gender gap in wages

The gender wage differential increased from 29 percent in 1995 to 37 percent in 2000. Differences in endowments and in occupational, industrial, and sectoral affiliation, including segregation to low-paid industries, account for 56–61 percent of the gross differential (Fakhrutdinova 2002) (box table). The higher educational endowment of women counterbalances the increase in the gender gap. Women's advantages in human capital, however, are overwhelmed by the disadvantages caused by gender-specific occupational and industrial employment segregation into low-paid sectors. Different rewards for the same endowments appear to be responsible for 39–44 percent of the wage gap in 1995–2000, which signals the continuation of gender discrimination in wages.

Box table. Gender wage gap decomposition

	1995		*1996*		*1998*		*2000*	
Measure	*Value*	*Percent*	*Value*	*Percent*	*Value*	*Percent*	*Value*	*Percent*
Total differential in log	0.2558	100	0.2713	100	0.2435	100	0.3167	100
as ln gap percent	29		31		27		37	
Of which difference in endowments:	0.1434	56.05	0.1544	56.91	0.1367	56.15	0.1924	60.76
Education	–0.0191	–7.47	–0.0307	–11.32	–0.0236	–9.69	–0.0507	–16.01
Occupation	0.0803	31.39	0.0784	28.90	0.0718	29.49	0.1183	37.36
Feminization of industry	0.0815	31.86	0.1021	37.63	0.0801	32.90	0.1033	32.62
Megapolitan areas	–0.0102	–3.99	–0.0008	–0.29	–0.0004	–0.16	–0.0016	–0.51
State enterprises	0.0109	4.26	0.0054	1.99	0.0088	3.61	0.0231	7.29
Of which difference in returns	0.1124	43.95	0.1169	43.09	0.1068	43.85	0.1243	39.24

Source: Fakhrutdinova (2002).

Fiscal Stabilization Has Helped Raise Public Sector Wages

The public sector is a major employer. Public sector employment attracts a significant share of labor and provides an important benchmark for wage setting. Moreover, the mechanism of wage setting in the public sector is still used as a model by many private employers (Kapeljushnikov 2003). Total employment in public services (broadly defined) amounts to 37 percent of the Russian workforce.

Public sector wages are fairly compressed and many jobs are low paid. The incidence of low pay was about 44 percent among public service workers in 2000, with 11.5 percent very low paid (table 5.7). In comparison, about 25 percent of private sector employees were low paid, with 8 percent very low paid. There were several increases in public sector salaries between 2000 and 2002 (figure 5.7). The wage of a particular public sector employee in a given grade is linked through a "grade coefficient" to the "minimum wage tariff," which is the base wage rate for the lowest grade. By 2002 public sector wages exceeded their value in 1997 in real terms.

Social assistance in the form of monthly benefits barely exists in Russia, and there is practically no unemployment assistance provision. This is a major difference between Russia and Eastern Europe, where social assistance is common and the unemployed receive unemployment assistance of infinite duration and nonnegligible magnitude. While the Russ-

Table 5.7. The percentage of low-paying jobs is higher in the public sector

Type of enterprise	*Percent of all employees*	*Percent who are low paid*[a]	*Percent who are very low paid*[b]	*Percent with no pay*
Wholly government owned	48.5	39.9	14.5	18.4
Public service workers	13.3	43.9	11.4	15.8
Private/joint ventures	36.2	24.6	8.2	14.3
Foreign owned	4.1	15.0	3.5	7.3
Do not know/ will not say	15.3	29.4	10.5	18.8
All employees	100.0	32.6	11.6	17.0

Source: Klugman, Micklewright, and Redmond (2002).

a. Earnings of less than two-thirds of median earnings.

b. Earnings of less than one-third of median earnings.

Figure 5.7. Both the minimum wage tariff and the minimum wage have increased since 2000

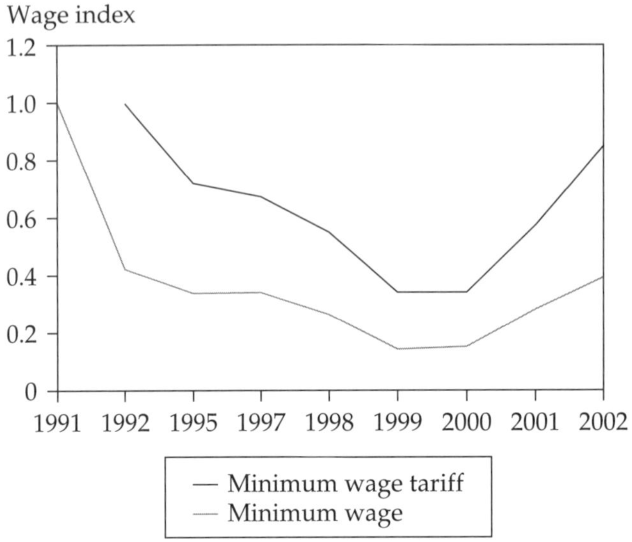

Source: Goskomstat (2003c).

ian system provides almost no distortions to the incentives to work, it does not prevent the unemployed from falling into poverty. The unemployment benefit system in Russia also fails to provide unemployment insurance for either skilled or unskilled workers. Although the formal replacement ratios are comparable to those in developed countries, high inflation at the beginning of the 1990s, payment arrears afterward, and the upper cap of the regional average wage level are responsible for the low effective replacement ratios of unemployment benefits. Moreover, there is a very loose connection between the labor market history of the unemployed and the benefit. The disincentives to search for a job are probably negligible in this case, but they come at the expense of the complete failure of the insurance function.

The New Labor Code Has Had Only a Limited Effect on Increasing the Flexibility of the Job Market

The Russian Labor Code remains restrictive relative to codes in OECD countries. Formally, the Code puts strong restrictions on an employer's adjustment to technological changes and economic shocks through labor shedding or wage reduction, significantly increasing the cost of doing business. If formal rules had been respected, the response to high separation and hiring costs would have been a decrease in the demand for labor and a decline in turnover.

The Russian labor market, which is formally rather restrictive, is in fact fairly flexible. Indeed, many restrictive norms of the Labor Code, including the new Code, are not enforced, which allows labor market participants to overcome the restrictions. Informal employment without contract specification and forced "voluntary" resignations are among the most frequently cited ways of overcoming the high turnover costs stipulated in the Labor Code. Formal contracts are often violated without penalty.

Institutional restrictions nevertheless affect the formal labor market. Gimpelson (2004) argues that the observed decrease in employment in large and medium-size enterprises in recent years is due to the high turnover costs for enterprises in the formal sector. It is the informal sector that has increased employment.

The new Labor Code introduced some changes aimed at lowering turnover costs. In particular, trade unions no longer have the right to veto separation decisions. The financial costs of separation remain high, however. The new Code specifies fixed-term contracts, which are expected to replace life-long contracts and reduce labor turnover costs, but such contracts can be entered into only under limited circumstances. The Code preserves significant obligations for the employer with respect to tenured employees (those with infinite contracts).

Consequently, few managers believe that the new Code makes labor relations more flexible. Gimpelson, Kapeljushnikov, and Khakhulina (2003) interviewed managers of about 300 enterprises. They found that only 26 percent believe that the new Code introduces more flexible labor relations, 36 percent believe that it introduces additional problems for managers, and the rest do not see any changes. The new Labor Code is regarded as more flexible mainly by new small private enterprises in good financial positions located in small towns. As far as enforcement is concerned, only 24 percent of managers expect the Code to stimulate better compliance, about 70 percent do not expect any changes, and 5 percent expect even worse compliance. On the positive side, almost one-third of managers indicate that it is now easier to use fixed-term contracts, and more than 18 percent find it easier to fire employees. More than half of the managers surveyed do not believe the Code has led to any improvements, however.

Collective bargaining institutions remain weak. Trade unions do not reflect the interests of employees, and employers' organizations lack support from employers. Better representation of workers in the bargaining process would increase labor's share of value added, increase the amount of on-the-job training, and improve working conditions.

Minimum wage setting does not reduce poverty. Wage regulation in Russia is undertaken mainly by setting a minimum wage level and a minimum wage tariff, which is the base rate for the lowest grade in the public sector. The minimum wage is not binding. The ratio of the minimum wage to the average wage fell from 23 percent in 1990 to 5 percent in 1999. During the recent period of economic growth, both the minimum wage and the minimum tariff increased in real terms, exceeding the precrisis level by 2002 (see figure 5.7).

Wage regulation instruments play a role in economywide wage-setting. Kapeljushnikov (2003) reports that more than half of the enterprises in his sample use the minimum wage, the minimum tariff, or the regional subsistence level in setting the lowest wages. A large share of enterprises use either the old Soviet or the current Russian tariff system to establish their compensation schemes for both blue-collar (45 percent of respondents) and white-collar (34 percent of respondents) staff.

Economic recovery has increased labor demand, leading to increased employment, higher productivity, and higher wages. Higher earnings have raised living standards and reduced poverty. The sustainability of wage increases will depend on the extent of future increases in productivity. The poverty reduction trends are addressed in the next chapter.

6
Poverty, Growth, and Inequality in Russia

Poverty reduction depends on two factors: economic growth and the extent to which the benefits of growth accrue to the poor. Economic growth has been robust, and labor earnings have risen significantly in the postcrisis period. The rapid and solid recovery in economic output and labor earnings contributed significantly to improved living standards and a broad-based reduction in poverty since 1999. In particular, higher wages in the private and public sectors, increased aggregate and private sector employment, reduced arrears in the payment of wages and social benefits, higher pensions, and increased public spending on the social sector contributed to broad-based improvements in living standards.

This chapter documents trends in living standards between 1997 and 2002, as measured by per capita consumption; analyzes the increase in poverty resulting from the Russian crisis; and examines the subsequent steep reduction in poverty that accompanied economic recovery. It addresses the extent to which poverty reduction can be attributed to growth and examines the potentially undermining effect of increasing inequality on the impact of growth on poverty. It closes by assessing the scope for further reductions in poverty given various scenarios for growth in consumption.

Poverty Increased and Then Declined between 1997 and 2002

Mirroring changes in output and labor earnings, per capita consumption fell sharply between 1997 and 1999, followed by a sharp increase between 1999 and 2002.[1] Real per capita consumption lost more than a quarter of its value in two years (1997–99) as a result of the financial crisis (table 6.1). This depression was followed by an impressive rebound. Consumption per capita was 5 percent greater in 2002 than in 1997.

The pattern of food and nonfood consumption confirms the aggregate trends in living standards. Because food is a necessity, households tend to adjust to adversity by cutting down more on nonfood items than on food items; when conditions improve, they increase their spending on nonfood items. Food consumption did not fall as sharply as nonfood consumption

Table 6.1. Consumption of nonfood items fluctuated more than consumption of food

Year	*Food*	*Nonfood*	*Total consumption*	*Share of food in consumption (percent)*
Rubles per person per month				
1997	1,107	909	2,016	54.9
1998	1,111	716	1,827	60.8
1999	893	578	1,471	60.7
2000	916	673	1,588	57.6
2001	1,031	847	1,877	54.9
2002	1,084	1,036	2,120	51.1
Indexes of per capita real consumption (1997 = 100)				
1997	100	100	100	100.0
1998	100	79	91	110.7
1999	81	64	73	110.6
2000	83	74	79	105.0
2001	93	93	93	100.0
2002	98	114	105	93.1
Growth rates of per capita real consumption (percent)				
1998	0.3	–21.2	– 9.4	n.a.
1999	–19.6	–19.3	–19.5	n.a.
2000	2.5	16.5	8.0	n.a.
2001	12.6	25.8	18.2	n.a.
2002	5.1	22.4	12.9	n.a.

Source: Bank staff calculations based on data from Household Budget Survey 1997–2002 (Goskomstat).
n.a. Not applicable.

between 1997 and 1999. In the postcrisis period, nonfood consumption increased more sharply than per capita food expenditure.

Growth Caused Poverty to Fall

The crisis had a severe impact on the poor. During 1997–98 the consumption of the poorest segment of the population experienced a far more significant drop than that of the population as a whole (top panel of figure 6.1). Consumption declined for every percentile between 1997 and 1998. The poor, like the rest of the population, became poorer. However, between 1998 and 1999, while the entire population again suffered a decline in consumption, the decline this time was much steeper for the richest segment of the population (bottom panel of figure 6.1).

Figure 6.1. The crisis had a severe impact on the poor

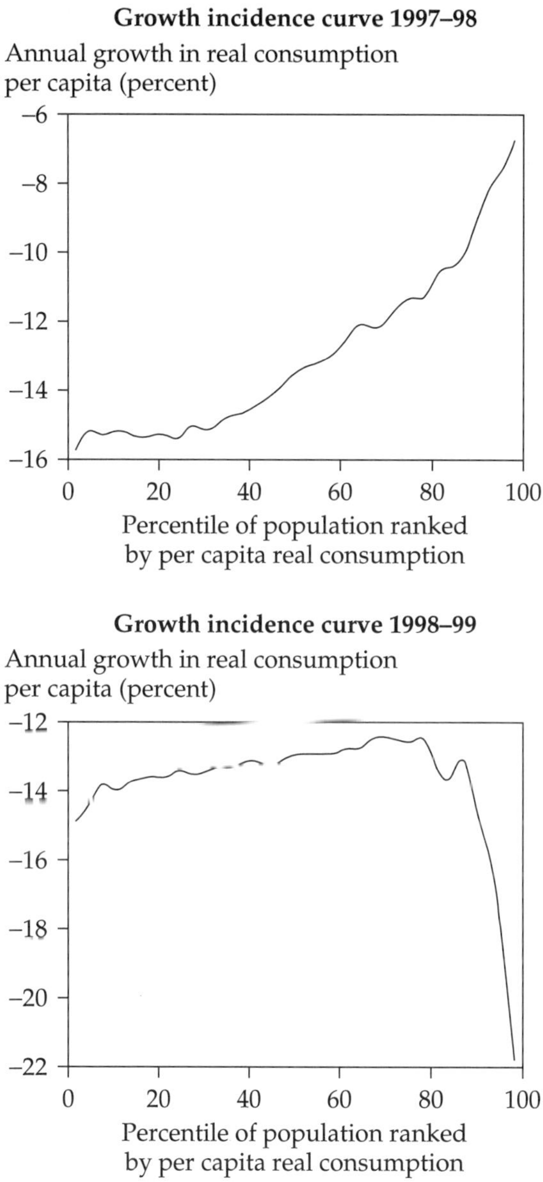

Source: Bank staff calculations based on data from Household Budget Survey 1997–1999 (Goskomstat).

Figure 6.2. Economic growth in 1999–2002 was pro-poor

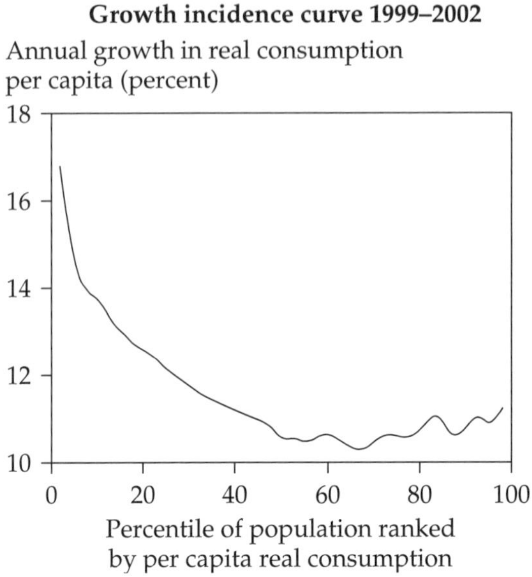

Source: Bank staff calculations based on data from Household Budget Survey 1999–2000 (Goskomstat).

Economic growth between 1999 and 2002 was pro-poor, with consumption of the poor growing more rapidly than that of the better off (figure 6.2).

All poverty measures show that poverty increased substantially from 1997 to 1999 (table 6.2). As a result of the decline in consumption by more than a quarter during this period, various measures of poverty increased significantly. The fraction of the population in poverty increased from 24.1 percent to 41.5 percent, throwing about 25 million people into poverty in two years. The severity index—which is more sensitive to the ultra poor—more than doubled, indicating that the ultra poor were hurt even more severely than the average poor during this period.

Poverty was cut in half during 1999–2002. The substantial increase in poverty during 1997–99 was more than fully offset by the significant reduction in poverty during 1999–2002. As household consumption recovered strongly, all poverty measures declined. The fraction of people with consumption below the recommended poverty line fell from 41.5 percent in 1999 to 19.6 percent in 2002. This decline meant that 32 million people were pulled out of poverty during this period. The poverty gap index was reduced at an even greater rate than the headcount index, and

Table 6.2. Poverty soared between 1997 and 1999 but has since declined to below precrisis levels

Year	*Headcount*	*Gap*	*Severity*
1997	24.1	7.0	3.0
1998	31.4	9.7	4.3
1999	41.5	14.1	6.6
2000	35.9	11.3	5.1
2001	26.2	7.5	3.2
2002	19.6	5.1	2.0

Source: Bank staff calculations based on data from Household Budget Survey 1997–2002 (Goskomstat).

the severity of poverty index was reduced at a still greater rate (figure 6.3). This indicates that the ultra poor benefited even more than the average poor during the recovery period. By the end of 2002, all measures of poverty were lower than they had been in 1997.

Figure 6.3. All indexes of poverty rose until 1999 and declined thereafter

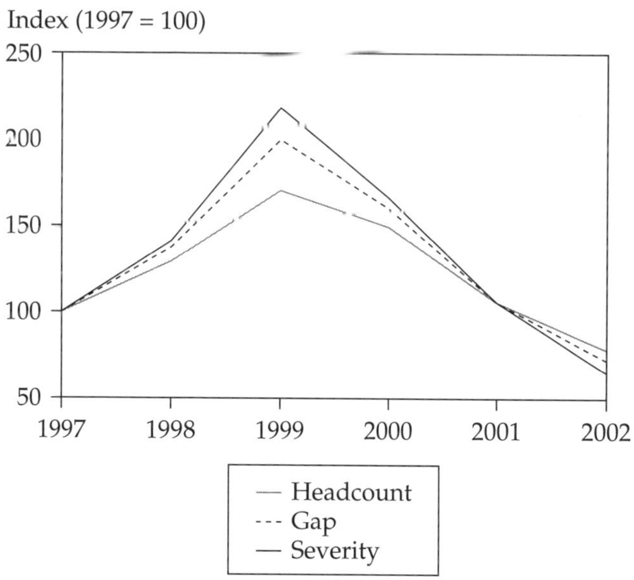

Source: Bank staff calculations based on data from Household Budget Survey 1997–2002 (Goskomstat).

GDP fell to its lowest level in 1998. GDP grew in 1999, but consumption continued to decline, reaching its lowest point, and poverty peaked. The financial crisis hit the economy in the second half of 1998, but households felt the full force of its impact mostly in 1999 (see table 5.6 in the previous chapter, which shows that the average wage rate reached its lowest level in 1999). The short lag between the low point for GDP (1998) and the low point for household consumption (1999) is plausible, as households were probably able to postpone the effects of the crisis for a short time.

Although the levels differ, the trends in poverty shown above are similar to those in the official poverty estimates, as well as those in poverty estimates using international poverty lines (table 6.3). All series show a significant increase in poverty between 1997 and 1999 and a significant reduction in poverty in the subsequent period. For example, using the $2 a day international poverty line, 12.3 million people were thrown into poverty in Russia between 1997 and 1999, and 15 million people escaped poverty in 1999–2002. The increase and subsequent decline in poverty are

Table 6.3. Various measures of poverty show the same trend: Steadily rising poverty followed by a steady decline during the recovery

Measure	*1997*	*1998*	*1999*	*2000*	*2001*	*2002*
Headcount index (percent of population)						
Official poverty estimates	20.7	23.3	28.3	28.9[a]	27.3	24.2
Recommended methodology	24.1	31.4	41.5	35.9	26.2	19.6
$1.075 a day poverty line	1.0	1.6	2.7	1.8	1.0	0.5
$2.15 a day poverty line	8.0	11.6	16.4	12.8	8.6	6.3
$4.30 a day poverty line	34.4	42.9	51.9	46.5	38.4	33.0
Number of poor people (millions)						
Official poverty estimates	30.3	34.0	41.2	41.9[a]	39.4	35.8
Recommended methodology	35.3	45.8	60.5	52.1	37.8	28.1
$1.075 a day poverty line	1.5	2.4	4.0	2.6	1.5	0.7
$2.15 a day poverty line	11.6	16.9	23.9	18.5	12.4	9.0
$4.30 a day poverty line	50.4	62.6	75.6	67.4	55.5	47.3

Source: Bank staff calculations based on data from Household Budget Survey 1997–2002 (Goskomstat).

Note: The 2000 purchasing power parity conversion factors were used for the international poverty lines.

a. The official poverty line was changed as of 2000; hence data before and after that date are not comparable.

sharper using the recommended poverty line of $3.54 in purchasing power parity (see chapter 1).

Inequality Has Declined since 1999

Aggregate changes in poverty are driven by changes in average consumption as well as changes in the inequality in consumption. Thus it is important to analyze trends in inequality.

Although the Gini index showed little change, growth was pro-poor between 1999 and 2002 because of the increasing share of welfare of the bottom quintile. Inequality increased in the aftermath of the 1998 crisis. Since then, it has fallen more or less monotonically. During the economic crisis, employment and particularly real wages declined. These changes

Table 6.4. Inequality has declined since 1999

Year	*Gini index*	*Quintile 1*	*Quintile 2*	*Quintile 3*	*Quintile 4*	*Quintile 5*
Per capita nominal consumption						
1997	37.0	6.5	11.3	16.0	22.4	43.8
1998	39.2	6.1	10.7	15.4	22.1	45.8
1999	37.3	6.3	11.1	15.9	22.8	43.9
2000	36.3	6.6	11.4	16.1	22.9	43.0
2001	36.8	6.6	11.3	15.9	22.6	43.7
2002	36.8	6.7	11.3	15.7	22.4	43.9
Per capita real consumption						
1997	36.1	6.7	11.6	16.2	22.6	43.0
1998	37.5	6.4	11.1	15.8	22.4	44.2
1999	35.5	6.6	11.5	16.4	23.2	42.2
2000	34.2	7.0	11.9	16.6	23.2	41.3
2001	34.5	7.0	11.8	16.4	23.0	41.7
2002	34.4	7.2	11.8	16.3	23.0	41.8
Per capita welfare						
1997	34.6	7.0	11.9	16.6	22.7	41.8
1998	36.1	6.7	11.5	16.1	22.6	43.0
1999	34.0	6.9	11.9	16.8	23.4	41.0
2000	33.0	7.2	12.2	16.9	23.4	40.3
2001	33.1	7.3	12.2	16.8	23.2	40.5
2002	33.0	7.5	12.2	16.6	23.1	40.6

Source: Bank staff calculations based on data from Household Budget Survey 1997–2002 (Goskomstat).

Note: Real consumption is nominal consumption adjusted for regional price differences. The "welfare" variable is real consumption divided by the poverty line. Quintile figures are percentages of the total.

Figure 6.4. Inequality in consumption peaked in 1998

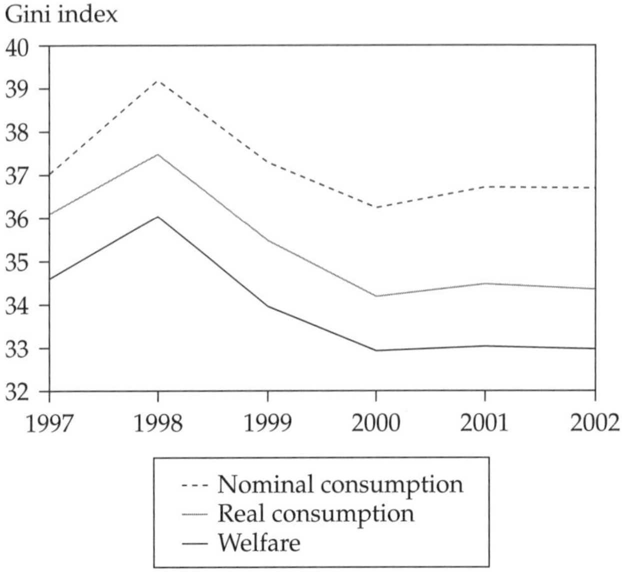

Source: Bank staff calculations based on data from Household Budget Survey 1997–2002 (Goskomstat).

affected the poor much more than the nonpoor, because the income of the former group depends more heavily on wage employment. Inequality began to decline in 1999. In 2000 there was a sharp decline in the unemployment rate and a very sharp increase in the real wage, which led to a further decline in inequality. Between 2000 and 2002, the decline in unemployment slowed, but the real wage continued to increase rapidly. The Gini index remained more or less constant during this period, but the welfare share of the bottom quintile continued to increase (figures 6.4 and 6.5). The share of the bottom quintile in total real consumption increased from 6.4 percent in 1998 to 7.2 percent in 2002 (table 6.4). These trends suggest that changes in the unemployment rate and in real wages are important determinants of changes in inequality.

Changes in Poverty Can Be Decomposed into Growth and Redistribution Components

The poverty level depends on two factors: the average level of consumption or welfare and the extent of inequality in the consumption distribution. An increase in average consumption reduces poverty; an increase in inequality increases poverty. The total change in poverty can be decom-

Figure 6.5. Consumption share of the bottom quintile has increased steadily since 1998

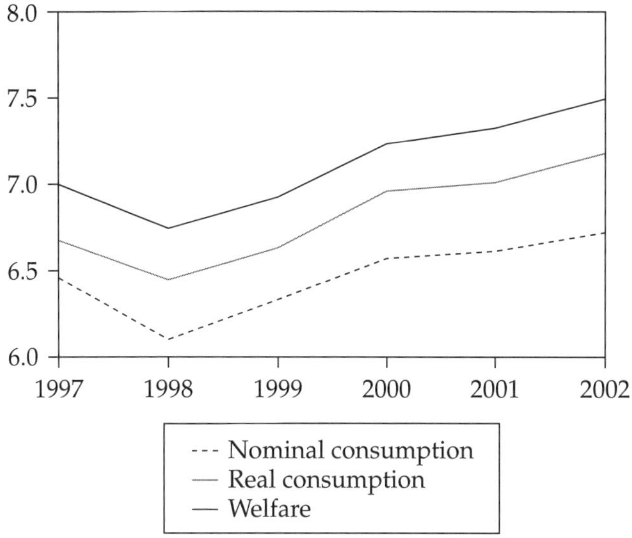

Source: Bank staff calculations based on data from Household Budget Survey 1997–2002 (Goskomstat).

posed as the sum of the growth and inequality components. The growth component measures the change in poverty assuming no change in the inequality. The inequality or redistribution component measures the change in poverty that is due strictly to the change in inequality, assuming that the average consumption of the whole distribution has not changed. The total change in poverty between any two years is the sum of these two components.

The crisis in Russia hurt the poor proportionately more than the non-poor. The percentage of poor people in Russia increased by 30.1 percent in 1998, of which the decrease in average expenditure accounted for 21.5 percent and the change in inequality contributed 8.7 percent (table 6.5). If inequality had not changed, the incidence of poverty would have increased only 21.5 percent. A similar conclusion emerges when other poverty measures (gap, severity) are considered.

The real wage declined in 1999, but the increase in employment offset its adverse effect. The incidence of poverty increased 32.2 percent in 1999. If inequality had not changed, the incidence of poverty would have increased 38.9 percent. This means that the consumption of the poor grew

Table 6.5. Changes in poverty can be decomposed into growth and redistribution components

Year	*Growth component*	*Redistribution component*	*Total percent poverty change*
Headcount ratio			
1998	21.5	8.7	30.1
1999	38.9	–6.7	32.2
2000	–11.3	–2.2	–13.4
2001	–27.3	0.1	–27.1
2002	–24.4	–0.7	–25.1
1997–2002	–11.8	–7.0	–18.7
Poverty gap ratio			
1998	27.2	10.6	37.8
1999	53.2	–8.2	45.1
2000	–14.0	–5.7	–19.7
2001	–32.4	–1.4	–33.8
2002	–27.3	–4.4	–31.6
1997–2002	–13.1	–14.3	–27.4
Severity of poverty			
1998	30.6	11.7	42.4
1999	62.8	–8.5	54.3
2000	–15.6	–8.2	–23.8
2001	–35.2	–2.4	–37.6
2002	–28.7	–7.7	–36.5
1997–2002	–13.7	–19.9	–33.6

Source: Bank staff calculations based on data from Household Budget Survey 1997–2002 (Goskomstat).
Note: Numbers may not add up due to rounding errors.

disproportionately more than that of the nonpoor, contributing to a reduction in poverty of 6.7 percent. The poor particularly benefited from growth during this period because of a large decline in the unemployment rate.

Between 1997 and 2002, the poverty headcount ratio declined 18.7 percent, of which growth contributed to a reduction of 11.8 percent and lower inequality contributed to a reduction of 7.0 percent. This means that growth favored the poor during this period.

The Poverty Profile Is Changing

The rural-urban gap narrowed until 1999, when it began to widen. Per capita welfare in 1997 in urban areas was about 28 percent higher than in rural areas (table 6.6). The gap between rural and urban areas increased

Table 6.6. The gap in welfare between urban and rural areas has increased since 1997

	Urban		*Rural*	
Year	*Per capita welfare*	*Growth rate (percent)*	*Per capita welfare*	*Growth rate (percent)*
1997	199	n.a.	156	n.a.
1998	180	– 9.4	141	– 9.4
1999	145	–19.6	117	–17.0
2000	158	8.7	123	5.3
2001	189	19.5	141	14.4
2002	215	13.9	155	9.8

Source: Bank staff calculations based on data from Household Budget Survey 1997–2002 (Goskomstat).
n.a. Not applicable.

Table 6.7. Inequality between urban and rural areas declined during the crisis years but increased during the recovery period

		Within-group inequality			
Year	*Total inequality*	*Urban*	*Rural*	*Between-group inequality*	*Share of between-group inequality in total (percent)*
1997	20.5	19.3	21.9	0.6	2.8
1998	22.1	21.5	21.6	0.6	2.6
1999	19.9	20.0	17.8	0.4	2.2
2000	18.5	18.3	16.9	0.6	3.2
2001	18.6	18.3	16.3	0.8	4.3
2002	18.3	17.8	15.9	1.0	5.5

Source: Bank staff calculations based on data from Household Budget Survey 1997–2002 (Goskomstat).
Note: Except where indicated otherwise, figures are Theil index values.

between 1997 and 2002: by 2002 per capita welfare in urban areas was about 38 percent higher than in rural areas.

Inequality between two groups can be decomposed into within-group inequality and between-group inequality using a standard inequality index called the Theil index. Use of the Theil index shows that the share of between-group inequality in total inequality decreased from 2.8 percent in 1997 to 2.2 percent in 1999 before increasing to 5.5 percent in 2001 (table 6.7). This is an expected phenomenon. When an economy is on the downturn, people in urban areas suffer more severely than those in rural

Table 6.8. Poverty has fallen among all demographic groups since the crisis, but the incidence of child poverty remains high

	Active population			*Children*		
Year	*Men*	*Women*	*Elderly*	*0–6*	*7–15*	*All*
Poverty incidence (percent)						
1997	23.9	22.8	17.9	33.6	29.9	24.2
1998	31.5	29.6	25.4	41.0	38.4	31.4
1999	40.6	39.8	37.7	49.8	48.8	41.6
2000	35.0	33.9	32.5	42.6	43.9	35.9
2001	25.6	24.8	21.5	32.5	33.7	26.2
2002	19.4	18.3	15.1	26.2	26.8	19.6
Percentage change in poverty						
1998	31.9	29.7	42.0	22.1	28.3	29.9
1999	29.0	34.3	48.5	21.6	27.2	32.3
2000	–13.8	–14.7	–13.7	–14.4	–10.0	–13.6
2001	–26.8	–26.9	–33.8	–23.8	–23.2	–27.1
2002	–24.5	–26.3	–29.8	–19.4	–20.4	–25.1
1997–2002	– 4.1	– 4.3	– 3.3	– 4.8	– 2.1	– 4.1

Source: Bank staff calculations based on data from Household Budget Survey 1997–2002 (Goskomstat).

areas, but during the upturn people living in urban areas benefit more than those in rural areas.

Poverty among children is high and poverty among the elderly low. The standard procedure is to assume that if a household is identified as poor, everyone living in that household is poor. This is not necessarily the case in practice, but it is justified by the lack of data on the distribution of resources within a household. Using this assumption, the incidence of poverty among different types of individuals can be measured (table 6.8). The incidence of poverty among older children was the highest of any demographic group by 2002, and it declined less than any other group between 1997 and 2002. Women and younger children benefited most from the recovery, with the incidence of poverty falling 4.3 percent among women and 4.8 percent among younger children—more than the average decline of 4.1 percent for the population as a whole.

Halving Poverty Is an Attainable but Difficult Goal

Cutting poverty in half between 2002 and 2007 is a potentially attainable but very challenging goal. Meeting the goal requires creating a diversified economic base and implementing deep structural reforms. WTO accession will generate medium-term gains for welfare and poverty reduction, but the implementation of a broad array of reforms is needed in other areas as well (see chapter 4).

Sustained and broad-based growth is the key element of a strategy to fight poverty. Growth was the driving force behind the significant poverty reduction that took place between 1999 and 2002. However, as poverty declines, consumption needs to grow more rapidly to achieve the same percentage point reduction in poverty. For example, for every 5 percentage points of uniform growth in consumption, poverty would decline by about 3 percentage points if 30 percent of the population lived in poverty, but it would decline by only 2 percentage points if the incidence of poverty was 15 percent.

The impact of different scenarios of consumption growth on the incidence of poverty can be simulated (figure 6.6). The simulations start from the poverty level of 19.6 percent in 2002. If uniform growth in consumption is constant at 3 percent a year, the incidence of poverty would be cut by about a third, falling to 13.4 percent in 2007. If consumption were to grow uniformly by 4 percent a year, the incidence of poverty would be cut by about 40 percent, reaching 11.7 percent by 2007. Uniform consumption

Figure 6.6. Uniform consumption would have to grow 5 percent a year to cut poverty in half by 2007

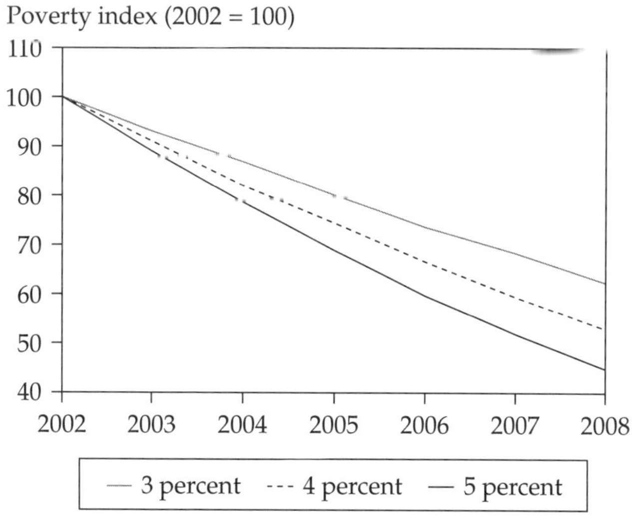

Source: Bank staff calculations based on data from Household Budget Survey 2002 (Goskomstat).

Figure 6.7. Rapid growth in consumption would have a dramatic effect on the poverty gap and poverty severity indexes

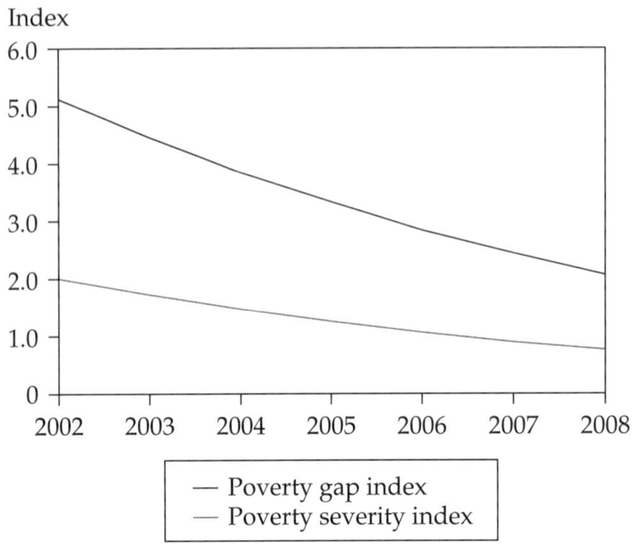

Source: Bank staff calculations based on data from Household Budget Survey 2002 (Goskomstat).

growth of at least 5 percent a year is needed to halve the incidence of poverty by 2007 (10.2 percent of the population would be poor under this scenario). In this case the poverty gap index and poverty severity index, which capture the depth and severity of poverty, would also decline by about half of their 2002 values (figure 6.7).

Increasing inequality would substantially diminish the poverty reduction impact of growth. If future growth were accompanied by increasing inequality—through higher returns to education and increasing decompression of wages, for example—inequality would likely rise. Increased inequality would lessen the poverty reduction impact of growth, and while average growth rates might be achieved, poverty reduction targets could be missed. It is important, therefore, to monitor inequality and develop a better understanding of its determinants and the policy levers that could influence it.

To achieve sustained growth of 5 percent a year in consumption, GDP would have to increase by more than 5 percent a year. As the economy grew from its depressed state in 1998, households responded by strongly increasing their consumption, particularly for nonfood items.

This rapid growth may not continue in the future. Growth was facilitated by substantial underutilized capacity, which meant that firms could expand with little extra investment. With several years of expanding output, capacity utilization is at a high level; additional output increases will require expanding the capital stock and devoting a larger share of output to investment rather than consumption. In addition, consumption is likely to rise less than incomes, as households start increasing their savings rate. While this would be good for achieving and sustaining growth in the long run, it implies that GDP will have to grow at a faster rate than the required 5 percent consumption growth to cut poverty in half by 2007.

Note

1. The analysis in this chapter relies on the recommended methodology outlined in chapter 1, with a derived poverty line and a measure of welfare as consumption with regional adjustments for the cost of living. The consumption measure includes both cash and in-kind consumption expenditures. Cash consumption expenditures include expenditures on food, alcohol, nonfood goods, and services. In-kind consumption includes the value of in-kind inflows, discounts, and subsidies. To reflect significant spatial price variations, the consumption measure is adjusted to reflect cost of living differences among regions.

7
The Impact of Accession to the World Trade Organization on Living Standards and Poverty

Accession to the World Trade Organization (WTO) is likely to generate substantial benefits for Russia—about 7 percent of the value of consumption in the medium term and considerably more in the long term. These benefits would come from increased foreign direct investment by multinational service providers, which would rise as a result of commitments to open up the services sectors to foreign investors; from increased productivity, which would occur as a result of the inflow of imported technology once Russian tariff barriers were reduced; and from the improved treatment of Russian exporters in antidumping cases. The export-intensive sectors are likely to experience the greatest expansion. Sectors that export little and that have relatively high import protection are likely to contract in the medium term. In the long term an increase in the return to investment should expand the capital stock and incomes considerably more. In the medium to long term, the vast majority of households will gain from WTO accession, and the poor will gain at least as much as the average household. Rural households are expected to gain slightly less, on average, than urban households, and workers are likely to gain more than capital owners.

In the medium to long term, the vast majority of Russian households will gain from Russia's membership in the World Trade Organization (WTO). During a transition period, however, many households may lose. Displaced unskilled workers will suffer losses from transitional unemployment and are likely to incur expenses related to retraining or relocation. Thus, despite the substantial improvement in the standard of living that is likely for almost all Russians after accession to the WTO and adjustment to the new equilibrium, the transition will require strong public policy. Government safety nets will be crucial in helping mitigate the short-run adverse impact of WTO accession, especially for the poorest members of society (see chapter 8).

The Challenge of Global Integration

By some measures, Russia is already well integrated with the global economy: the trade-to-GDP ratio in 2002 was almost 50 percent, for example. But much of Russia's exports are energy commodities, which represent 54

Table 7.1. Foreign direct investment in Russia is much lower than in other emerging economies

	Net FDI inflow ($ billion)							*Net FDI as % of GDP*						
Country	*1995*	*1996*	*1997*	*1998*	*1999*	*2000*	*2001*	*1995*	*1996*	*1997*	*1998*	*1999*	*2000*	*2001*
Russian Federation	**2.0**	**2.5**	**6.6**	**2.8**	**3.3**	**2.7**	**2.5**	**0.6**	**0.6**	**1.5**	**1.0**	**1.7**	**1.1**	**0.8**
Czech Republic	2.6	1.4	1.3	3.7	6.3	4.6	4.9	4.9	2.5	2.4	6.5	11.6	9.0	8.7
Hungary	4.5	2.3	2.2	2.0	2.0	1.7	2.4	10.1	5.0	4.7	4.3	4.1	3.7	4.6
Poland	3.7	4.5	4.9	6.4	7.3	9.3	8.8	2.9	3.1	3.4	4.0	4.7	5.9	5.1
Argentina	5.6	6.9	9.2	7.3	24.0	11.7	3.2	2.2	2.6	3.1	2.4	8.5	4.1	1.2
Brazil	4.9	11.2	19.7	31.9	23.6	32.8	22.5	0.7	1.4	2.4	4.1	5.4	5.5	4.5
China	35.9	40.2	44.2	43.8	38.4	38.8	46.8	5.1	4.9	4.9	4.6	3.9	3.6	4.0
Mexico	9.5	9.2	12.8	11.3	11.9	13.3	24.7	3.3	2.8	3.2	2.7	2.5	2.3	4.0

Sources: World Bank (2002b); UNCTAD (2001).

percent of total exports. Foreign direct investment inflows remain low compared with those of most transition economies (table 7.1). Net foreign direct investment in Russia was 0.8–1.7 percent of GDP between 1997 and 2001 (less in earlier years). Attracting more foreign direct investment is important to promote growth, boost competitiveness through the transfer of technology and management expertise, and diversify the economy. Doing so requires an environment in which multinationals view Russia as a country in which investment can give them a global competitive advantage. An open trade regime is a prerequisite for WTO accession. So too are low policy and administrative barriers to investment and trade facilitation (see chapter 4).

WTO accession must be a central pillar of Russia's strategy for global integration. Accession would improve access for Russian exporters, enable Russia to help shape the future of the global trading environment, and spur progress in the domestic reform agenda in many dimensions. Toward that end, Russia would benefit from taking the following steps:

- Reduce tariff peaks for certain products and move toward tariff uniformity. Russia's average tariff rate of 11 percent for Most Favored Nations (MFN) is lower than the average tariff in many non-OECD countries. However, tariffs on some important products are high. These tariff peaks distort the tariff system. Their reduction and movement toward uniformity would improve efficiency.
- Continue recent initiatives to improve the investment climate.
- Improve services in ways that encourage investment by foreign service providers.[1]
- Make further progress on customs, trade facilitation, and standards.[2]

The Aggregate Benefits of WTO Accession

Although WTO accession will benefit Russia significantly, accession is likely to have differential impacts on different layers of Russian society and on the economy. Liberalization of trade and foreign direct investment is likely to have a significant positive impact on growth—and hence on the sustained reduction of poverty. But policymakers are concerned that effects that have been positive in many countries may not be so in Russia. They are concerned not only with the aggregate effects and the impacts on the productive and service sectors but also with the effects on labor markets and the poor. To address these concerns, this chapter evaluates the

Table 7.2. The impact of WTO accession can be decomposed into various types of effects

Measure	Aggregate impact of WTO accession	*Of which:* Impact of improved market access	Impact of tariff reform	Impact of reform of foreign direct investment barriers
Aggregate welfare				
Consumption (equivalent variation as percent of consumption)	7.3	0.7	1.3	5.3
GDP (equivalent variation as percent of GDP)	3.4	0.3	0.6	2.5
Government budget				
Tariff revenue (percent of GDP)	0.9	1.4	0.8	1.4
Tariff revenue (percent change)	-32.9	8.8	-38.1	11.4
Aggregate trade				
Real exchange rate (percent change)	2.7	-0.5	2.1	1.2
Aggregate exports (percent change)	14.5	2.3	8.1	3.7
Returns to mobile factors				
Unskilled labor (percent change)	3.8	0.1	0.5	3.2
Skilled labor (percent change)	5.5	0.6	1.7	3.0
Capital (percent change)	1.7	-0.5	1.1	1.1
Share of mobile factors that will have to adjust				
Unskilled labor (percent)	1.3	0.3	1.3	0.3
Skilled labor (percent)	1.2	0.4	0.5	0.6
Capital (percent)	0.9	0.5	0.2	0.5

Source: Rutherford, Tarr, and Shepotylo (2004) based on Household Budget Survey (Goskomstat, various years) and Russia Longitudinal Monitoring Survey (UNC, various years).
Note: Government revenue surplus is assumed to be distributed proportionally to income.

Box 7.1. Overview of the model and dataset

The analysis uses a computable general equilibrium model of the Russian economy. The primary factors of production are capital, skilled labor, and unskilled labor. There are five types of capital, 35 sectors, and three types of sectors: competitive goods and services, imperfectly competitive goods, and imperfectly competitive business services. (A detailed description of the model is presented in Jensen, Rutherford, and Tarr [2004a], which provides confidence intervals for the estimates.)

Goods produced subject to increasing returns to scale are differentiated at the firm level. Firms in these industries set prices so that marginal cost equals marginal revenue, and free entry drives profits to zero. The standard Chamberlinian large group monopolistic competition assumption is used, which results in constant mark-ups over marginal cost.

Aggregate productivity is affected by the number of varieties of goods using the standard Dixit-Stiglitz formulation. The effective cost function for users of goods produced subject to increasing returns to scale declines with the total number of firms in the industry. For simplicity the model assumes that the composition of fixed and marginal cost is identical in all sectors facing increasing returns to scale. This implies that the ratio of fixed to marginal cost is a constant. In a standard Chamberlinian large-group model, this assumption ensures that output per firm for all firm types remains constant—that is, the model does not produce rationalization gains or losses.

Manufactured goods are assumed to be imported or produced domestically, and the cost structure of domestic firms is defined by observed primary factor and intermediate inputs to that sector in the base year data. The cif import price of foreign goods is defined by the import price, and, by the zero profits assumption, in equilibrium the import price must cover the fixed and marginal costs of foreign firms. In the services sector characterized by increasing returns to scale, two types of firms provide services to the Russian economy: Russian firms, which employ primary factors and intermediate inputs, and multinational firms, which provide services using imported inputs (foreign direct investment and foreign expertise), together with primary factors and intermediate inputs.

The model assumes that the structure of both the marginal costs and the fixed costs of services firms are identical, so that (as was the case in goods production) output per firm is fixed and there are no rationalization gains. For multinational service providers, both the fixed and variable costs of service supply are assumed to be a convex combination of the domestic supply price in the same sector and the cost of imported inputs.

Households are modeled endogenously, primarily based on the 49,000 households in the Household Budget Survey. The major shortcoming of the Household Budget Survey for the purposes of the analysis is that it does not contain information on the sources of income. These data are taken from the Russia Longitudinal Monitoring Survey (UNC, various years), which contains extensive information on individual and household sources of income: wages and profits from first, second, and third jobs; pensions and unemployment benefits; and profits and dividends from accumulated assets.

Recent advances have proposed techniques for combining data from different survey sources. Econometric techniques known as small area estimation and matching have been proposed to produce synthetic datasets that combine survey data with comprehensive census information. The model used here employs both techniques to generate sources of income data for all 49,000 households in the Household Budget Survey. The model thus draws on household characteristics that are common to both datasets and that are expected to influence the factor shares of income.

likely impact of WTO accession on the poor and on different layers of society and the economy.

The analysis relies on an innovative model combining the households surveyed in the Household Budget Survey with a computable general equilibrium model (box 7.1). Using the model and data from the Household Budget Survey and the Russia Longitudinal Monitoring Survey (UNC, various years), this chapter assesses the distributional and poverty implications of WTO accession and provides intuitive explanations for the principal policy conclusions, including the macroeconomic, sector, labor market, poverty, and distributional results (table 7.2). Overall, the Russian economy is projected to gain about 7.3 percent of the value of consumption (about 3.4 percent of GDP) from WTO accession in the medium term. The potential gains in the long run are much larger: about 24 percent of Russian consumption.

Improved market access is valuable, but it is the least important of the three effects of WTO accession. Improved market access accounts for only 0.7 percentage point of the overall gain of 7.3 percentage points (see table 7.2). Russia has already attained either bilateral MFN status or preferential status (in the CIS) from almost all of its trading partners. Hence the MFN status accorded to WTO members will not significantly help Russian exporters increase market access. Russian exporters will enhance their legal status to challenge the application of antidumping duties, but this is not likely to lead to significantly lower duties, on average. Only a small improvement in market access for Russian exporters is thus likely to result from WTO accession.

Tariff reduction will lead to significant gains, but it is not the most important effect of WTO accession. Tariff reduction would increase consumption by 1.3 percentage points. It should improve the allocation of resources in Russia, as resources are induced to shift to sectors in which they are more highly valued at world prices. More important, tariff reduction would make it easier for Russian businesses to import products that contain new and diverse technologies, which would increase productivity. Since the Russian tariff is already moderate, however (1.6 percent of GDP, or about 7 percent of the value of imports), the reduction would not produce a large macroeconomic effect, although it would be important for a few sectors.[3]

Liberalization of the barriers to foreign direct investment in the services sectors is the most important source of gains from WTO accession. About 5.3 percentage points of the estimated increase in consumption would stem from liberalization of the barriers to multinational providers of services. Barriers under negotiation include the monopoly on long-distance telephone services, the restraints on multinational banks opening affiliates in Russia, and the quotas on multinational providers of insurance services. Russian commitments to multinational service providers would encourage more foreign direct investment in Russia. This would increase access by Russian businesses to the services of multinational service providers in such sectors as telecommunications, banking, insurance, and transportation, lowering the cost of doing business and increasing the productivity gains of firms using these services.

Confidence intervals of the estimates indicate that the medium-term gains should be substantial under a wide range of parameter and modeling assumptions. The potential long-term growth effects of improvements in the investment climate could result in much larger gains: since long-term improvement in the investment climate should expand the capital stock, the long-term gains in consumption could be three or four times the medium-term gains.[4]

Impact on Sectors and the Labor Market

Employment and output in some sectors will contract, but total unemployment will not change. Despite overall gains to the economy, some goods and services sectors will contract in the medium run. However, despite fears that widespread unemployment will follow from increased imports due to the liberalization of tariff barriers, not all sectors will contract. Russia will have to pay for increased imports, and foreigners will demand hard currency for their goods and services. Exports will have to expand in order to pay for imports.[5] The exchange rate will depreciate to encourage both an increase in exports and a decline in imports, so that additional exports can pay for additional imports. International experience indicates that trade liberalization causes no aggregate change in employment in the medium term (Rutherford, Tarr, and Shepotylo 2004). No change in employment is therefore expected in Russia as a result of WTO accession.

Protected manufacturing sectors that export little are likely to contract. In manufacturing the greatest fall in employment will be in the food industry, light industry, construction materials, and machinery and equipment. Exports as a share of output are low in these sectors, and food, light industry, and construction materials are the only sectors with tariff rates of about 10 percent.

More sectors will expand than contract, and export-intensive manufacturing sectors are likely to experience the largest expansion. Outside of services, the sectors that will experience the greatest expansion in employment are nonferrous metals, ferrous metals, and chemicals. These sectors are among those that export the highest percentage of their output and will thus benefit most from the real exchange rate depreciation that should accompany tariff reduction. In addition, these sectors are among the seven sectors that will benefit from improved treatment in antidumping cases.

Most services sectors that receive foreign direct investment will expand employment. Many of the key business services sectors, in which Russian service providers will be subject to increased competition from multinational service providers, will expand their employment. These sectors include telecommunications, financial services, trucking, and trade. Multinationals that invest in Russia in these sectors employ 90–98 percent Russian labor. Consequently, foreign direct investment in these sectors will increase demand for Russian skilled workers in these sectors, even if there is a decline in demand for labor from Russian-owned companies.

In services sectors in which there will be little or no foreign direct investment, employment will decline slightly. These sectors will lose from the depreciation of the real exchange rate. The price of traded goods will thus increase relative to the price of the output of their sectors.

Returns to Factors of Production

The model estimates that the wage rate of skilled labor will rise 5.5 percent, the wage rate of unskilled labor will rise 3.8 percent, and the rate of return on capital will increase 1.7 percent. Although the returns to all factors of production should increase, the return on capital will increase less than the return on wages, because owners of "specific" capital in sectors that are subject to increased competition from imports or from foreign direct investment will see a reduction in the value of their returns. Owners of capital that is mobile across sectors will experience an increase in their returns of more than 6 percent. The average increase in return to owners of specific and mobile capital is 1.7 percent.

The impact on Russian owners of "specific" capital in sectors that compete with foreign direct investment will depend on their ability to participate in joint ventures. Despite an overall decrease in the returns to "specific" capital owners, all Russian specific capital owners are not expected to lose. Notably, the model estimates that there will be a significant increase in foreign direct investment and an increase in multinational firms operating in the business services sectors in Russia, which will result in a more competitive environment for Russian capital owners in these sectors. Multinationals, however, will often look for a Russian joint venture partner when they want to invest in Russia. The Russian firms that become part of a joint venture with foreign investors are likely to increase the value of their investments. Russian capital owners in business services that remain wholly independent of multinational firms, either because they avoid joint ventures or because they are not desired as joint venture partners, are likely to see the value of their investments decline.

Skilled labor in the services sectors should gain from foreign direct investment, but capital owners will experience diverse impacts. The estimates suggest that labor should find it in its interest to support the liberalization of foreign direct investment, even if capital owners in the sector oppose it. But capital owners themselves may have diverse interests, depending on their prospects for acquisition by multinationals.

Distribution of Gains at the Household Level

The vast majority of households are expected to gain from WTO accession, increasing consumption 2–25 percent in the medium term (figure 7.1).[6] In the long run, when the positive impact on the investment climate and productivity materializes, the gains will be larger.

The poorest 10 percent of households gain 7.8 percent of consumption, slightly more than the average gain of 7.3 percent of consumption (see table 7.3). As a percent of consumption, the gains are distributed rather evenly across households at different income levels. The richest 10 percent of households gain 6.7 percent of consumption, slightly less than the average for all households. The reason for the differences is that the return to capital increases less than the return to unskilled labor, and poor households have proportionately more unskilled labor and less capital. Skilled labor in Russia is remarkably evenly distributed across income levels. This reflects the fact that skilled workers, such as teachers and researchers, often earn low wages.

Rural households are expected to benefit from WTO accession, albeit by less than urban households. Consumption by the poorest rural households is expected to rise 7.2 percent, while consumption by the poorest urban households is expected to rise 8.5 percent. Rural households are generally less endowed with skilled labor than urban households, and skilled labor will gain more than unskilled labor.

Figure 7.1. Distribution of estimated welfare gains from Russian WTO accession

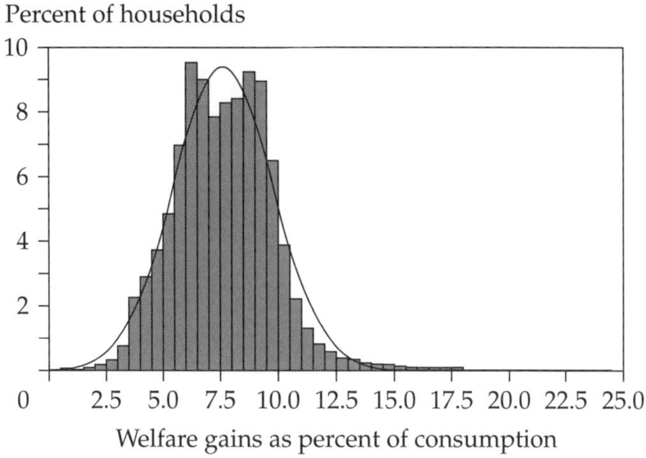

Source: Rutherford, Tarr, and Shepotylo (2004).
Note: Figure is truncated: 13 observations with losses and 7 observations with gains of more than 25 percent are not shown.

Impact on Potential Government Transfers and the Safety Net

Government revenue will increase as a result of WTO accession. Despite the loss of tariff revenue (about 0.7 percent of GDP), the economy is estimated to expand, and other indirect taxes, such as the value-added tax, will more than compensate for the loss of tariff revenue. If the government were to distribute the additional revenue from WTO accession to households in equal ruble amounts for each household, the average gain for the poor would increase from 7.8 percent to 9.0 percent of consumption (table 7.3).

Government safety nets are very important in buffering the impact of accession, especially for the poorest members of society, who can ill afford a harsh transition. Despite gains in the medium to long term, during a transition period it is possible that many households will lose. Some unskilled workers will be displaced and will have to find new employment. They will suffer losses from transitional unemployment and are likely to incur expenses related to retraining or relocation. Thus, despite a likely substantial improvement in the standard of living for almost all households after accession to the WTO and adjustment to a new

Table 7.3. The impact of WTO accession on Russian households

	WTO accession		*Partial reforms*[a]		
Household type	*Revenue surplus distributed proportionally to income*	*Equal ruble transfers*[a]	*Improved market access only*	*Tariff reform only*	*Reform of foreign direct investment barriers only*
Bottom decile					
Total	7.8	9.0	0.9	1.0	5.8
Rural	7.2	8.5	0.8	0.8	5.6
Urban	8.5	9.5	1.0	1.3	6.1
Decile 2					
Total	7.7	8.4	7.7	1.1	5.7
Rural	6.9	7.6	0.8	0.8	5.3
Urban	8.3	9.0	1.0	1.3	6.0
Decile 3					
Total	7.9	8.3	7.9	1.2	5.7
Rural	6.8	7.3	0.8	0.8	5.2
Urban	8.4	8.8	1.0	1.4	5.9
Decile 4					
Total	7.9	8.1	7.9	1.2	5.7
Rural	6.8	7.1	0.8	0.8	5.2
Urban	8.3	8.6	1.0	1.4	5.8
Decile 5					
Total	7.8	8.0	7.8	1.2	5.6
Rural	6.6	6.8	0.7	0.8	5.0
Urban	8.2	8.4	0.9	1.4	5.8
Decile 6					
Total	7.6	7.7	7.6	1.3	5.5
Rural	6.3	6.4	0.6	0.8	4.9
Urban	8.1	8.2	0.9	1.4	5.7
Decile 7					
Total	7.6	7.6	7.6	1.3	5.5
Rural	6.4	6.4	0.6	0.8	4.9
Urban	7.9	7.9	0.8	1.4	5.6
Decile 8					
Total	7.6	7.5	7.6	1.4	5.4
Rural	6.2	6.1	0.6	0.8	4.7
Urban	7.9	7.9	0.8	1.5	5.5

Table 7.3. The impact of WTO accession on Russian households (continued)

	WTO accession		Partial reforms[a]		
Household type	*Revenue surplus distributed proportionally to income*	*Equal ruble transfers*[a]	*Improved market access only*	*Tariff reform only*	*Reform of foreign direct investment barriers only*
Decile 9					
Total	7.2	7.1	7.2	1.3	5.3
Rural	6.2	6.0	0.5	0.8	4.9
Urban	7.4	7.2	0.6	1.4	5.3
Top decile					
Total	6.7	6.4	6.7	1.3	5.0
Rural	5.6	5.3	0.3	0.9	4.4
Urban	6.8	6.4	0.4	1.3	5.0

Source: Rutherford, Tarr, and Shepotylo (2004).
Note: Figures are welfare change as percent of consumption.
a. Government revenue surplus is distributed in equal ruble values for each decile. In all other columns, the surplus is distributed proportionately to income.

equilibrium, there is a strong role for public policy, especially in helping the poorest members of society to adjust to the transition. (Social safety net policies are discussed in chapter 8.)

These results are consistent with international experience of the past 20–30 years, which shows that rapid and sustained economic growth has occurred only in countries that progressively liberalized import protection and provided incentives to exporters that offset the tax that import protection imposes on exports (Rutherford, Tarr, and Shepotylo 2004). All of the "development miracle" countries of the past 20–30 years progressively opened their markets. This is true for Chile, Hong Kong (China), and Singapore, which pursued classical free market principles; it is true for Mauritius, which used export processing zones to encourage exports and provide exporters with equivalent incentives as importers; and it is true for the Republic of Korea and Taiwan (China), which started with significant import protection but progressively lowered it. Since import protection implicitly imposes a tax on exports, the Republic of Korea and Taiwan (China) implemented complicated programs (such as indirect duty drawbacks) to provide exporters with incentives equivalent to sectors that received import protection. Diverse and rapid export growth characterized the experiences of all these countries and appears crucial for sustained rapid economic growth. Since import protection penalizes exporters, it appears that lowering protection is a crucial necessary (but not sufficient) condition for sustained, rapid economic development.

Notes

1. Relative to Russia's tariff barriers on goods, the barriers to foreign direct investment by multinational companies in areas such as banking, insurance, securities, accounting, telecommunications, maritime transportation, and aviation appear to be quite high. Services remain one of the most contentious issues in accession discussions with the WTO.

2. Trade facilitation refers to procedures that allow goods to enter and exit the country without undue delays, based on transparent, nondiscriminatory rules. Progress on standards requires reducing technical barriers to trade and sanitary and phyto-sanitary barriers that are discriminatory or that limit the flow of goods. Greater reliance on international certification agencies is needed for the certification of the safety of goods.

3. Seven percent is an effective tariff rate (that is, the value of collected import duties divided by imports). This figure differs from the average statuary rate of 11 percent, cited earlier, because of the application of various preferential customs regimes.

4. All estimates are subject to a margin of error, due to parameter specification and modeling assumptions. The long-run estimates are subject to a much larger margin of error.

5. Russia has a trade surplus, but it reflects capital investment decisions. As long as Russians continue to want to send capital abroad, the trade surplus cannot be used to pay for imports.

6. The Household Budget Survey dataset contains 55,531 households, but only 49,239 households are in the sample. The difference is due to the fact that Goskomstat split 6,292 households into two households, with the weight of the original household split between the two households. If the household was on the border between deciles i and i + 1, it was duplicated and the weight assigned to the household was divided between the original and the duplicated household so that the weight-adjusted number of households per decile remained the same. The model worked with the 55,531-household version of the dataset.

Part III
Reforming Sectoral Policies for Alleviating Poverty

Although recent poverty trends have been encouraging, further progress is not likely to come as easily as it did during the years of rapid catch-up growth in real wages. Moreover, Russia will have to implement some reforms that may have a negative welfare impact on some households, at least in the short run. Most prominent among them will be the reform of the housing and communal sector and structural reforms triggered by WTO accession. Hence the government's ambitious plans on poverty alleviation, as emphasized in President Putin's address to the nation in May 2004, will have to depend not only on promoting growth but also on creating a more efficient system of wealth redistribution. This puts reforms of the social protection policies at the top of the government agenda.

This part of the report starts with a discussion of the existing system of social benefits and the reforms required to improve its relevance to the poverty alleviation goals. It then reviews social policies affecting the non-cash aspects of poverty. Increasing inequity in access to health care and education not only deprives the poor of good-quality services, it also lowers their chances of increasing their welfare. Reforming the education and health care sectors by developing the human capital of socially vulnerable groups is thus an important part of fighting poverty today and preventing it from reemerging in the future.

Chapter 8 assesses the targeting performance of noncontributory social assistance programs. The amount of resources channeled through noncontributory social assistance programs is substantial, but the impact of these programs on poverty alleviation is small. Five factors have contributed to this outcome: the procyclical nature of overall spending; the fact that by design only a small fraction of these resources is targeted to the poor; the mediocre ability of the social assistance administration to identify the poor, which results in substantial leakage even from funds that are targeted; the small size of benefits transferred by these programs compared with the income deficit of the poor beneficiaries; and the widespread duplication of programs.

The report suggests that the system of privileges be reformed to ensure equitable access to subsidized goods and services and that the scope of occupation-related privileges be reduced. The resources freed up by these reforms could be reallocated to poverty alleviation programs. If these resources simply augment the budget of existing targeted programs, however, without reforming targeting practices, the poverty reduction outcome will be modest. The effectiveness of targeted social assistance programs can and should be substantially improved by using a proxy means test instead of the formal income test, which is a weak predictor of the true poverty status of a household in Russia. Finally, it is highly desirable that government spending on social policy become countercyclical.

Chapter 9 analyzes the current system of housing and utility services subsidies and the policy measures required to mitigate the negative poverty impact of moving to full cost recovery, including expanding the take-up of the housing allowance program among the poorest.

Chapter 10 presents evidence that inadequate educational opportunities and poverty are mutually reinforcing in Russia. The educational challenges faced by the poor in Russia are twofold: access to education is increasingly determined by income and wealth, with poverty reducing access to noncompulsory education and high-quality modern educational programs, and funding for education in Russia is inequitably allocated. It is recommended that targeting of education expenditures be improved, students rather than schools be financed, the relevance of secondary vocational programs be increased, and the education administration's capacity to monitor poverty and its relationship with education be developed.

Chapter 11 studies the health situation of the Russian poor and the adequacy of the health care system to address the poverty challenge. It finds that nearly half of people in the lowest consumption quintile report bad or very bad health status. Moreover, the poor are more likely to engage in risky behaviors that contribute to the poor health status. Although defining causality is difficult, the decline in health status roughly parallels the decrease in public sector health care expenditures in real terms. Lack of affordable medicines is a serious impediment to preserving good health for the poor. The chapter suggests formalizing informal payments through a standardized copayment system and developing explicit protection from copayments for the poor and medically vulnerable groups. Major changes will also be required to improve efficiency, equity, and access to medical services. In particular, allocation of government expenditures based on population and criteria such as need and levels of poverty could enable a redistribution of funds and a cross-subsidization from richer regions to poorer ones as well as from the healthy to the sick.

8
Improving the Targeting of Social Transfers

This chapter assesses the targeting performance of noncontributory social assistance programs. After providing an overview of the whole social protection system, including pensions and other social insurance programs, it examines noncontributory programs. The volume of resources channeled through noncontributory social assistance programs is substantial, but the impact of these programs on poverty alleviation is small. From the perspective of both equity and efficiency, the chapter suggests that the system of privileges be reformed to ensure equitable access to subsidized goods and services and that the scope of occupation-related privileges be reduced. The resources freed up by these reforms could be reallocated to poverty alleviation programs. However, if these resources are used simply to augment the budget of the existing targeted programs, without reforming the targeting practices, the poverty reduction outcome will be modest. The effectiveness of targeted social assistance programs can and should be substantially improved by the use of a proxy means test instead of the currently used formal income test, which is a weak predictor of the true poverty status of a household in Russia.

The Role of Social Protection in Reducing Poverty

Social protection programs, including pensions, are an important component of the government's poverty reduction strategy. This is demonstrated by the large volume of resources the government redistributes, the share of the population covered by such programs, and the importance of the transfers for the consumption of beneficiaries, particularly the poor. These programs reach about 79 percent of the population directly or indirectly. On average, social protection transfers represent about one-fifth of household consumption. For the poorest quintile, the value of these transfers was equivalent to 41 percent of their current consumption. The most important transfer income is pensions. The importance of other, noncontributory social assistance transfers in household consumption is small.

These transfers represent 4.4 percent of the consumption of the average household and 7.6 percent of the consumption of households in the poorest quintile.

The social protection system is a combination of old and new programs. Russia has a modern pension system, complemented by other social insurance and unemployment benefit programs, and an extensive system of cash and in-kind benefits for privileged citizens and, to a lesser extent, poor and vulnerable groups. A large segment of the system consists of old programs inherited from the socialist past that need to be reformed, such as the extensive and costly system of privileges and the inefficient system of institutionalized care. (Appendix F presents an overview of the main programs, in terms of target groups, eligibility criteria, benefit determination, financing, and administration.)

Overall Spending and Composition

Consolidated government spending for social protection programs accounted for 12.6 percent of GDP in 2002 (table 8.1 and box 8.1). And the scope of the social protection system extends beyond public spending. Many citizens are eligible for subsidies whose costs are partly covered by the budget and partly by providers (parastatals in housing and utility services, transport, health, and some other sectors). The quasi-fiscal cost of these subsidies adds another 2.0 percent to the overall social protection bill, bringing overall spending for social protection to 14.6 percent of GDP—more than twice as much as the combined spending for health and education (7.1 percent).

The largest share—about two-thirds—of social protection spending finances social insurance programs. The social insurance system consists of pensions for former employees or farmers (for old age and disability) and their dependents (survivorship) and of other programs providing benefits in case of sickness, maternity, or unemployment. Total spending on social insurance programs accounted for 8.7 percent of GDP in 2002 (table 8.1). While these programs do not have an explicit poverty alleviation mandate, some components are designed to reduce the risk of poverty among contributors or beneficiaries (minimum pension provisions) or cover vulnerable groups (for example, social pensions for the disabled elderly without other sources of income).

Noncontributory social assistance programs and subsidies channel an additional 5.9 percent of GDP, of which 3.9 percent is through the enlarged budget of the government and 2.0 percent is in quasi-fiscal subsidies. There are three broad categories of noncontributory social assistance programs: subsidies for privileged citizens, social assistance programs targeted to the poor, and other programs.

Box 8.1. How much does the Russian Federation spend on social protection?

A review of social protection spending was conducted to determine its magnitude, trends, and functional composition (Morozov 2004). This proved to be a daunting task, given the federal structure of the budget, the large number of programs operated by various levels of government, the widespread financing of social programs from multiple sources, and the use of both fiscal and quasi-fiscal mechanisms to finance benefits.

Although it covers the most important programs, the review is not exhaustive. In particular, spending on social protection programs administered by line ministries other than the ministries for social protection, health, and education was not included. Subsidized transport is omitted, for example. Social protection programs financed from subnational budgets but not identified as such in the standard reporting documents are also omitted. The quasi-fiscal component of the subsidies provided to privileged citizens in areas other than housing and utility services is also excluded. Administrative data are combined with information from two household surveys, the Household Budget Survey (1997–2002) and the 2003 National Survey of Household Welfare and Program Participation (NOBUS) to obtain a complete picture of the magnitude and composition of social protection spending.

QUASI-FISCAL SOURCES

For a large number of consumer subsidies for privileged citizens, a part of the subsidy is covered by providers. In the heating and utility, transport, health, and other sectors, the state uses parastatals to finance social protection activities by quasi-fiscal means. There are no administrative data on these subsidies, but survey data suggest that they represented 1–2 percent of GDP in 2002.

PUBLIC SPENDING ON SOCIAL PROTECTION

The magnitude of social protection spending from public sources is easier to estimate. This spending is financed transparently from government budgets at all levels: federal, subnational, and state social extrabudgetary funds. Known as the "enlarged" budget of the government, it covers cash benefits for the population (such as pensions or child allowances), financing for the provision of social services (such as orphanages), social security institutions (such as the administration of extrabudgetary funds), and producer subsidies to the housing and communal services sector, which are provided from the budget for compensation for below-cost tariffs. Many government and extrabudgetary fund flows need to be eliminated to arrive at true consolidated public spending. To the extent possible, double counting of social expenditures in the enlarged budget was eliminated. This included netting of transfers from the federal budget to the pension fund for

(continued)

Box 8.1 *(continued)*

labor and military pensions and transfers from the federal budget to subnational budgets. As mentioned above, although the review captures the largest component of spending, amounting to 12.6 percent of GDP in 2002, it is not exhaustive, since spending by other line ministries and by subnational governments is not accounted for.

FUNCTIONAL COMPOSITION OF PUBLIC SPENDING

It is even more difficult to identify the composition of social protection spending by main programs, as many programs are cofinanced from republican or local subnational budgets but not reported as individual line items (programs) in the subnational budgets. Official reports on the execution of the federal and subnational budgets and the budgets of state social extrabudgetary funds do not provide sufficient information on specific social protection programs. In addition, the presentation of some budget expenditures does not follow the Government Finance Statistics principles of functional classification. For example, food benefits to parentless children are shown in the budget under the category "Expenditures on Education," and cash compensation to the elderly for Sberbank deposits eroded by hyperinflation in the early 1990s is presented under the category "Internal Sources of Budget Deficit Financing."

Source: Morozov (2004).

Table 8.1. Pensions represent half of all public spending on social protection (percent of GDP)

Social Insurance	*8.7*
Pensions	6.3
Unemployment benefits	0.0
Other social insurance	2.4
Noncontributory Programs	*3.9*
Privileges for housing and utility services	2.3
Housing allowances	0.1
Child benefits	0.2
Other social protection programs	1.3
Total public spending	12.6
Other privileges not covered above and quasi-fiscal subsidies	2.0
Total social protection spending	14.6

Source: Morozov (2004).

SUBSIDIES FOR PRIVILEGED CITIZENS

Privileges protect vulnerable groups (such as the disabled, war invalids, dependents of war victims, people affected by radiation); grant reparations to those unjustly oppressed under the communist dictatorship (rehabilitated people and their dependents); and reward citizens for exceptional services (war veterans, labor war veterans, citizens awarded the title of Hero of the Russian Federation or the Soviet Union, holders of the full Order of Glory, Heroes of Socialist Labor). This report refers to these privileges as *merit based.*

The government also provides numerous privileges to labor veterans and people working in agencies with occupational benefits. This report refers to these privileges as *occupational privileges.* Privileged citizens enjoy subsidized or free access to a wide range of services and goods, such as exemptions from or discounts for rents or utility payments; telephone services; medicines, medical appliances, and medical services; urban, commuter, and long-distance transport; and vouchers for sanatoriums, spas, child care facilities, and summer camps (table 8.2). Some categories of citizens are exempted from or eligible for discounted real estate taxes, receive substantial financial support to repair their homes, or are given plots of land.

Overall, slightly more than half of privilege holders belong to the merit-based category, with the remaining 47 percent enjoying occupational privileges. The fiscal and quasi-fiscal cost of these subsidies in 2002

Table 8.2. Coverage and type of privileges

	Coverage		*Type of privileges (% of total)*	
	% of population	*Millions of people*	*Merit*	*Occupational*
Housing and utility services	20	29.7	57	43
Telephone	11	15.8	52	48
Medical	9	12.6	29	71
Transport	20	29.0	61	39
Spa and holidays	1	1.5	34	66
Others	2	2.9	53	47
All privileges	27	145.3	53	47

Source: Bank staff calculations based on data from NOBUS (Goskomstat 2003b).
Note: Coverage includes the number of direct beneficiaries who used the benefit at least once during the past three months. Each type of benefit includes multiple categories.

is estimated at 4.3 percent of GDP. The largest part of these subsidies accrues for housing and utility services (2.9 percent of GDP).[1] Although only 27 percent of the population are privilege holders, the number of people who benefit is higher, since everyone living in their household benefits from the subsidy. Taking into account indirect beneficiaries extends the coverage of the system to 45 percent of the population.

Social assistance programs targeted to the poor

The system of targeted social assistance includes three main programs: child allowances, allowances for housing and utility services, and targeted social assistance programs provided by subnational governments (regional and local).[2] In 2002 these programs channeled only 0.4 percent of GDP, of which 0.2 percent was for child allowances, 0.1 percent for housing and utility services allowances, and an estimated 0.1 percent for decentralized social assistance programs.[3]

Other programs

Other social protection programs channel 1.3 percent of GDP. Included in this category are institutionalized care (estimated at 0.5 percent of GDP [World Bank 2002a]) and the administrative costs of the system (estimated at 0.5 percent of GDP). It is legitimate to ask whether these tax-financed noncontributory social assistance programs are equitably distributed or—given the emphasis placed by the government on reducing poverty—well targeted toward the poor.

Coverage of Social Protection Programs

Most Russian citizens benefit from social protection transfers or subsidies. This extensive coverage is found in the European Union and in many countries in Central and Eastern Europe, which share common features with the Russian Federation, such as an extensive pension system and a broad policy of child or family allowances. About 55 percent of the population benefits from social insurance, mostly pensions (51 percent) (table 8.3). Noncontributory programs, such as privileges, directly or indirectly cover 45 percent of the population, and targeted social assistance covers 42 percent. Among the social assistance programs targeted to the poor, the child allowance system has the largest coverage (32 percent of the population and about two-thirds of households with children), followed by the social assistance programs financed and implemented at the subnational level (11 percent of the population) and the targeted housing and utility services allowance program (6 percent).

The importance of social protection programs to household consumption is substantial. Pensions make the greatest contribution,

Table 8.3. Coverage of selected social protection programs (percent of population)

Social Protection, of which:	*79*
A. Social Insurance, of which:	55
Pensions	51
Allowances	5
Unemployment benefits	2
B. Targeted Social Assistance, of which:	42
Child allowances	32
Housing and utility services allowances	6
Decentralized social assistance	11
C. Privileges, of which:	45
Transport	25
Housing and utility services	32

Source: Bank staff calculations based on data from NOBUS (Goskomstat 2003b).
Note: Coverage includes both direct and indirect beneficiaries of social programs.

accounting for 12.9 percent of total consumption of the average household and 27.1 percent of the consumption of the bottom 20 percent of the population (table 8.4). The second most important group of programs is subsidies for privileged citizens. The subsidies on heating and utility services

Table 8.4. Importance of social protection transfers in household consumption (percent of total consumption)

	Average household	*Poorest quintile*
Social Protection, of which:	**19.6**	**41.0**
Social insurance, of which:	*15.2*	*33.4*
Pensions	12.9	27.1
Allowances	2.1	5.4
Unemployment benefits	0.2	0.8
Targeted Social Assistance, of which:	*1.6*	*4.2*
Child allowances	0.5	2.0
Housing and utility services allowance	0.5	0.8
Decentralized social assistance	0.3	1.0
Scholarship	0.2	0.3
Privileges, of which:	*2.8*	*3.4*
Transport	1.0	1.0
Housing and utility services	1.8	2.4

Source: Bank staff calculations based on data from NOBUS (Goskomstat 2003b).

and transport amounted to 2.8 percent of average household consumption and 3.4 percent of the consumption of the bottom quintile.

In contrast, programs explicitly targeted to the poor play only a marginal role in the consumption of either the average household or households in the poorest 20 percent of the population. Despite its extensive coverage, the system of targeted social assistance, which includes child allowances, housing and utility services allowances, and targeted social assistance programs provided by subnational governments (decentralized social assistance), has relatively low benefit adequacy. On average, these programs contribute only 1.6 percent of the consumption of the average household and 4.2 percent of the consumption of the poorest 20 percent. Although they receive less funding than privileges, targeted programs are more important to the consumption of the bottom 20 percent of the population.

Impact of Social Protection Transfers on Poverty Reduction

How much do government benefits contribute to poverty reduction? Estimating the poverty rate that would exist in the absence of government benefits provides an idea of the impact of various social programs on aggregate poverty. This is a simplified approach that ignores people's behavior in the absence of the social protection system.

Absent government programs, 19 million more people in Russia would have been poor in 2002 (table 8.5). Pensions had the largest impact on poverty (90 percent of the total impact) because of the higher level of funds channeled to pensioners and because of the redistributive function that has gained prominence in the past few years. The impact of noncontributory social assistance programs is substantially smaller. The child allowance programs, for example, lifted only 0.9 million people out of poverty, less than 2 percent of the overall impact. Other benefits, notably subsidies granted to privileged persons, were substantially less effective in reducing poverty.

Pulling a person out of poverty in Russia costs 9.4 times what it would if targeting were perfect. The total cost of all social protection programs is 46.79 billion rubles a month, or 2,464 rubles per person per month. Under perfect targeting, a person could be pulled out of poverty by receiving an amount equal to the difference between his or her actual consumption and the poverty line. The 2002 Household Budget Survey shows that average per capita consumption of the poor was 747 rubles per month, while the average poverty line was 1,009 rubles per month. This means that the average cost of pulling a person from the poverty line would be only 262 rubles per month. While perfect targeting is impossible to achieve, this comparison illustrates that the Russian welfare programs are excessively costly and their efficiency could be improved by better targeting.

Table 8.5. Impact of social protection on poverty reduction

	Number of poor (millions)		*Impact*	*Cost of program per person*
	Actual	*Without the program*	*Millions of people*	*Rubles/ month*
Old-age pension	28.1	43.2	15.1	2,568
Disability pension	28.1	29.6	1.5	2,434
Loss of breadwinner pension	28.1	28.8	0.7	1,813
Social pension	28.1	28.3	0.1	1,960
Care for children under 18 months	28.1	28.3	0.2	2,200
Child allowance	28.1	29.1	0.9	1,564
Unemployment benefit	28.1	28.3	0.1	2,164
Other benefits	28.1	28.2	0.1	2,032
Scholarship	28.1	28.4	0.2	2,274
All benefits	28.1	47.1	19.0	2,464

Source: Bank staff calculations based on data from Household Budget Survey 2002 (Goskomstat).
Note: Privileges are not included.

Factors That Diminish the Effectiveness of Noncontributory Social Transfers in Reducing Poverty

Despite the massive resources spent on social protection, the impact on poverty reduction is relatively low. The most important factors contributing to this outcome are the procyclical nature of overall spending; the fact that by design only a small fraction of these resources are targeted to the poor; the mediocre ability of the social assistance administration to identify the poor, which results in a significant leakage of funds; the fact that the benefits transferred by these programs are small compared with the income deficit of a poor beneficiary; and the widespread duplication of programs.

Procyclical Social Spending

In the aftermath of the 1998 crisis, the needed fiscal consolidation in Russia was achieved primarily at the expense of social spending. Social spending, including spending on social protection, education, and health, failed to act as an automatic stabilizer during the financial crisis in 1998. Instead, social spending was procyclical, failing to protect the poor during the crisis, when they were most in need. Social expenditures followed a U-curve, declining from their precrisis level (in percentage of GDP terms) until 2000–2001 and quickly recovering thereafter (table 8.6). Both

Table 8.6. Enlarged budget expenditures as percentage of GDP, 1997–2002

	1997	*1998*	*1999*	*2000*	*2001*	*2002*
			Percent of GDP			
Noninterest expenditures	*40.4*	*36.2*	*31.1*	*30.0*	*31.5*	*34.6*
Education	4.6	3.6	3.0	2.8	3.1	3.9
Health	3.5	3.4	2.9	2.8	2.9	3.2
Social protection	16.0	13.3	9.7	8.9	10.9	12.6
Other	16.3	15.9	15.5	15.5	14.6	14.9

Source: Morozov (2004).

the downward and upward sloping parts of the curve are very steep, pointing to significant fluctuations in social expenditures. All major categories of social expenditures (health, education, social protection) experienced the same U-curve dynamics. In this respect, they differ from the nonsocial (other) noninterest expenditures of the budget, which demonstrated surprising stability, declining only moderately after the 1998 crisis. Although total noninterest expenditures were cut by more than 10 percentage points of GDP between 1997 and 2000, this cut was achieved almost entirely through a reduction in spending on social protection, education, and health.

Inefficient Budget Allocation within Noncontributory Social Assistance Programs

The budget allocation among various noncontributory social assistance programs is an inefficient system of privileges that marginalizes programs targeted to the poor. While the amount of public resources redistributed by the system is very large compared with other countries at a similar level of economic development, the share of resources targeted toward the poor and vulnerable is very small, at just 7 percent of total social assistance spending.[4]

From a static perspective, current programs channel insufficient resources toward the neediest people because they overemphasize regressive subsidies; set an overly generous minimum subsistence level for the minority of targeted programs, which dilutes the allocation of scarce resources by targeting too large a group; and use targeting methods that yield mediocre performance. From a dynamic perspective, the current program mix focuses too much on coping with rather than preventing poverty or vulnerability. Social work and community care programs are underdeveloped, social workers spend too much time verifying program eligibility (income) and too little managing the cases of their clients, and the policy toward orphans relied until recently on costly institutionalization, ignoring preventive services and family-based care.

The system of subsidies for privileged citizens needs to be reformed. Privileges—targeted subsidies to certain categories of citizens for a wide range of services and goods—are the most important noncontributory transfers in terms of spending. In 2003 two types of privileges—for housing and utility services and for transport—channeled more than six times the resources allocated for transfers targeted to the poor. These privileges are governed by a complex system of federal, regional, and local laws and regulations. At the federal level alone, an estimated 156 types of privileges were granted to 236 types of beneficiaries (IISP 2002). A review of the social protection system in three regions (Komi Republic, Nizhniy Novgorod Oblast, and Moscow Oblast) revealed that regional and local governments complement the system by granting privileges to new categories or granting more generous discounts to those legislated federally.

This program archipelago is overly complex, hindering basic functions such as adequate budgeting or monitoring. According to the World Bank (2002a), the system of privileges covers 70 percent of the population, but the government can honor only part of its obligations. In 2000 only 36 percent of households received privileges. Thus privileges continue to operate as an unfunded mandate, with adverse consequences for budgetary planning (without knowing the number of beneficiaries and the level of the benefit, it is hard to estimate the volume of the subsidy required to cover this mandate), as well as for the financial position of service providers.

About 45 percent of the population benefits directly or indirectly from at least one type of privilege. Irrespective of their type, the largest share of occupational privileges accrues to the richest strata of the population (figure 8.1). The share of households from the poorest quintile in the overall utilization of such subsidized services (in terms of the number of services, not the total amount of the subsidy) is 7–14 percent. In contrast, the richest 20 percent of the population captures 22–33 percent of the number of services. The capture of the subsidy by the richest quintile is particularly acute for a few categories with narrower coverage, such as telephone services, spas and holidays, and tax exemption for home repair. For merit-related privileges, the distributional pattern is similar, but the criterion of pro-poorness is not relevant.

Occupational privileges are an expensive and highly regressive way to complement the wages and pensions of benefit holders. These types of benefits are contrary to the social protection principles of a market economy. The system represents inequitable use of scarce resources, as it does not explicitly benefit the poor and vulnerable. The fact that most benefits are captured by well-off beneficiaries is only one of the factors

Figure 8.1. Utilization of occupational privileges is highly regressive

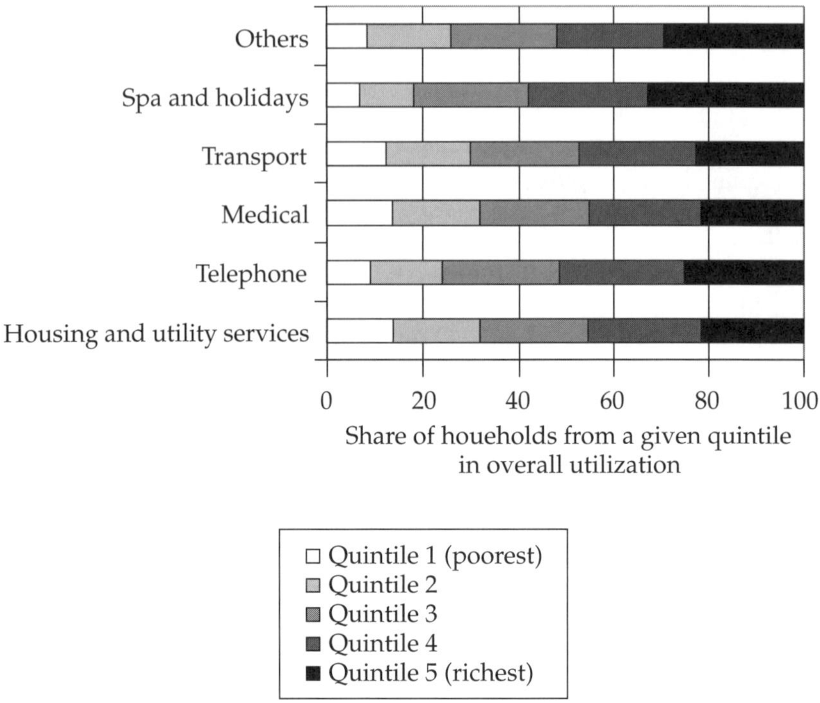

Source: Bank staff calculations based on data from NOBUS (Goskomstat 2003b).

that determines the highly regressive outcome of the occupational privileges. The other, equally important factor is the regressivity of the benefit—the fact that the amount of subsidy captured by richer households is many times larger than that captured by poor households. The regressivity of the benefit is embodied in the design of the system. As privileges are subsidies for the consumption of services with high income elasticity of demand, better-off households tend to consume both a larger quantity of services and better quality (hence more expensive) services, if available.

A first step toward reforming the current system of privileges is to ensure equitable access to both occupational and merit-based privileges. According to this principle, all privileged people would be entitled to an equal amount of subsidy. For example, all war veterans would receive the same per capita compensation for transport based on average utilization rates and tariffs. One way to enforce such equitable access is to migrate from the current system of open-ended subsidies to quota-based subsidies (under which each privileged citizen receives a voucher redeemable up to its face value) or replace them with flat cash benefits. Information on the utilization of these services and the appropriate tariffs could be obtained from a sample of providers (supply-side information), from a household survey (demand-side information), or from both (allowing a cross-check).

The effect of such a reform is shown for transport-related privileges. According to the 2003 NOBUS survey, 55.3 million people benefited, directly or indirectly, from free or discounted (assumed at 50 percent) urban, commuter, or long-distance transport services. The total amount of the subsidy is 3,155 million rubles per quarter. The distribution of beneficiaries is not very regressive—about 17 percent of users belong to the poorest 20 percent of the population—but the distribution of the subsidy is very regressive: beneficiaries from the poorest quintile received about 8 percent of the total subsidy, while the richest 20 percent captured 30 percent.

Under the current system, the average per capita benefit of this subsidy for a recipient household ranges from 123 rubles for the poorest quintile to 303 rubles for the richest quintile (table 8.7). Replacing the current subsidy

Table 8.7. Reduction in the fiscal and quasi-fiscal cost of transport privileges (if monetized at the level of the subsidy earned by the second quintile)

	Quintiles					
	1	*2*	*3*	*4*	*5*	*Total*
Actual Distribution of the Transport Privileges						
Beneficiaries						
Millions of people	9.2	11.8	12.1	12.2	10.0	55.3
Shares	17%	21%	22%	22%	18%	100%
Current Subsidy						
Millions of rubles	246	475	732	755	947	3,155
Shares	8%	15%	23%	24%	30%	100%
Mean Subsidy, Rubles per capita	*123*	*146*	*200*	*200*	*303*	*199*
Simulation: Replacing the current subsidy with a flat per capita benefit of 146 rubles						
Millions of rubles	291	475	535	551	455	2,308
Relative to current subsidy (%)	119%	100%	73%	73%	48%	73%

Source: Bank staff simulation based on data from NOBUS (Goskomstat 2003b).

with a flat per capita benefit of 146 rubles would be income neutral for the second quintile, raise the subsidy received by the poorest quintile by 19 percent, and reduce the value of the subsidies in the richer quintiles. It would reduce the total cost of the program by more than one-quarter, freeing up substantial resources to increase the budget of other, poverty-targeted benefits. Given that the cost of the housing and utility services benefit is almost twice that of the transport benefit, potential budget savings from their rationalization would be even greater.

Inadequate Targeting Performance

The two programs with the largest share of poor among their beneficiaries are the child allowance program and the decentralized social assistance program (table 8.8). About 30 percent of beneficiaries of the child allowance program and 28 percent of beneficiaries of the decentralized social assistance program come from the poorest quintile.

Programs not targeted to the poor have even worse targeting performance. Programs that include a smaller share of poor recipients among their beneficiaries include transport privileges (13 percent), housing and utility services privileges (17 percent), and targeted housing and utility services allowance (20 percent). There is substantial leakage for all programs, irrespective of the poverty line (official or alternative). About half

Table 8.8. Beneficiary incidence, by type of social protection program (share of direct and indirect beneficiaries from a given quintile in percent)

	Quintiles					
	1	*2*	*3*	*4*	*5*	*Total*
Targeted Social Assistance, of which:	*26*	*23*	*21*	*18*	*13*	*100*
Child allowance	30	24	20	16	11	100
Housing and utility services allowance	20	25	25	18	11	100
Decentralized social assistance	28	22	20	17	12	100
Privileges, of which:	*17*	*21*	*22*	*22*	*18*	*100*
Transport	13	20	23	24	20	100
Housing and utility services	17	22	22	23	17	100

Source: Bank staff calculations based on data from NOBUS (Goskomstat 2003b).

Figure 8.2. Rich households receive higher benefits than poor households, except in the case of the child allowance

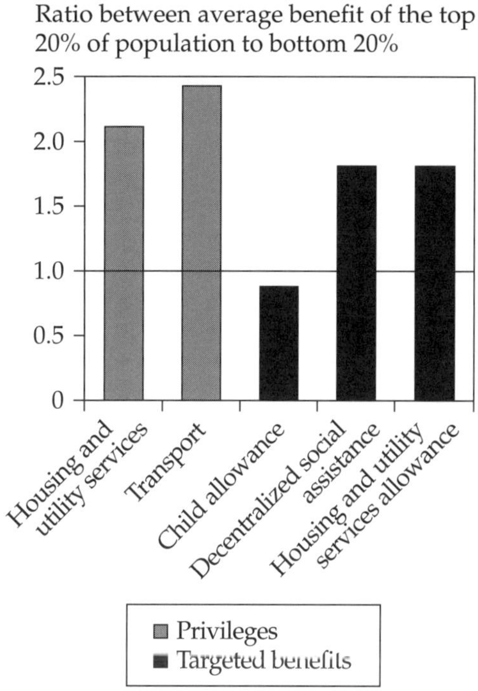

Source: Bank staff calculations based on data from NOBUS (Goskomstat 2003b).

of beneficiaries of targeted social assistance programs come from the richest 60 percent. This share is even higher for privileges, where 62 percent of beneficiaries are from the richest 60 percent of the population.

Almost all programs transfer more benefits to richer households: the incidence of the benefit is regressive. Among pro-poor programs, only the child allowance program transfers larger amounts to households from the poorest quintile than to the richest quintile (figure 8.2). This outcome is due to the benefit formula, which provides higher amounts for very vulnerable beneficiaries (the benefit is doubled for a single-parent household). The average benefit received by a household from the richest quintile is 80 percent higher than that received by the poorest quintile in the housing and utility services allowance and 100 percent higher in the decentralized social assistance program. The subsidies for privileged citizens for housing and utility services and for transport are the most regressive.

Figure 8.3. Compared with other countries, targeting of programs in Russia is poor

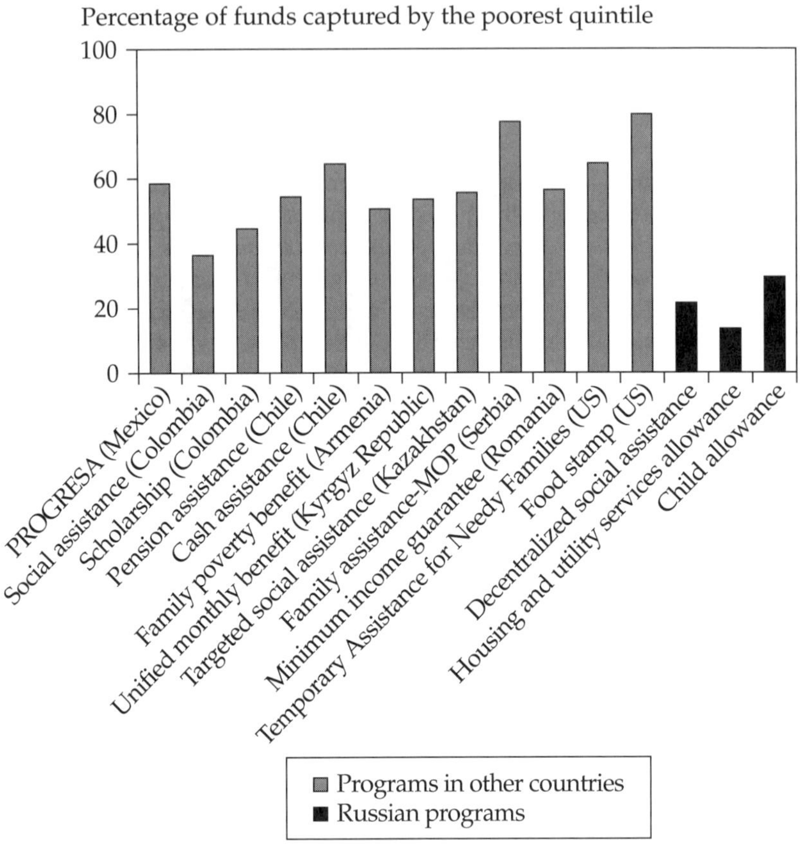

Sources: For Latin America and the United States, Castañeda and Lindert (2005); for Europe and Central Asia, various World Bank poverty assessments.
Note: Figure shows share of funds captured by poorest quintile.

The targeting performance of targeted social assistance programs in the Russian Federation is substantially lower than in good practice programs in countries that use either a means test or a proxy means test. All programs implemented in Russia rank well below their comparators in terms of the share of funds captured by the poorest quintile of the population (figure 8.3). The program with the best targeting performance, the child allowance program, channels only 30 percent of funding to beneficiaries from the poorest quintile, while most comparator programs transfer 40–60 percent of their funds to the bottom quintile.

The targeting techniques used by the comparator programs are similar but not identical to the one used in the Russian Federation, where an income test verifies both formal and informal income. The administration can verify de facto only formal income, which is known to be plagued by underreporting. Computerized checks are performed only in a few regions and only for other social protection incomes (pensions, unemployment benefits, and other targeted social assistance programs). Income from second jobs, in-kind income from agricultural self-employment, and entrepreneurial income are infrequently declared, hard to check, and seldom verified. This income test is thus an incomplete test of a household's true welfare level, as shown below.

Given the lack of reliability of income information and the mediocre targeting performance of the targeted social assistance programs, a proxy means test formula can provide better targeting outcomes. The main

Box 8.2. Targeting methods in selected countries

Among comparator welfare programs in other countries, only the food stamps and Temporary Assistance for Needy Families programs in the United States rely on a verified income test, supplemented by a limited asset test (benefits are denied if bank savings exceed a certain threshold, if the household owns an expensive car, and so forth). However, the infrastructure used to verify the accuracy of the information supplied by applicants is much more sophisticated than in the Russian Federation.

Facing the same problems as the Russian Federation—the impossibility of verifying all sources of income of applicants in an economy in which the informal sector and underground economy are large—other countries have successfully applied two alternative targeting mechanisms. In Central and Eastern Europe and the former Soviet Union, successful programs use a combination of an income and an assets test, in an attempt to identify the "economic potential" of households. Such a technique is similar to experiments performed in the Russian Federation in 1998 in Komi and Voronezh. To ensure that able-bodied individuals do not receive state support, Bulgaria and Romania supplement the means test with a workfare requirement. In Armenia, Turkey, and many Latin American countries, targeting is based on a proxy means test. Program eligibility is determined using a synthetic score based on easily observed characteristics (household structure, location, housing, ownership of durable goods, and so forth). Such a technique was implemented in the Russian Federation in parts of the Volgograd Oblast in 1998.

Sources: For Latin America and the United States, Castañeda and Lindert (2005); for Europe and Central Asia, various World Bank poverty assessments.

challenge for the social assistance administration in Russia is improving the means test formula. Under a proxy means test program, eligibility is based on a synthetic score, which is based on observable household characteristics—variables that are simple to report and hard for applicants to manipulate (box 8.2).

The results of a simulated proxy means test based on the NOBUS data (Gaskomstat 2003b) suggest that this method can substantially improve the targeting results of targeted social assistance programs.[5] The simulation shows that such a scoring formula would correctly identify 67 percent of beneficiaries (table 8.9). Moreover, the distribution of program beneficiaries by quintiles would improve substantially (table 8.10). About 61 percent of the proxy means test beneficiaries would come from the poorest quintile, followed by another 25 percent from the second quintile.

Table 8.9. Simulated targeting performance using proxy means test

	Proxy Means Test Score		
	Nonpoor	*Poor*	*Total*
Nonpoor	86	33	77
Poor	14	67	23
Total	100	100	100

Source: Bank staff simulation based on data from NOBUS (Goskomstat 2003b).

Table 8.10. Distribution of proxy means test beneficiaries by quintiles

	Proxy Means Test Score		
	Nonpoor	*Poor*	*Total*
Poorest quintile	11	61	20
2	19	25	20
3	22	10	20
4	23	4	20
Richest quintile	24	1	20
Total	100	100	100

Source: Bank staff simulation based on data from NOBUS (Goskomstat 2003b).

Hence the application of the proxy means test would generate a substantial reduction in poverty, under the same program envelope, by almost doubling the resources that could be channeled to the poorest quintile of the population.

Policy Recommendations

Resources need to be reallocated from untargeted, regressive privileges toward targeted social assistance programs. Untargeted programs cost the state an estimated 4.3 percent of GDP in 2002, while targeted programs received just 0.4 percent of GDP.

The scope for a reform of the system of privileges is large. Opposition to the reform of the system of privileges is traditionally fueled by the argument that these rights are merit based. But about half of existing privileges are unrelated to merit. These privileges could be reformed. The government could choose between several reform options, such as grandfathering privileges for existing beneficiaries while ceasing to grant new privileges; monetizing privileges by using a flat benefit for reasonable consumption norms or quotas (for example, the level of current consumption in the second quintile) or replacing them with vouchers (quota-based as opposed to open-ended consumer subsidies); and eliminating very regressive privileges.

The system of decentralized social assistance programs should be strengthened through improved financing and better targeting of instruments. The current system of decentralized financing and implementation generates substantial regional inequities, which hurt the poor from poorer regions. The following steps could be considered:

- Transform the unfunded mandate of the decentralized social assistance programs into one core program that is federally funded, is locally monitored and implemented, and fulfills the role of safety net of last resort for the very poor and destitute.
- Implement a program eligibility threshold aligned with budgetary resources (targeting, for instance, the poorest decile).
- Determine a reasonable program budget based on the poverty gap of the first decile and reasonable assumptions about program leakage.
- Earmark expenditures for this program through the Federal Equalization Fund and distribute these funds to the regions (or retain earmarked funds at the regional level) proportional to the share of the regional poverty gap of the target group in the national poverty gap. This share could be obtained using nationally representative surveys, such as the Household Budget Survey or the NOBUS.

- Consider developing poverty maps to further refine the allocation of program funds at the subregional level.
- Use proxy means testing to determine who is eligible for the program. Such a method would substantially reduce current leakage rates. Alternatively, improve the targeting performance of the existing formal income test by considering additional criteria for program eligibility related to housing conditions or endowment with key durables or real estate.
- Monitor the program, using a combination of administrative and survey techniques, and improve program dissemination and access.

The adequacy and targeting performance of the child allowance program should be strengthened. The child allowance program has the best targeting performance among targeted social assistance programs, largely because of the high correlation between poverty and the presence of children in a household. Currently, the program channels about 0.2 percent of GDP, and its adequacy is very low—only about one-fourth what it was in 1998.

To improve the poverty alleviation outcomes of the child allowance programs, the following measures could be considered:

- Improve program adequacy by raising the level of the benefit to the 1998 level and indexing the program benefit to inflation, in order to maintain its adequacy over time.
- Improve the targeting of the program benefit by granting higher benefits to vulnerable households.
- Improve the targeting of program beneficiaries. The resources of the program could be targeted toward very poor children by using a more conservative eligibility threshold.
- Use proxy means testing to determine who is eligible for the program.

Notes

1. The cost of housing and utility services for the enlarged government budget was 2.3 percent of GDP. In addition, providers lost an estimated 0.6 percent of GDP equivalent to the revenue gap of the utilities that provide such services below cost and the net increase in household arrears (quasi-fiscal cost).

2. Targeted social assistance programs provided by subnational governments include a set of income-tested one-time or monthly benefits, in cash or in kind, provided by regional and local governments in accordance with the provisions of the Federal Law on Government Social Assistance and financed from their respective budgets. According to NOBUS (2003), the largest programs in terms of coverage are cash assistance programs (8.8 percent of the population), food assis-

tance programs (3.2 percent), and subsidized access to health services (7.0 percent).

3. Spending for decentralized social assistance was estimated based on the NOBUS survey (Goskomstat 2003b) by comparing the total benefits received by households from this source with the amount of child allowances or housing and utility services allowances.

4. The allocation for all targeted social assistance programs represented 0.4 percent of GDP, equivalent to 10 percent of total public spending on noncontributory social programs (3.9 percent of GDP) or 7 percent of overall (fiscal and quasi-fiscal) spending on noncontributory social programs (5.9 percent of GDP).

5. A log-linear regression of household consumption on selected household characteristics was used to predict household consumption. The dependent variables in the regression are variables that are easily observable or verified and not easily manipulated: household demographics, education and employment status of the household head, characteristics of the dwelling, and ownership of other real estate or major durables. Predicted consumption was then compared with the household-specific poverty line to determine the proxy means test poverty status.

9
Reforming Housing and Utility Services and Protecting the Poor

*Reforming the housing and utility services sector is a priority item on the policy agenda. This chapter reviews the current system of housing subsidies, the rationale for reforming these subsidies in light of their sizable budgetary cost, and the links between reforming these subsidies and reform of the energy sector. It examines the required policy measures to mitigate the negative poverty impact of moving to full cost recovery, including expanding the take-up of the housing allowance program among the poorest.**

The Current System of Housing Subsidies

The system of housing and utility services has been and continues to be an important area for reform. Tariffs for housing and utility services were far below international prices in Russia at the beginning of the transition. Both rents and utility tariffs were subsidized to the point of being provided practically free of charge. Reform of housing and utility tariffs is essential, not only to relieve the budget of the unsustainable burden and to reduce energy losses and waste but also to revitalize the country's housing stock. The inefficient allocation and poor maintenance of the housing stock is a major barrier to the development of housing and labor markets in Russia.

Since 1992 the government has stated that the goal of the reform of housing and utility tariffs is to achieve full coverage of costs by residents while protecting low-income families. This principle has continued to be affirmed, although the deadline for achieving the goal has been pushed back and a clear program defining how it is to be accomplished remains to be agreed on. Initially, it was thought that the goal could be achieved in stages over a five-year period, but the full transition to the new system has repeatedly been moved to a later date. The current date for moving to full cost coverage is 2008. Almost a decade after the start of the reform, the average cost coverage for housing and utility services increased substantially, to 54 percent in 2000, up from 10 percent in 1992 (figure 9.1).[1]

The increase in housing and utility services expenditures was particularly hard for the poorest quintile. Evidence from the Russia Longitudinal Monitoring Survey (UNC, various years) shows that the poor pay a

Figure 9.1. Cost coverage of housing and utility services rose between 1992 and 2000

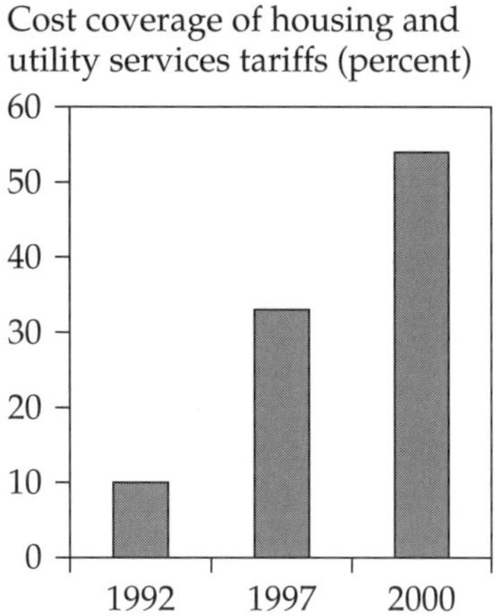

Sources: World Bank (1998); Decoster and Puzanov (2004).
Note: Cost coverage is the ratio of tariffs to production costs.

higher share of expenditures for these services than the rich, and the difference increased over time, peaking in 1998–99 (Hamilton, Banerjee, and Lomaia 2004) (figure 9.2). In relative terms, the largest increase in the share of housing and utility services expenditures from 1995 to 2001 was recorded in Moscow and St. Petersburg (where it increased by a factor of six), followed by other cities (where it doubled) and rural areas (where it almost doubled). Regardless of location, the highest income groups pay little for housing and utility services, with an effort ratio of less than 5 percent.

The government relies on two subsidization mechanisms—tariff discounts for privileged citizens and housing allowances targeting low-income families—to mitigate the effects of the increases in rents and utility prices on household welfare. A system of subsidies for privileged citizens, granting access to goods or services free of charge or at a fraction of their costs, has existed in Russia since Soviet times. Originally, the system was designed to reward certain categories of citizens for their civic merits (or to protect certain vulnerable strata of the population). During the transition the system was expanded. A large number of housing and utility privileges were introduced after 1992, supporting various occupational groups. Privileges were provided to people in particular occupations, such as customs officers, militiamen, police prosecutors, army officers, judges,

Figure 9.2. Poor households spend a higher share of total expenditures on housing and utility services

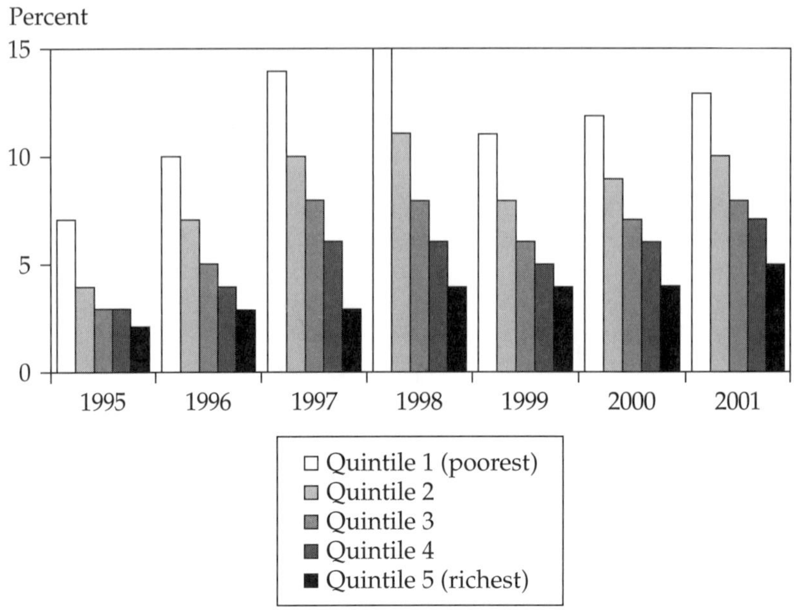

Source: Bank staff calculations based on data from Russia Longitudinal Monitoring Survey 1995–2002 (UNC).

and others. The criteria of merit, poverty, and vulnerability played no role in this subset of privileges. More than 10 new laws and more than 30 amendments providing for a reduction in rents and utility rates for particular groups of citizens were introduced between 1991 and 2002. Households receiving privileges pay only part of their housing bill—typically 50 percent and sometimes nothing at all. About one-third of the population benefits from subsidized access to housing and utility services because of this privileged status.

Targeted housing allowances are subsidies introduced since 1994 to limit the burden inflicted by rising utility expenditures. Among the three main housing subsidy mechanisms used in Central and Eastern Europe or the former Soviet Union—life-line tariffs, cash transfers, and the notional-burden approach—the Russian Federation opted for the notional-burden approach.[2] The formula for calculating the allowance has undergone some revisions over the past decade. Currently, housing allowances are available to households if their rent and utilities (based on norms) exceed 22 percent of their total income (the threshold is lower in certain regions).

Box 9.1. Determination of the housing allowance

The federal norms for the housing allowance (set until 2008) are as follows:

- 33 square meters for single-person households
- 42 square meters for two-person households
- 18 square meters per person in households with three or more people.

Utility service consumption norms are different in each of three climatic zones. To calculate the housing allowance, formal and informal (for example, family plot) household income and assets are divided by the number of household members. Living standards are measured by household expenditure per capita, excluding housing expenditures. An increase in housing costs is assumed to be offset by a decrease in other expenditures. Thus the change in living standards is calculated as the change in housing costs post-benefit. If average household per capita income is greater than the minimum subsistence level, the housing allowance is equal to either zero or the cost of housing and utility services based on social standards minus 22 percent of family income, whichever is greater. If average family per capita income is less than the minimum subsistence level, the housing allowance is determined in one of two ways:

Option 1: housing allowance = cost of housing and utility services based on social standards – [(0.22 × total family income/minimum subsistence level) × total family income]

Option 2: housing allowance = cost of housing and utility services based on social standards – 0.5 × official minimum wage × number of household members

Local housing offices or other local authorities are in charge of collecting applications for housing allowances, which are directly transferred to the housing or utility provider.

Source: Decoster and Puzanov (2004).

An amendment to the housing and utility services legislation in 2003 improved the poverty alleviation outcomes of the housing allowance. If the household's per capita income is below the regional minimum subsistence level, the admissible burden is adjusted downward by a coefficient equal to the ratio of family income to the minimum subsistence level (box 9.1).

Federal standards were set in 1997 for the social norm of housing floor area, which is used in interbudgetary relations. This standard is currently adopted in most regions in the Russian Federation. Other federal standards relate to the level of cost coverage (currently 90 percent), to production costs for housing and utility services (differentiated by the subjects of the Federation and updated through special government decrees every year) and to the maximum contribution to housing costs of the household (currently 22 percent of income). Within the federal norms, local administrations are allowed some discretion in administering the allowances, particularly in setting the maximum household contribution to housing costs.

The Need to Reform the System of Housing and Utility Subsidies

Reform of the system of housing and utility payments remains important for a number of reasons. First, subsidies by various levels of government absorb a large share of their resources. Second, a number of unfunded mandates compromise efforts to reform the energy sector. While the federal government has mandated reductions in housing and utility costs for various population groups, it has not provided sufficient funds for local authorities to do so. The result is that utility providers have to subsidize part of the cost reductions. This is in addition to what they absorb in the absence of full cost coverage not directly reimbursed by the government. Third, while transfer payments play a role in mitigating poverty, they are neither well targeted nor very effective in reducing poverty. Most of the subsidies for housing services pay for privileges that do not go to the poor. The household allowances that go to poor households are incomplete in coverage due to low take-up and poor targeting.

The amount of subsidies earmarked for housing and utility services constitutes an important drain on scarce government resources. Housing allowances and privileges are funded at both the federal and local levels and administered at the local level. The budgetary cost of discounted housing and utility services tariffs for privileged citizens was 2.3 percent of GDP in 2002—half the amount spent on pensions and six times what was spent on all targeted social assistance programs (including housing allowances). In contrast, the budget for housing allowances represented only 0.1 percent of GDP. In addition, providers lost an estimated 0.6 percent of GDP owing to the revenue gap of utilities that provide such services below cost and the net increase in household arrears (quasi-fiscal cost). The total fiscal and quasi-fiscal cost associated with the housing and utility services subsidization policy represented about 3 percent of GDP in 2002.

Unfunded mandates are a problem, particularly for local governments but also for utilities, which are forced to absorb the costs of the unfunded mandates. Federal and local funds do not completely cover the liabilities associated with the complex set of allowances and privileges decreed under federal or subnational laws. Municipalities have not been able to

Table 9.1. Coverage of social protection programs, by type (persons in recipient households benefiting directly or indirectly from the program)

		Postbenefit quintile				
Program	*Total*	*1*	*2*	*3*	*4*	*5*
Housing allowances	6	6	8	8	6	4
Housing privileges	32	26	35	35	36	28

Source: Tesliuc and Zotova (2004).
Note: Figures are percentages of the total population. Estimates were weighted by household weights and household size.

afford the federally mandated reductions in household and utility rates for certain privileged occupational groups. The financing of the implementation of the most costly law (the Law on Veterans) is entrusted to the governments of the subjects of the Russian Federation, which are unable to fulfill their financial obligations. Even if the budgets of higher levels of government provide compensation for reductions in utilities payments, some of the allocated funds never reach service providers. Most often, they disappear in local budgets. The end result is that the utility sector absorbs part of the cost of the privileges and allowances decreed by the government. The utilities also absorb part of the cost of providing services at prices that do not fully cover their costs.

The system of housing allowances and privileges covers a large share of the population and is not limited to the lower quintiles. The system of housing privileges covers about 32 percent of the population, while housing allowances cover only 6 percent of the population (table 9.1). The coverage of both sets of subsidies is fairly evenly spread across the population, but the poorest quintile is the least well covered, even for housing allowances, which are in principle a poverty-targeted program.

The Distributional Impact of Existing Housing and Utility Services Subsidies Is Anti-Poor

Household budget data record information on household expenditures after the allowance or subsidy has been factored in. To determine if these allowances or subsidies reach a particular income stratum (consumption decile), it is necessary to determine the household's income in the absence of these benefits. A first step is to estimate the housing and utility bill in the absence of allowances or subsidies and to add the estimate to household consumption net of housing and utility services costs. The household's housing bill in the absence of the benefit is estimated based on information on the various utilities that a household consumes, the type of housing, and the surface area of the housing. Using data from the Household Budget Survey for the fourth quarter of 2000, additional information on household income and benefits from the discount, and information on the various regional cost and norm parameters, the household's housing and utility bill is calculated on a net basis. For households receiving a housing allowance, the allowance is calculated as the maximum social rent less the marginal tax rate multiplied by the household's money income. Privileged households are assumed to pay only 50 percent of the calculated gross housing bill.

With information on both gross and net housing costs, the distributional impact of housing payments can be calculated. The welfare measure used is household expenditure per capita. Since there are some economies of scale in housing costs and poorer individuals tend to live in larger households, per capita housing costs are expected to rise with income. In addition, as income increases, households tend to occupy more surface area per capita. Indeed, gross housing costs per capita tend to be higher in the upper deciles than in the lower deciles (figure 9.3).

The simulated housing and utility services subsidies and allowances are regressive, with most of the benefits going to the upper deciles (figure 9.4). The subsidy declines steeply from the first to the second decile, then levels out and starts to rise again from the fourth decile on, only to fall again in the tenth decile. It would appear that the housing allowances are most heavily concentrated in the poorest decile. But the reductions in housing costs are quite substantial from the fourth decile on, with the seventh and ninth deciles benefiting even more than the first decile. Except for the bottom decile, the share of total spending (estimated by the benchmark simulation) that goes to the housing subsidy increases sharply from the fourth decile on (table 9.2). The largest share of the total subsidy goes to the top decile. All in all, housing allowances account for only about a quarter of the housing subsidies, with privileges accounting for the other three-quarters.

Distributional Impact of Proposed Reforms

Some key parameters in the benchmark model were altered to assess the poverty and fiscal impacts of the two major elements of reform under consideration: removing privileges and increasing cost coverage. The model was also used to examine what would happen if all households eligible for the allowance took advantage of it. Various simulations were carried out (table 9.3).

Eliminating privileges would substantially reduce the cost of the housing subsidy and have little impact on poverty. Simulation A1 indicates that the cost of the housing subsidy could be reduced by about 75

Figure 9.3. Although the level of housing expenditures is higher for richer households, the share of housing in total expenditures is greater for poor households; the housing subsidy significantly reduces that expenditure share for the bottom quintile

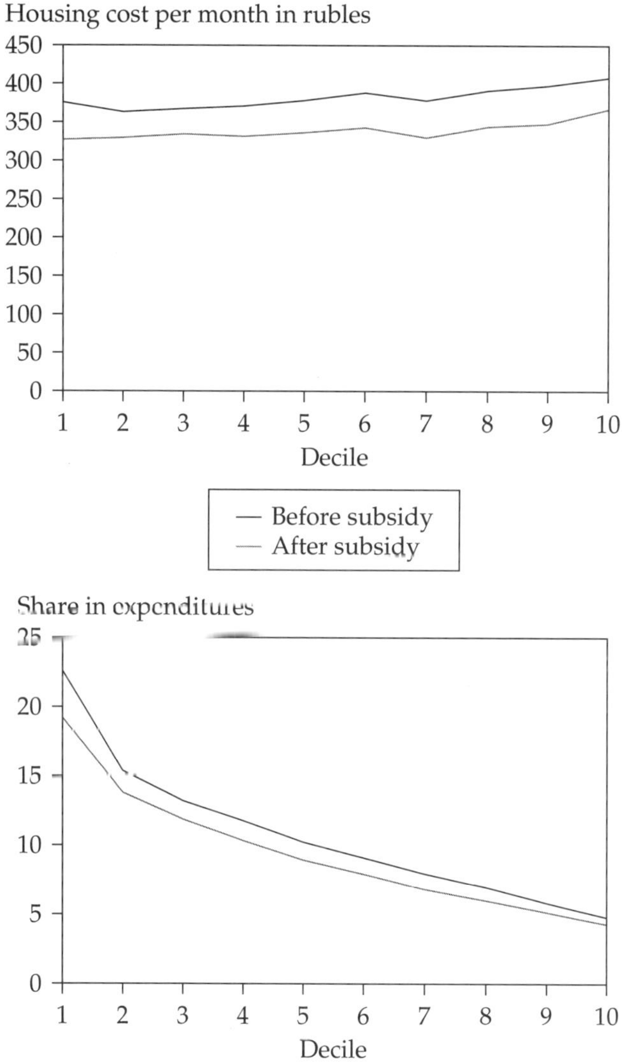

Source: Decoster and Puzanov (2004).

Figure 9.4. Housing and utility subsidies appear to be regressive

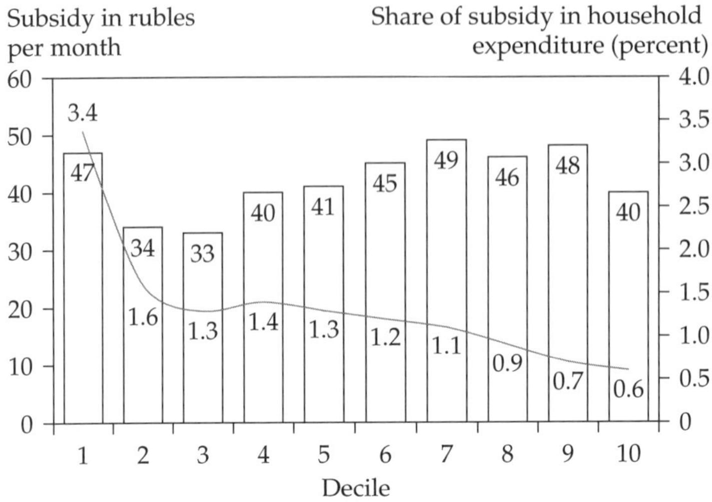

Source: Decoster and Puzanov (2004).

Table 9.2. The size of the housing subsidy rises with income

Income decile	*Share of budgetary cost (percent)*
1 (lowest)	8.1
2	6.7
3	7.1
4	9.2
5	9.7
6	10.6
7	11.9
8	11.4
9	12.1
10 (highest)	13.2
All households	9.7

Source: Decoster and Puzanov (2004).

percent if privileges were eliminated (table 9.4). Eliminating privileges would have little impact on poverty, as virtually all of the housing subsidy goes to households in the upper deciles. The incidence of poverty would rise very slightly, from 22.6 percent to 22.9 percent (table 9.5). The elimination of privileges is generally a progressive scenario: while all

Table 9.3. Description of the simulations

Simulation	*Description*
A1	Eliminate privileges.
A3	Increase the burden limit to the federal standard of 22 percent.
A4	Assume that all households that were eligible for a housing allowance in the benchmark situation but did not apply for it receive the housing allowance (full take-up).
B1	Move to full cost recovery. The maximum social rent increases with higher prices for utilities, inducing changes in the housing allowance, which increases. However, only households receiving the housing allowance in the base case are assumed to receive the housing allowance.

Source: Decoster and Puzanov (2004).

Table 9.4. Budgetary effects of simulations

	Housing household expenditures (billions of rubles per year)			*Change in cost of reductions*	
Simulation	*Before subsidy*	*After subsidy*	*Cost of subsidy*	*In billions of rubles*	*As percentage of benchmark cost of reductions*
Benchmark situation in 2000	209.5	185.4	24.1	n.a.	n.a.
Simulation					
A1 Eliminate privileges	209.5	203.6	5.9	–18.2	–76
A3 Increase burden limit to 22%	209.5	187.8	21.7	– 2.4	–10
A4 Full take-up of allowances	209.5	165.1	44.5	20.4	85
B1 Full cost recovery	369.7	318.3	51.4	30.0	125

Source: Decoster and Puzanov (2004).
n.a. Not applicable.

deciles experience a loss in living standards (as measured by the percentage change in household expenditure per capita), the loss increases through the sixth decile (table 9.6). The top four deciles also experience a loss that is greater than that experienced by the bottom three deciles (the population that falls roughly below the poverty line).

Table 9.5. Effect of simulated reforms on poverty and inequality

	Poverty		
Situation	*Incidence (percent)*	*Depth (percent)*	*Gini coefficient*
Benchmark situation in 2000	22.6	6.6	0.350
Simulation			
A1 Eliminate privileges	22.9	6.7	0.350
A3 Increase burden limit to 22%	22.8	6.7	0.351
A4 Full take-up of allowances	21.0	5.5	0.340
B1 Full cost recovery	27.0	8.9	0.365

Source: Decoster and Puzanov (2004).

Table 9.6. Simulations of a change in living standards, by decile

Decile	*A1*	*A3*	*A4*	*B1*
1 (lowest)	–0.07	–0.66	17.1	–17.5
2	–0.30	–0.61	5.5	–10.6
3	–0.56	–0.44	2.6	–9.1
4	–1.01	–0.29	1.2	–7.9
5	–1.09	–0.16	0.6	–7.0
6	–1.17	–0.06	0.3	–6.5
7	–1.14	–0.03	0.1	–5.7
8	–0.91	–0.02	0.1	–4.9
9	–0.77	0.00	0.0	–4.2
10 (highest)	–0.58	0.00	0.0	–3.5
All households	–0.76	–0.23	2.8	–7.7

Source: Decoster and Puzanov (2004).

Moving to the federal standards would yield a modest cost savings, with some declines in welfare. Many regions have not moved to the federal standard of 22 percent for the marginal tax rate on income applied in calculating the maximum social rent. The average implicit tax rate in 2000 was 17.3 percent. Moving uniformly to federal standards would reduce the allowances received by households. Since most households receiving allowances fall in the bottom of the distribution, living standards of the poor would be reduced and poverty increased. The results from simulation A3 show that incomes would decline by about 0.6 percent in the first two deciles and by about 0.4 percent in the third decile. The changes would not be sufficient to affect the poverty rate, however, which would remain virtually unchanged (tables 9.5 and 9.6). The savings would be small—about 10 percent of the benchmark cost of the reductions (see table 9.4).

Improving the take-up so that every eligible household benefits from the allowance would improve living standards at the bottom of the distribution and reduce poverty, but doing so would come at a high cost. The take-up of housing allowances is very low. Many households that are eligible for an allowance do not apply for it. In fact, only 23 percent of eligible households took the allowance in 2000.

To determine the impact of a larger take-up, a simulation (A4) was carried out in which every household whose money income made it eligible for an allowance received it. Spending increased 85 percent, to about 10 percent more than the amount spent on privileges (see table 9.4). Financing a substantial improvement in the take-up rate would thus require the elimination of privileges if the cost of the housing allowances were held constant.

Moving to full take-up of housing allowances would substantially improve living standards at the bottom of the distribution, particularly in the first and second deciles. Living standards in the first decile would improve 17 percent (see table 9.6), and poverty rates would fall 1.6 percentage points (see table 9.5). However, while the increase in the number of households receiving the allowance would substantially benefit those in the first decile, it would not be sufficient to move many households out of poverty.

The transition to full cost recovery by the utilities would significantly increase public spending on housing subsidies, but it would yield substantial revenues in the form of additional housing and utility payments. This simulation (B1) is modeled by multiplying current utility prices by the inverse of the cost coverage level in each region. The average cost coverage level for all utilities combined was about 54 percent in 2000; for electricity it was 81 percent. Moving to full cost coverage raises the gross housing bill for all households. At the same time, it increases the amount of the allowances that poor households receive, as well as the amount of the housing subsidy privileged households receive. The total cost of the subsidies (both allowances and privileges) more than doubles relative to the benchmark case (see table 9.4). However, the revenues generated from the increase in cost recovery (the difference in gross housing costs between this simulation and the benchmark) are more than three times the cost of the subsidy (allowances and privileges) in the full coverage scenario. In the benchmark case, however, price subsidies were not included in the cost of the housing subsidy, which comprised only the cost of the housing allowance and privileges. To the extent that various levels of government are explicitly subsidizing housing and utilities service providers, the subsidies (estimated in the benchmark model at 160.2 billon rubles) saved by moving to full cost coverage could be used to offset the additional costs imposed by the higher allowances and privileges.

Full cost recovery would significantly lower standards of living and increase poverty. All deciles would suffer a decline in living standards (see table 9.6) under the full cost recovery scenario. In principle, households already receiving a housing allowance would not pay more, as the allowance would increase to cover the growth in housing costs. However, poor households that do not benefit from an allowance would be especially hard hit, since their housing costs—which already constitute a large share of their expenditures—would increase substantially. Privileged households would be forced, according to the assumptions used in calculating the benchmark case, to shoulder half the increase in housing costs. Better-off households that are not privileged would also have to bear the full brunt of the increase, but as housing costs account for a relatively smaller share of their expenditures, their welfare loss would not be as great. The decline in living standards would be particularly acute in the bottom deciles, where a substantial number of poor households are not receiving housing allowances. To pay for the increased cost of housing, households in the first decile would need to decrease other expenditures by 17.5 percent, households in the second decile would need to decrease other expenditures by 10.6 percent, and households in the top decile would incur a loss of welfare of 3.5 percent (see table 9.6). The poverty headcount would increase 4.4 percentage points (see table 9.5).

Policy Recommendations

Housing privileges have remained substantially intact in the reforms adopted, though there appears to be some flexibility at the regional level. The amendments to the Law on Fundamentals approved in May 2003 provide for some changes in the system of privileges for rents and utility rates.[3] According to the new law, most privileged groups will retain their current privileges at the current amounts. But the law mandates that part of these privileges must be financed from the federal budget, with the rest financed from the budgets of subjects of the Russian Federation. The law also contains a provision allowing each subject of the Russian Federation to determine whether to grant public social assistance and how much to provide from its budget. This provision came into effect in early 2005. Though the new version of the law contains a number of positive improvements, it does not resolve the main problem: optimizing and reducing government obligations to subsidize housing and utility rates for different social and occupational groups.

Reducing the amount spent on privileges will be key if the housing allowance benefit is expanded for the poor as full cost coverage takes effect. As the simulations show, expanding the take-up of housing allowances by the poor will require eliminating spending on privileges if the impact on the budget is to remain more or less neutral. Moving to full cost recovery without eliminating privileges will impose an even greater burden on the various levels of government. Reining in costs in a socially progressive manner is important to ensure that the government is able to afford the cost of the housing allowances. Otherwise, it is likely that the benefits of increased cost recovery that would go to the utility and housing providers will be undercut by the inability of the government to pay for housing allowances and privileges.

Various means are available for reducing privileges. Chapter 8 proposes several avenues to achieving this, including monetizing privileges by means of a flat benefit. At the same time, measures will be needed to mitigate the negative poverty impact of moving to full cost recovery, including expanding the take-up of the housing allowance program among the poorest. As incomes continue to grow, poorer households will be in a better position to shoulder the impact of moving to full price coverage. But in the short run, measures will be needed to deal with the negative consequences for poverty. While those receiving housing allowances would be largely protected from the move to full cost coverage to the extent that their housing costs are limited to a share of their income, the poor who do not benefit from housing allowances would be most vulnerable to the move to full cost coverage. The analysis of household data for 2000 suggests that more than three-quarters of households that are eligible for the housing allowance do not currently receive it. Expanding the program to include them would help cushion some of the negative impacts of moving to full cost recovery.

Revising the formula used to calculate the housing allowance is desirable. The analysis of the distribution of beneficiaries presented in table 9.1 shows that the beneficiaries are more or less evenly spread out by quintile. Most likely, the income concept in calculating the housing allowance—which is tightly linked to forms of income that can be easily checked—needs to be revised. The government may want to consider using a proxy means test to determine who is eligible for the program. As illustrated in chapter 8, this method would substantially reduce current leakage rates. Alternatively, the targeting performance of the existing formal income test may improve by considering additional criteria for program eligibility related to housing conditions or to endowment of durables or real estate. In the run-up period, further income growth, especially among the poor, will be important in cushioning the impact of the transition to full cost coverage.

Notes

*. This chapter draws on Decoster and Puzanov (2004).

1. Estimates for 2000 are from Decoster and Puzanov (2004). Estimates for 1992 and 1997 are from World Bank (1998).

2. Life-line tariffs restrict the price subsidy to an initial block of consumption (sometimes called the basic need level), providing a less costly alternative to across-the-board price subsidies. The mechanism is relatively simple to administer. It was implemented during the early 1990s in many countries in Central and Eastern Europe. Cash transfers—earmarked for housing and utility services or not—are an alternative to tariff subsidization. Bulgaria and Romania operate a guaranteed minimum income program that includes an energy benefit component provided monthly to eligible families during the cold season. The notional burden approach is commonly found in countries of the former Soviet Union. The admissible share of housing and utility services expenditures in household consumption tends to vary between 15 and 30 percent. A similar program is found in the United States, where the burden limit is 50 percent.

3. Earlier the Russian government proposed to the Duma to abolish privileges in their current form and introduce targeted allowances instead, but the proposal was not supported by legislators.

10
Improving the Poor's Access to Good-Quality Education

Inadequate access to education and poor-quality education are contributors to poverty, and poverty is often a contributor to children not being enrolled in school, discontinuing their education, or being enrolled in low-quality or irrelevant programs. A poorly educated population is a constraint to increasing the productivity and flexibility of the workforce and therefore a constraint to economic growth. This chapter shows that the mutually reinforcing relationship between poverty and inadequate educational opportunities is a serious problem in Russia—a problem that has been worsening and may continue to worsen unless steps are taken to break the cycle. The educational challenges faced by the poor are twofold: access to education is increasingly determined by income and wealth, with poverty having a negative impact on access to noncompulsory education and high-quality modern educational programs, and funding for education is inequitably allocated. The chapter provides a list of poverty-related policy recommendations.

Transition Has Increased Inequality in Education Attainment and Outcomes

Russia inherited an educational system from the Soviet Union that provided broad access to education regardless of ethnic background, gender, or geographical location. While there is no comparative measurement of education outcomes during the Soviet era (the capacity for objectively assessing learning outcomes is only now being developed), it is generally accepted that there was no significant variation across income groups or geographic areas in terms of the quality of education, especially in comparison with many OECD countries. Nearly all students received a basic education, reflected in an adult literacy rate that was reportedly near 100 percent (Rashid and Posarac 2002). The Soviet Union was among the first countries to introduce a complex system of affirmative action, which supported students from peasant and working class families in higher education. That system collapsed over the past 10 years, with only orphans continuing to receive regular support from preschool to higher education. Some regions continue to provide free school meals, textbooks, and even summer school grants for students based on poverty level, although these subsidies are not universal and tend to be irregularly provided.

Declining birth rates and increasing in- and out-migration rates have influenced the structure of the school-age population across the Federation, a factor that should be taken into consideration when per capita indicators for developing Russia's education system are calculated. Between 1989 and 1997, the number of school-age children decreased by 3.6 million; by 2010 an additional decline of 7.8 million is expected. The regions in the North West, Far East, and Siberia experienced the largest enrollment declines, owing to out-migration, while the Central region saw the largest enrollment increases (World Bank 1999). The peripheral areas of the North West, Far East, and Siberia are likely to face even greater declines in the demand for education because of net out-migration in the coming years, while the Volga, Ural, and Central regions will experience increased demand for education as a result of net in-migration.

Despite Russia's strong position in terms of compulsory enrollment and completion, children from poor households have less access to preschool and noncompulsory education, which is increasingly determined by income and wealth.[1] Data from the 2003 NOBUS survey show that the net compulsory education enrollment rate (the percentage of children 7–15 who are enrolled in compulsory education) for all income levels is 94–96 percent, which is high by most transition economy standards and close to Western European levels. Nearly 100 percent of Russian children eventually complete compulsory education. However, the rate of enrollment of six-year-olds in kindergarten is nearly 90 percent for the highest income deciles and only about 75 percent in the lowest-income decile. Children from poor households show a slightly higher tendency to enroll in compulsory education at age six, possibly reflecting lack of access to kindergarten. Yet six-year-olds from poor households are also more likely than higher-income children not to be enrolled in any educational program.

The more limited access of the poor to kindergarten and preschool programs is a serious policy concern. Lack of early childhood care and education, which is often combined with other problems, such as sporadic attendance, absenteeism, and underachievement, increases the chances that a child will begin compulsory education behind his or her peer group. As few teachers are trained to deal effectively with different ability levels in the classroom and few schools have the resources to fund remedial programs, children who start out behind are very likely to continue to lose ground as they progress through compulsory education. The life prospects of the poor could increasingly be determined before the child begins compulsory education.

Children from lower-income households in Russia are also more likely to discontinue their education after the compulsory levels are completed. Russia's net secondary enrollment rate for 16- to 17-year-olds of about 78 percent (NOBUS 2003) is significantly below net secondary enrollment for

Western Europe and North America (UNESCO 2000–02), both of which average 89 percent, and below most comparable transition economies (figure 10.1).[2] There is a significant correlation between poverty and nonenrollment in secondary education (figure 10.2). While only 5 percent of 16- to 17-year-olds from the highest-income decile are not enrolled in secondary education, more than 16 percent of 16- to 17-year-olds from the lowest-income decile are not enrolled. Furthermore, while more than 16 percent of 16- to 17-year-olds from the lowest-income decile are still enrolled in compulsory education—reflecting a late start or grade repetition—only about 7 percent of 16- to 17-year-olds from the highest-income decile are still enrolled in compulsory education, and more than 6 percent are enrolled in tertiary education. The trend continues in tertiary education, where about 42 percent of 18- to 24-year-olds in the highest-income decile but less than 17 percent of those from the lowest-income decile are enrolled.[3]

On average, the lowest-income group has two to three years less schooling than the highest-income group (table 10.1). Rural population

Figure 10.1. Net secondary enrollment rate in Russia is lower than in other transition economies

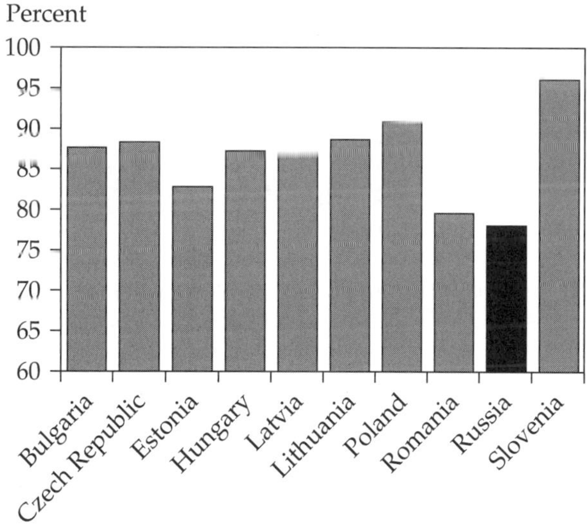

Sources: UNESCO 2000; Bank staff calculations based on data from NOBUS (Goskomstat 2003b).

Note: Figure compares the NOBUS (2003) estimate of Russia's net secondary enrollment for 16- to 17-year-olds to net secondary enrollment data for other countries in 2000, the most recent data point available for cross-country net enrollment rates from UNESCO.

Figure 10.2. Enrollment in noncompulsory education is lower among the poor

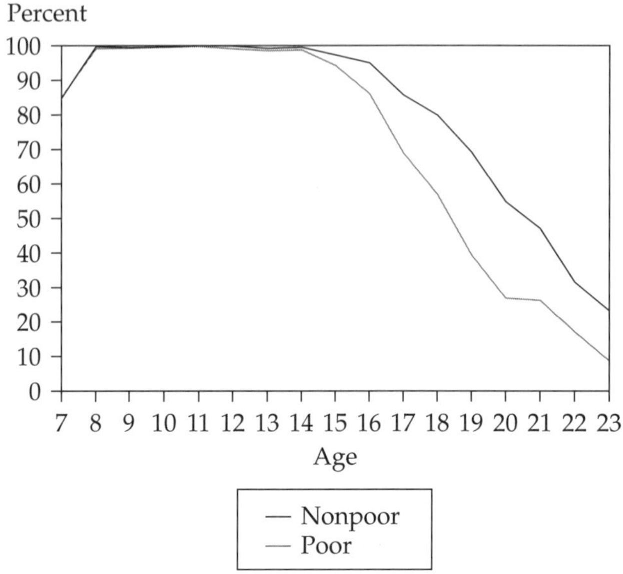

Source: Bank staff calculations based on data from NOBUS (Goskomstat 2003b).

has fewer years of schooling than urban population, irrespective of income group. According to the NOBUS data, 15 percent of adults in rural areas and just 6 percent in urban areas terminated their education following primary education, and slightly more than 8 percent of adults in rural areas and 22 percent in urban areas completed higher education. A tendency for women to have fewer years of schooling than men is pronounced only in lower-income groups. The Russia Longitudinal Monitoring Survey (UNC, various years) data show a similar trend.

Regional variations reveal the dependence of educational attainment on income. In the South—by far the poorest region in Russia, with a GRP per capita in 2001 of only 28,000 rubles—more than 10 percent of adults left school following primary education. In contrast, in the North West, where per capita GRP was 53,000 rubles, and the Far East, where per capita GRP was 56,000 rubles, only about 4–5 percent of adults left school after primary education. In the comparatively affluent Ural region, with per capita GRP of 97,000 rubles, just 7 percent of children discontinued their education after primary school; in the Central region, where per capita GRP was 70,000 rubles, the figure was 8 percent. There is also variation in the com-

Table 10.1. Mean years of schooling for adults rise with consumption

	Consumption decile									
Item	*1 (lowest)*	*2*	*3*	*4*	*5*	*6*	*7*	*8*	*9*	*10 (highest)*
Rural	9.5	9.4	9.3	9.7	9.9	10.2	10.1	10.6	10.9	11.4
Urban	10.4	10.9	11.2	11.2	11.5	11.8	11.9	12.3	12.6	13.2
Male	10.4	10.7	11.0	11.1	11.3	11.6	11.8	12.1	12.5	13.0
Female	9.6	10.0	10.3	10.6	11.0	11.3	11.4	11.9	12.3	13.0
Total	10.0	10.3	10.5	10.8	11.1	11.4	11.5	12.0	12.4	13.0

Source: Bank staff calculations based on data from NOBUS (Goskomstat 2003b).
Note: Sample includes all individuals 23 and older.

pletion of university-level education across regions, ranging from about 16 percent in the Volga region to nearly 22 percent in the North West.

The tendency of children and young adults from low-income groups to discontinue their education after the compulsory level and to have lower levels of educational attainment has a direct negative impact on their life chances (table 10.2). In nearly all countries, higher levels of education are associated with a higher probability of employment and higher earnings. Goskomstat data show that in 2002, 83 percent of the population with a tertiary or professional education was in the labor force, while the corresponding percentage for compulsory education graduates was 38 percent (Roshtchina 2004). The unemployment rate of compulsory education graduates was 19.7 percent in 2002, while that of higher education graduates was only 4.2 percent. According to Goskomstat, more than 70 percent of higher education graduates between 18 and 65 are employed. This share gradually falls with lower levels of education attainment, to 43.7 percent among those with only a compulsory education and 20.5 percent among those with only a primary education.

Mean monthly net income also increases with the level of education in Russia. The NOBUS data show that the standard deviation is very large, revealing significant variation in income among workers—a common finding in transition economies. The 2002 Russia Longitudinal Monitoring Survey (UNC, various years) provides evidence that returns to education in Russia have become similar to those in Western economies. Higher education graduates between 18 and 25 earn more than 50 percent more than those with only a secondary education, and people 36–64 with higher education earn twice as much as people with only a secondary education.[4]

The need to make private contributions for education represents a serious poverty issue in Russia today. According to the 2002 Russia Lon-

Table 10.2. The nonpoor have higher education attainment than the poor (percent)

Education attainment	*Nonpoor*	*Poor*
No primary education	1.58	3.52
Primary	7.06	12.26
Lower secondary	10.69	16.80
Full secondary	16.85	22.65
Initial vocational without secondary certificate	3.64	3.53
Initial vocational with secondary certificate	6.31	7.81
Secondary vocational	29.14	24.05
Incomplete higher education	3.09	1.28
Higher education	21.28	8.05
Postgraduate	0.34	0.04
Total	100.00	100.00

Source: Bank staff calculations based on data from NOBUS (Goskomstat 2003b).
Note: Sample includes all individuals 23 and older.

gitudinal Monitoring Survey data, the top income quintile accounted for 46 percent of private spending on education, while the bottom income quintile contributed about 2 percent of all private funding. The rural population has a higher tendency to report the high costs of studying as a major constraint to continuing education, while the urban population is twice as likely to cite the need to find employment as a reason for discontinuing education, a finding that reflects the shift of employment opportunities to the cities. Across regions the percentage of people citing the high cost of education as a problem is much higher in the South (33.9 percent) and Siberia (31.6 percent), where per capita GRP is relatively low, than in the more affluent North West (9.7 percent) and Far East (11.6 percent).

Poverty in Russia has a growing impact on access to high-quality and relevant educational programs. Low income is preventing many students from gaining access to the type and quality of education that will promote better life chances and thus help break the cycle of poverty in Russia. As in most countries with open enrollment policies, children from wealthier households tend to enroll disproportionately in more competitive programs, in schools that tend to send more students on to higher education, and in schools with greater resources. The 2001 Access to Tertiary Education in Russia data (Roshtchina, Drugov, and Kuzina 2001), which surveyed urban secondary students in four regions, show that 40 percent of eleventh grade students from families in the highest income quintile attend a *lyceum* or *gymnasium* (as distinct from a general secondary school), while only 15 percent of those from families in the poorest quintile attend such schools.[5] Access to computers, the Internet, and foreign languages is also lower among low-income families. About 80 percent of students categorized as poor had three or fewer foreign language lessons a week, while the majority of students from high-income families had more than five such lessons per week. Although no country can be expected to ensure equality of educational outcomes with regard to the types of schools attended, Russia could do a better job of promoting access to educational opportunities, which would level the playing field in the competition for more elite schools.

Low income is a barrier to entering high-quality university programs. According to the 2001 Access to Tertiary Education data, only 15–50 percent of children from poor families were accepted into a higher education institution, while almost 80 percent of those from better-off families gained admittance. The characteristics of the secondary school attended play a strong role in admission. The better the school is in terms of the number of specialized academic subjects and the number of foreign language classes, the higher the chances its graduates have of entering a university or college. The 2003 VCIOM data show that 95 percent of entrants from high-income families enter a higher education institution upon their first application, while only about 10 percent of students from low-income families (those with household incomes of less than 5,000 rubles a year) succeed on their first try. Students from low-income families are also much more likely to attend a higher education institution that was not their first choice, and they are more likely to attend evening courses. The 2001 Access to Tertiary Education data (Roshtchina, Drugov, and Kuzina 2001) show a correlation between the choice of a university department by secondary graduates and economic factors. Students from higher-income families tend to be accepted into more competitive economics and law departments, while students from lower income families tend to be accepted into technical and engineering programs.

Deepening inequality in terms of access to better schools and programs is compounded by a rise in privately financed education and informal payments. Not surprisingly, high-income households tend to make larger private contributions to their children's education than lower-income households, although it is likely that lower-income households tend to contribute a higher share of their disposable income to their children's education. Of those households spending more than 15,000 rubles on their children's education during the previous school year, more than 80 percent were nonpoor (figure 10.3); while among those households spending less than 2,500 rubles on their children's education, nearly 80 percent were categorized as poor. This large disparity in nominal contributions is a concern because of the potential long-term negative impact on quality for schools with large numbers of students from poor households.

Figure 10.3. The poor spend less on education than the nonpoor

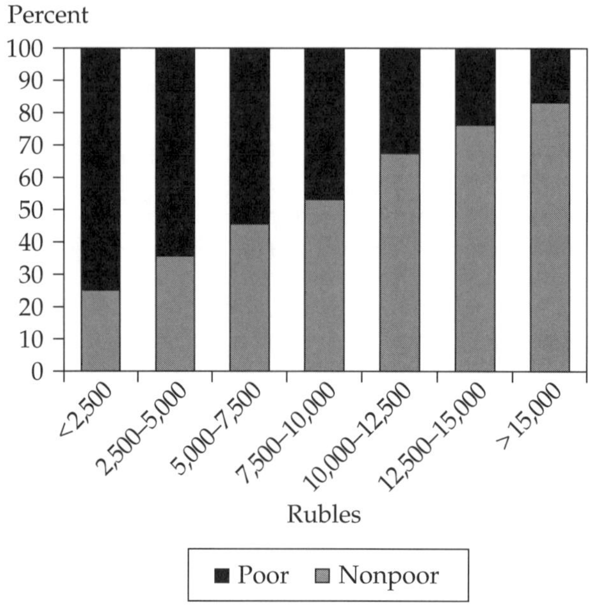

Source: Bank staff calculations based on data from NOBUS (Goskomstat 2003b).

There is also significant variation in spending on tutoring between the lowest- and highest-income households. The NOBUS survey shows that more than 40 percent of households from the highest-income decile spent more than 2,000 rubles on private tutoring in 2003, while 60 percent of households in the lowest-income decile made only negligible contributions to tutoring.

The cost of transportation reduces access to high-quality schools and programs. Spending on transportation varies markedly between the lowest- and highest-income households. Children from higher-income households have a clear advantage in terms of having access to better and more desirable types of schools. A large share of lower-income households spent less than 250 rubles for their children's transportation the previous year, while a large share of higher-income households spent more than 2,000 rubles a year on transportation.

Access to textbooks may be related to poverty. Mean household spending on textbooks was 472 rubles per year in 2003. But more than half of the households in the lowest-income decile spent less than 250 rubles on their children's textbooks, while 33 percent of households in the highest-income decile spent more than 750 rubles. This variance in private expenditure for textbooks could reflect the fact that some regions provide free textbooks to disadvantaged students. More research is needed to ensure that textbook subsidies, where they exist, are actually reaching the poor. Generally, spending on textbooks is higher in urban areas than in rural ones.

Funding for Education Is Inequitably Allocated

Public funding for education declined after 1997, as the fiscal consolidation following the 1998 financial crisis was achieved largely at the expense of social spending (figure 10.4). Although spending as a share of GDP has increased since 2000, it continues to be low in comparison with OECD countries, the Baltic states, and most Central and Eastern European countries (figure 10.5).

There is concern as well about the efficiency with which resources are used. In addition to the common problems associated with persistent underfunding of the system (decaying infrastructure, inadequate educational resources, undertrained and underpaid teachers, and so forth), inadequate and inefficiently used resources have meant that Russia has not been able to target funding to disadvantaged groups or to schools in which educational performance is low.

Figure 10.4. Education expenditures as a percentage of GDP fell until 2000, before rising

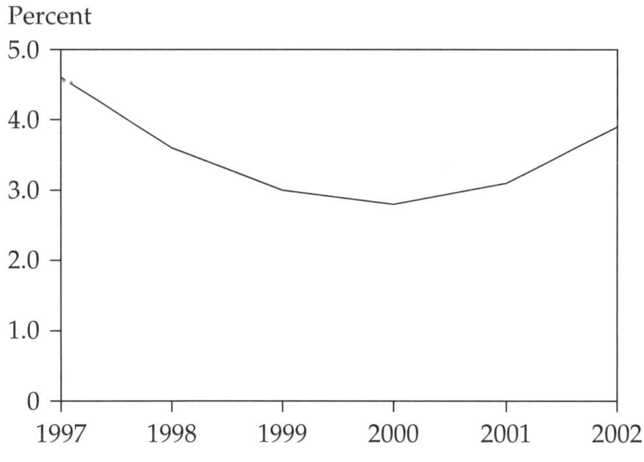

Source: Morozov (2004).

Figure 10.5. As a percentage of GDP, Russia spends less on education than other countries in Eastern Europe and OECD countries

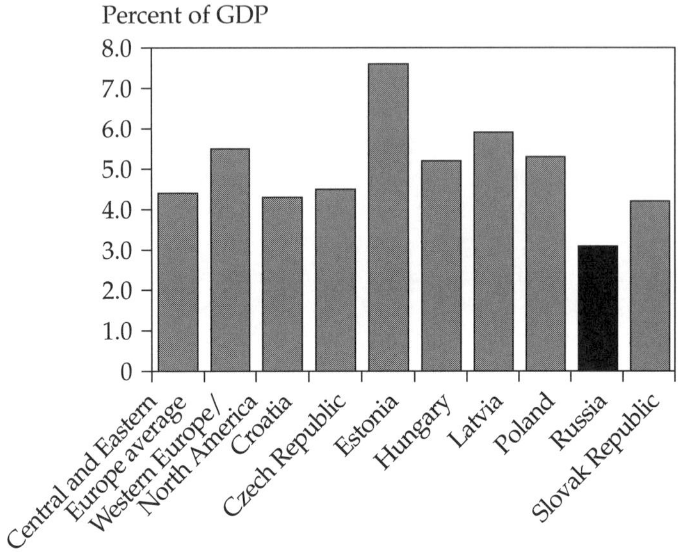

Source: UNESCO (2002).

Uneven regional funding for education has led to inequalities in access and quality. Russia's sheer size and diversity and the increasing fiscal decentralization since independence (only 0.7 percent of GDP spent on education comes from the federal government) have led to a steep rise in inequality in per capita spending for education across local governments. The majority of financing for education comes from municipal budgets (63.2 percent of the total in 2001), followed by regional budgets (19.0 percent) and the federal budget (17.8 percent, the bulk of which is for universities and vocational education). According to Roshtchina (2004), consolidated budget expenditure on education per student is positively correlated with the number of education institutions in the region and with per capita income levels (in other words, it is negatively correlated with the poverty level) (figure 10.6). Poorer regions provide more limited education opportunities, especially at higher education institutions, and regional variations are exacerbated by the fact that higher-income regions tend to spend more on education from both public and private resources.

Private spending on education also shows significant regional variation. In Moscow more than 59 percent of households spent more than

Figure 10.6. Budget expenditure per student is positively correlated with regional per capita income

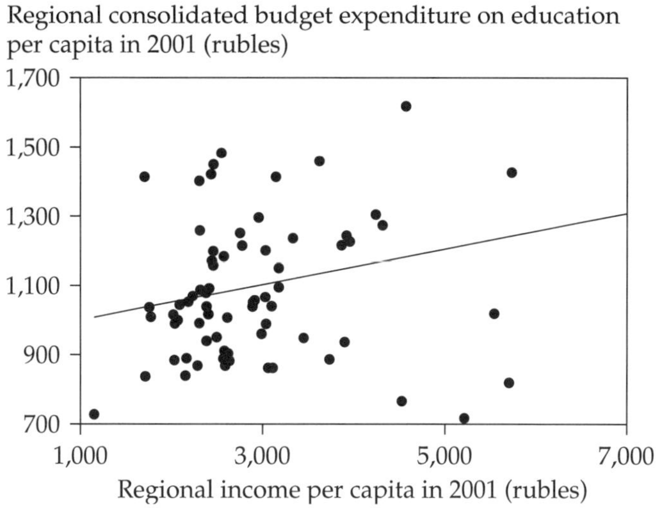

Source: Roshtchina (2004).

15,000 rubles per child in 2001, while in Ingushetiya Republic more than 63 percent of households spent less than 2,500 rubles per child. In regions such as the Far East and the Urals, household spending on children's education is high (more than 25 percent of the population spent more than 15,000 rubles). Households in the South spend much less on their children's education (more than 35 percent of the population spent less than 5,000 rubles). Overall, household expenditure on education as a percentage of total household expenditure is very low in Russia, with the average household spending on education slightly more than 1 percent of its household budget. The share of household spending on education is positively correlated with regional per capita income (figure 10.7).

Scholarships do not adequately target the poor. The NOBUS data reveal that the percentage of the population receiving scholarships in initial and secondary vocational and higher education is slightly higher among the poor than among the nonpoor (table 10.3). However, because the total number of poor students enrolled at these levels is significantly smaller than the number of nonpoor, scholarship funding is heavily skewed toward the nonpoor. The amount of scholarship funding awarded to individuals also seems to be skewed toward the nonpoor. Among those

Figure 10.7. The share of household spending on education is positively correlated with regional per capita income

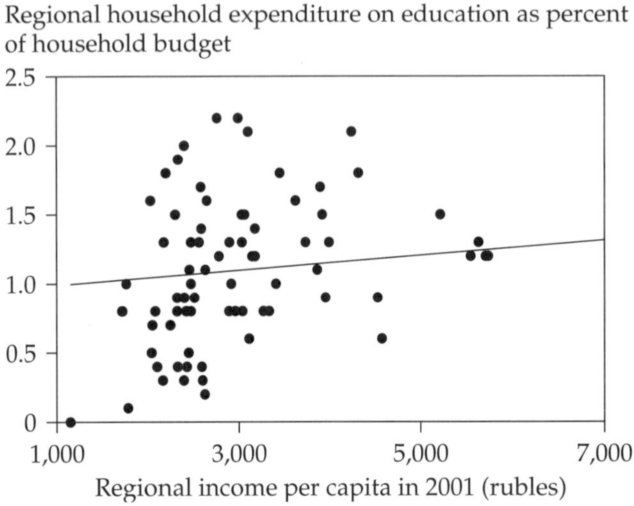

Source: Roshtchina (2004).

who receive scholarships in initial vocational education, only 2 percent of students from the lowest-income deciles received more than 500 rubles over a three-month period, while the corresponding percentage for students from the highest-income deciles was 36 percent. The trend for scholarships in secondary vocational and higher education is similar.

Table 10.3. A substantial fraction of the nonpoor receive scholarships

Education level	*Percent receiving scholarship*
Initial vocational education	
Nonpoor	65
Poor	72
Secondary vocational education	
Nonpoor	29
Poor	46
Tertiary education	
Nonpoor	23
Poor	35

Source: Bank staff calculations based on data from NOBUS (Goskomstat 2003b).

Policy Recommendations

This analysis leads to a number of policy recommendations:[6]

- *Provide adequate and equitably distributed public financing for education.* The education reforms and actions needed to increase educational access and improve the quality and relevance of education will be possible only with increased mobilization of financial resources for education. The 3.7 percent of GDP that Russia currently devotes to spending on education is much lower than the 5.5 percent spent by OECD countries and the 4.5 percent spent by countries in Central and Eastern Europe. Given demographic declines and internal migration, increased funding for education should be combined with measures—such as a per student funding mechanism—that provide incentives for more efficient use of resources.
- *Improve the targeting of remedial programs and other investments aimed at poor and disadvantaged groups.* Although neither the federal level nor any region should be expected to commit to equal per student recurrent funding across educational jurisdictions, much more could be done to target investment funding for remedial programs to groups, geographic areas, or schools where educational performance problems are identified. As a first priority, programs should be more explicitly targeted to support early childhood development (particularly by increasing access to preschool and kindergarten for the poor), as well as to support children with special learning needs and those from disadvantaged families. Although more research needs to be carried out in Russia, the payoff to expanding early childhood development programs for the poor has been convincingly demonstrated in many OECD countries. To the extent that transparent criteria for such targeting do not already exist, regional education authorities, together with social welfare institutions, should identify them. The free provision of services such as students' meals and textbooks consumes a significant part of the education budget, but these subsidies do not increase equality. Noneducational subsidies, such as school meals, transportation, and summer camps, should be provided free of charge only to disadvantaged students, as identified by local social welfare institutions, and consideration should be given to better targeting of educational materials and textbooks.
- *Although doing so may be politically difficult, challenge Russia's long-standing policy of granting free admission to higher education institutions only to the best students, who come predominantly from higher socioeconomic levels.* While admission to higher education institutions should continue to be granted on the basis of academic merit (standards should not be lowered in the name of more equitable admissions), the funding of higher education could be made more equitable. It should be a high priority

in Russia to bring transparency and consistency to the student fee system in higher education, as well as to spending for noneducational student subsidies, such as student board, housing, and transportation. As fees have become prevalent in the higher education system, making fees universal and allocating free admission based not only on merit but also on need would be an important element in creating a transparent fee and scholarship system. Defining a viable mechanism for means testing higher education applicants would be a key step in this university entrance reform process.

- *Finance students rather than schools.* The traditional process of allocating budget to schools, in which each school prepares its budget based on input norms, does not promote an efficient or equitable allocation of scarce resources for education in Russia. New per capita funding models, which have been successfully developed and implemented in several of Russia's regions, should be expanded to other regions. Such an objective measure of the funding devoted to education is a prerequisite for ensuring adequate resources for the system and for better targeting resources to disadvantaged groups.
- *Improve instructional quality in secondary schools by establishing standards and assessing performance against those standards.* As income has been shown to be a factor in access to and quality of postcompulsory education, more focus and more resources should be devoted to improving quality and relevance at this level. A consultative process is needed aimed at defining competence-based standards that are linked to measurable performance outcomes (as opposed to merely prescribing what teachers should teach). Following this process, priority should be given to developing curriculum materials (of which textbooks are only one part of the package); education technologies, including information and computer technology programs; and new teaching methodologies.
- *Increase the relevance of secondary vocational programs.* Reforming the secondary vocational education system is the highest priority for action in education and the one reform area that has the highest potential for short-term results. New broad-based curricula should be developed that provide all children with broad skills and competencies. Providing children with the tools needed for flexibility and labor mobility in Russia's dynamic economy is a much better poverty reduction instrument than training children for specific occupations, for which there may or may not be demand throughout their lives.
- *Develop the education administration's capacity to monitor poverty and its relationship with education.* The Russian education administration does not currently monitor the impact of poverty on education outcomes or

the impact of education on socioeconomic status. While the federal education administration should not establish its own capacity for collecting and monitoring poverty data, it should develop the capacity to analyze and use poverty data and indicators provided by other government or nongovernmental sources. One of the primary roles of the federal level in a decentralized system should be to develop the capacity to monitor the allocation of both public and private resources for education across socioeconomic groups and geographic areas and to promote a minimum level of spending per student across all groups and areas. Developing a poverty monitoring capacity in the Federal Ministry of Education is also linked to the recommendation to begin targeting remedial programs to regions, localities, or individual schools in which problems with quality or educational access have been identified. The development of a capacity for assessing student performance is a complementary action in terms of targeting resources to underperforming groups or areas.

Notes

1. Compulsory education in Russia includes primary and lower secondary grades 1–9. Data used in the analysis are drawn from the 2003 NOBUS survey (Goskomstat 2003b); the 2001 and 2002 Russia Longitudinal Monitoring Survey (UNC); the 2002 Education Economics Monitoring survey (Moscow State University); the 2001 Access to Tertiary Education in Russia survey (Roshtchina, Drugov, and Kuzina 2001); and the Russian Public Opinion Survey Center (VCIOM 2003). The NOBUS data are regionally representative and cover a population of just over 31,000 respondents between the ages of 6 and 24. While the Russia Longitudinal Monitoring Survey data are also regionally representative, the sample size is smaller (about 1,300 school-age respondents). The Access to Tertiary Education 2001 survey data represent 1,520 schoolchildren and their parents in four regions (Moscow, Pskov, Rostov, and Perm). The 2003 VCIOM data cover a population of 3,000 in a representative Russian sample. Regional comparisons cover selected regions, which were chosen based on high, medium, and low economic and social performance. All findings are discussed in terms of consumption deciles, the breakdown between poor and nonpoor (based on the poverty line measured by consumption aggregate), gender, and urban and rural location.

2. Given that there is no four-year secondary education standard in Russia, the net secondary enrollment rate for the 16- to 17-year-old age group is used to make cross-country comparisons of net secondary enrollment rates.

3. The 2002 Russia Longitudinal Monitoring Survey indicates an enrollment rate for 16- to 17-year-olds of 84 percent and an enrollment rate for 18- to 24-year-olds of 16 percent. According to the 2003 NOBUS data, these figures were 92 and 49 percent, respectively. As the NOBUS survey is more representative, the data from it are used here. The most important finding—the trend toward nonenrollment among lower-income groups—emerged from the data in both surveys.

4. The analysis also reveals gender disparity in wages: the salaries of men are 1.5–1.8 times higher than those of women with the same level of education. The salaries of women with higher education are about the same as salaries of men without higher education.

5. The 2001 Access to Tertiary Education data (Roshtchina, Drugov, and Kuzina 2001) cover urban areas in a small number of regions and are not representative of Russia. The data should therefore be interpreted with caution.

6. For a more in-depth review of education policy recommendations, see World Bank (2004b).

11
Restructuring Health Care to Decrease the Vulnerability of the Poor

Globally, poverty and poor health are intertwined: the poor are more likely to suffer from poor health, which reduces their economic prospects. This trend is evident in Russia, where health status is worse for the poor and lower-income groups are more likely to engage in risky behaviors. Poor people in every region in Russia are less healthy than wealthier people, and the gap between the two groups has widened since the 1998 crisis. To address the major health issues affecting people of productive age, the health care sector needs to be downsized and restructured, and funding, which is well below levels in most EU countries, needs to be reallocated across regions. Steps are needed to protect the poor as well as the nonpoor from falling into impoverishment due to demands for payment at the point of service.

Poverty and Health Status

The association of poverty and poorer health reflects causality in both directions: poverty breeds ill health, and ill health keeps poor people poor. Illness may have a substantial impact on income and may even make a difference between being above or below the poverty line. Ill health is also associated with substantial health care costs.

Health status and economic growth and development are also linked. Lagging health outcomes significantly reduce productivity, for example. Investments in health (along with education) are essential to increase labor productivity.

Poor people have worse health status in Russia (table 11.1). Nearly half of respondents from the lowest consumption quintile reported bad or very bad health status in the NOBUS survey. The upper quintiles reported much better health status. The differences between the two groups may be even larger than these findings reveal, given the considerable evidence in the literature that the poor systematically underreport their level of poor health (World Bank 2000b). By international standards, all quintiles score poorly. For example, 90 percent of Canadians reported good or very good health status in a 1998/99 survey (Statistics Canada 1999).

Table 11.1. Self-reported health status is better among the nonpoor (percent)

Consumption quintile	*Good or very good*	*Satisfactory*	*Bad or very bad*
1 (poorest)	38	16	47
2	39	20	41
3	39	20	41
4	43	21	35
5 (richest)	52	20	28

Source: Bank staff calculations based on data from NOBUS (Goskomstat 2003b).

Table 11.2. Alcohol use is higher among the poor (percent)

	Consumption quintile				
Frequency of use	*1*	*2*	*3*	*4*	*5*
Several times a week	31	19	19	17	14
Practically every day	40	22	13	13	12

Source: Bank staff calculations based on data from NOBUS (Goskomstat 2003b).

The poor are also more likely to engage in risky behaviors that contribute to poor health status (table 11.2). Lower-income groups are more likely to engage in heavy drinking. Heavy use of alcohol decreases as income increases.

Russia's health status compares unfavorably with that of many middle-income countries (table 11.3). Russia's poor health status reflects both communicable and noncommunicable diseases. But other factors are also linked to poor health status, including the socioeconomic turmoil caused by the transition (Field and Twigg 2000) and lifestyles involving such risk factors as tobacco use, heavy alcohol consumption, high-fat diets, nutritional deficits in poorer regions, and lack of exercise (Lock and others 2002; Malyutina and others 2002; Men and others 2003).

The general health status in Russia is also worse than in most transition economies. Life expectancy has been declining since the mid-1980s, with a sharp fall in the early 1990s and since the 1998 economic crisis (figure 11.1). In the 1950s and 1960s, life expectancy in Russia was similar to that in Europe. However, since the 1970s life expectancy has improved steadily in Western Europe, stagnated in Central and Eastern Europe, and deteriorated sharply in the former Soviet Union (Asvall and Alderslade 2002).

Figure 11.1. Life expectancy is much lower in Russia than elsewhere in Europe

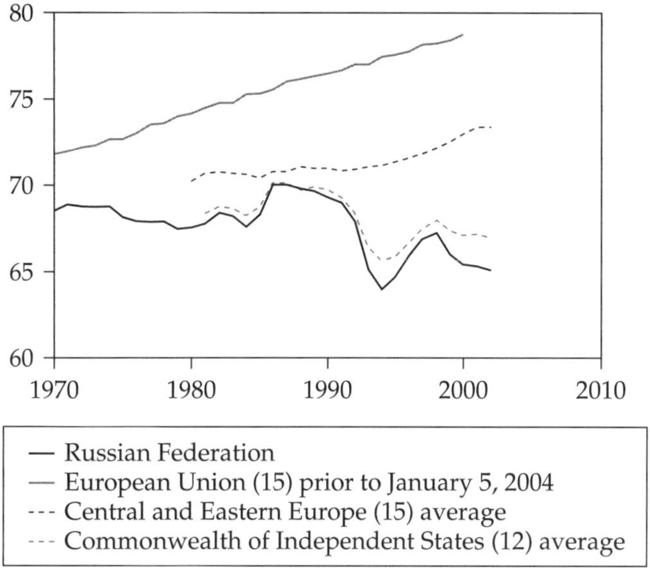

Source: WHO (2004).

More than three-fourths of the decline in life expectancy during the transition was due to an increased mortality rate among people 25–64. An increase in noncommunicable ailments, including cardiovascular diseases (heart disease and stroke) and injuries (often caused by abuse of alcohol), accounted for 65 percent of the decline in life expectancy. Chronic liver diseases and cirrhosis accounted for 2.4 percent of the decline and other alcohol-related causes for 9.6 percent. This was the case even though, according to the Russia Longitudinal Monitoring Survey (UNC, various years), alcohol consumption declined between 1992 and 1998. Cancer accounted for only 0.7 percent of the increase in mortality (Notzon and others 1998). Infectious diseases, including pneumonia and influenza, accounted for 5.8 percent.

Health status is particularly poor among Russian men. If the current death rate remains constant, about 42 percent of Russian men who were 15 years old in 2001 will be dead before the age of 60 (table 11.3). In Poland the equivalent figure is 23 percent; in lower-middle-income countries, the figure is 20 percent (World Bank 2003c). Russian men in the prime years of economic activity are falling sick and dying at a more rapid rate than in countries with which Russia competes, decreasing Russia's productivity.

Table 11.3. Economic and health status indicators are lower in Russia than in most comparable countries

Country	*GNP per capita (purchasing power parity, international dollars) (2001)*	*Incidence of tuberculosis per 100,000 (2000)*	*Prevalence of smoking–percent of adult men (2000)*	*Male life expectancy at birth (2001)*	*Percentage of 15-year-olds projected to die before the age of 60 (2001)*
Brazil	7,070	68	38	64	25.9
Kyrgyz Republic	2,630	153	60	62	33.5
Mexico	8,240	38	51	70	18.0
Poland	9,370	36	54	69	22.6
Russian Federation	6,880	132	63	59	42.4
Turkey	5,830	36	65	67	21.8
Lower-middle-income	4,700	119	59	67	20.5
Upper-middle-income	8,500	55	42	68	21.8

Source: World Bank (2003c).

Lower social and income status was correlated with increased mortality in Russia in the past decade (Plavinski and others 2003). In the 1990s there was no recorded increase in mortality in men with university degrees; the most pronounced differences were found among people with the lowest level of education. This pattern held for heart disease and deaths from cancer. Men in lower socioeconomic groups were most affected by the sharp increases in mortality in the 1990s.

Infectious diseases, thought to be under control in the late 1980s, have resurged in the Russian Federation since the transition. The increase is having a negative impact on growth. The incidence of tuberculosis is 10 times that of most EU countries, and the incidence of HIV/AIDS is growing. According to the Russian Federal AIDS Center, more than 1 million Russians are HIV-positive, and together with Ukraine, Russia has one of the highest HIV growth rates in the world.[1] Until recently, HIV was transmitted predominantly among intravenous drug users who share needles (high-risk core transmitters), but the disease is spreading rapidly to the general population through sexual contact (particularly via prostitution) and blood transfusions. The younger generation is disproportionately affected, with about 60 percent of people with HIV between the ages of 20 and 30. Overall, the female/male ratio is 1:3 among registered cases.

Figure 11.2. The number of officially reported cases of HIV is rising rapidly in Russia

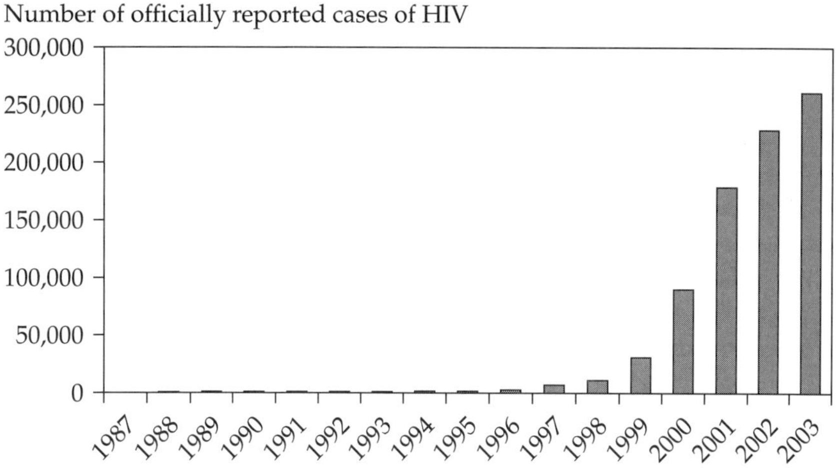

Source: Federal AIDS Center (2004).

This increase in the number of HIV cases represents a serious threat to Russia's long-term growth and welfare prospects (figure 11.2).[2] If no policy changes are made, by 2010 the death toll from HIV/AIDS may be very large, and the cumulative number of people infected with HIV may reach more than 2.3 million. Under conservative assumptions, this could lead to a decline in GDP of 10 percent by 2020 relative to a scenario in which HIV does not spread. The decline in GDP is likely to be accompanied by an even larger decline in the labor supply.

Regional Variation in Health Status

Summary national health statistics do not tell the full story. An equally fundamental issue is the variation in health outcomes by geographic region and socioeconomic variation (table 11.4). There are enormous interregional variations in terms of both mortality and illness. Infant and child mortality in regions with the worst outcomes is five times that in regions with the best outcomes (WHO 2003), and the incidence of tuberculosis varies by a factor of more than 12. Interregional male and female life expectancy varies by as much as 16 years (Tragakes and Lessof 2003).

This regional variation is growing (tables 11.5 and 11.6). Variations in the rates of infant mortality and in average life expectancy at birth increased after the 1998 economic crisis.

Table 11.4. Regional mortality rates vary dramatically in Russia

Region	*Infectious and parasitic diseases*	*Tuberculosis*	*Neoplasm*	*Diseases of blood/ blood-forming organs*	*Diseases of respiratory system*	*Digestive tract diseases*	*Accidents, poisoning, and injuries*
Russian Federation	25.0	20.6	205.5	849.4	70.5	44.6	219.9
Worst region	92.2	80.3	282.2	1,338.4	134.0	564.2	444.7
Best region	4.7	2.3	56.9	198.6	9.3	9.7	37.3
Median	22.9	19.0	189.8	719.6	66.3	43.4	53.8

Source: Regions of Russia 2000 (Goskomstat).
Note: Figures are number of deaths per 100,000 people.

Table 11.5. Regional differences in infant mortality rates in Russia are huge

Region	*1999*	*2000*	*2001*
Worst region	40.3	33.0	42.1
Best region	10.1	9.4	8.1

Source: Regions of Russia 1999–2001 (Goskomstat).
Note: Figures are number of deaths per 1,000 live births.

Table 11.6. Regional differences in average life expectancy at birth are large across the Russian Federation

	1999			*2000*			*2001*		
Region	*Total*	*Male*	*Female*	*Total*	*Male*	*Female*	*Total*	*Male*	*Female*
Longest life expectancy	73.4	68.1	78.6	74.0	68.6	79.0	74.6	70.0	79.1
Shortest life expectancy	56.0	50.7	62.1	56.1	50.4	63.0	56.4	51.1	62.8

Source: Regions of Russia 1999–2001 (Goskomstat).

Disparities in urban-rural areas may be growing. Life expectancy for men is two years lower in rural regions than in urban regions (Goskomstat 2003). There is a broad perception by rural regional leaders that alcoholism, drug use, suicide, and child malnutrition rates are rising dramatically in rural areas (World Bank selected focus group studies, unpublished data, 2003).

Russia's Ineffective Health Delivery System

Policies related to levels of funding for services, as well as distribution and uses of funding, play significant roles in improving health and reducing poverty. Russia's publicly financed health care system is plagued by gaps between what it promises to finance and actual allocations. Furthermore, allocations for services are inequitable and often poorly utilized.

Funding of Health Care in Russia

Could additional public funding reverse the trend in mortality and help the poor, or are other changes needed as well? The effectiveness of expenditures in improving health outcomes and reaching the poor depends on the policy and the institutional environment. Resources need to be carefully targeted and spent. If a weak policy and institutional environment is present, significant improvements in health outcomes will not be possible (World Bank 2003d). Investment in health has high returns, but only if investment is made carefully and concerns about quality and efficiency are built into the system. These conditions are not currently met in Russia.

There is some evidence that funding for health care improves health outcomes and should be directed toward protecting vulnerable populations. Ivaschenko (2003) examined the impact of poverty and public health spending on interregional and intertemporal variation in longevity in the Russian Federation. This study showed that regional poverty and real public health expenditure per capita correlated with observed variations in longevity across regions and over time. The longevity of males showed a significant correlation with changes in expenditures.

While it is difficult to determine causality, the decline in health status roughly parallels decreases in real public sector health care expenditures (figure 11.3). Government expenditures on health care declined in real terms by one-third in the past decade, particularly in the early 1990s and in 1998. Since 1998 public sector expenditures on health care have stabilized and increased slightly.

Public sector expenditures, measured as a share of GDP, have fluctuated between 3 and 4 percent since 1995, with some drops after the 1998 crisis. Health expenditures as a percentage of GDP followed a U-curve, declining from their precrisis level until 2000–01 before recovering (table 11.7). Health expenditures differed from the "nonsocial" noninterest expenditures of the budget, which declined only moderately after the 1998 crisis. Thus, in the aftermath of the 1998 crisis, the necessary fiscal consolidation in Russia was achieved primarily at the expense of health and other social expenditures.

Figure 11.3. Total public expenditures on health care fell during the 1990s

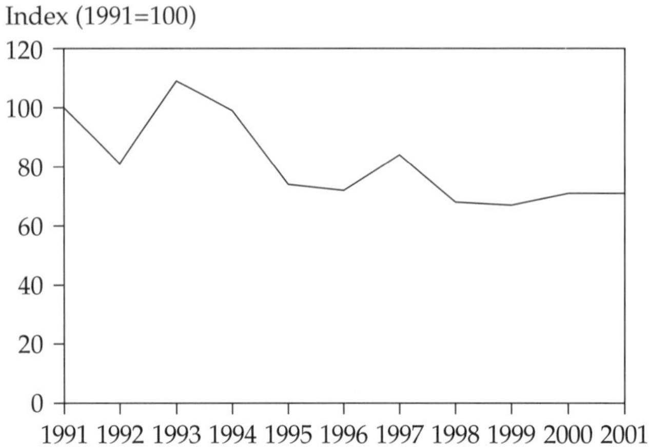

Source: Goskomstat database using index deflators of GDP.
Note: Includes budget and health insurance contributions.

Table 11.7. Social spending, including spending on health, suffered as a result of the 1998 crisis and postcrisis fiscal consolidation (percent of GDP)

Sector	*1997*	*1998*	*1999*	*2000*	*2001*	*2002*
Noninterest expenditures	40.4	36.2	31.1	30.0	31.5	34.6
Health	3.5	3.4	2.9	2.8	2.9	3.2
Education	4.6	3.6	3.0	2.8	3.1	3.9
Social protection	16.0	13.3	9.7	8.9	10.9	12.6
Other	16.3	15.9	15.5	15.5	14.6	14.9

Source: World Bank (2004a).

Russia's public sector spending for health care (measured as share of GDP) is low compared with EU countries, which spend 6–8 percent of GDP, on average. Public spending is similar to spending in other middle-income countries, however. Moreover, it is not clear whether overall expenditures—public plus private—are too low. Internationally, public plus private health spending as a share of GDP generally increases as GDP increases, with lower-middle-income countries (countries with a per capita GDP of less than $10,000) allocating less than 6 percent of GDP and higher-income countries spending more than 7 percent. In Russia public and private spending on health care represents 5.3 percent of GDP.

The implementation of mandatory health insurance has not generated additional funding or other expected favorable results. Under legislation passed in the early 1990s, the regions were supposed to collect a new payroll tax and allocate budget funds for the nonworking population. The equalization transfers were never earmarked for health, however, and most regions have been unwilling to pool necessary funds under the regional health insurance funds as legislated. This has effectively created two parallel health care financing systems, the insurance system and the regional budgetary allocations. Furthermore, mandatory health insurance has actually led to the erosion of budgetary allocations for health, as increases in payroll taxes have been offset by cuts in the budget.

Even more to the point is the relative lack of public sector funding to cover the cost of free medical services. The policy objective of free access to a basic package of services for all has not always been met. The poor often receive a different level and style of care. They visit outpatient clinics less often, and the duration of their hospital stays is shorter than that

Figure 11.4. Regional differences in per capita health expenditures are huge in Russia

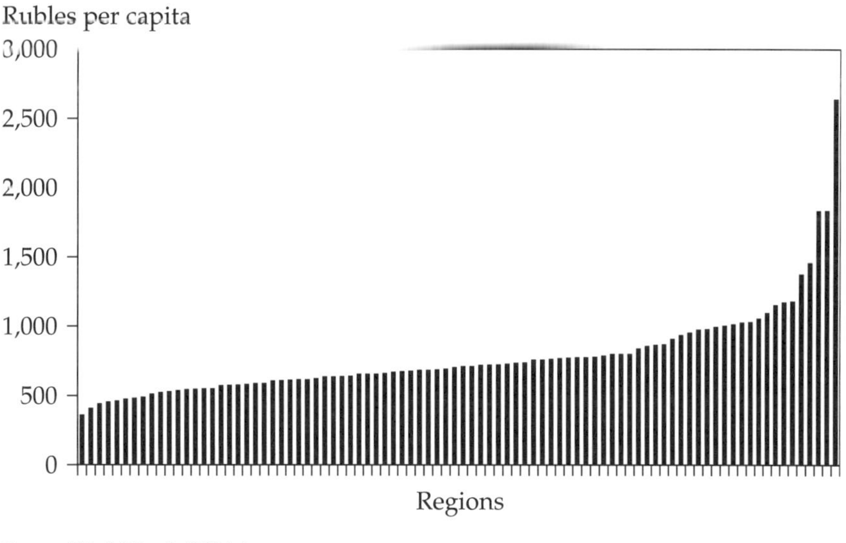

Source: World Bank (2004a).
Note: Figures are for 2001. They are adjusted using the Producer Price Index.

of upper-income groups (Shishkin 2000). The difference could be due to supply-side (provider) behavior or to differences in health-seeking behaviors. The health impact is not clear. (Survey results discussed later in this chapter address this issue in the context of the affordability and access of care.)

Allocation of Funding across Regions

Regional inequities are growing in Russia. Even when adjusted for variations in input prices, per capita public spending in Russia's 89 regions ranged from 355 to 2,635 rubles per capita in 2001 (figure 11.4). Rather than basing allocations on population or health needs, the budget allocation formula across and within regions tends to be based on inputs (such as the number of beds or staff), as it was in the Soviet era. For example, if unneeded beds or facilities are eliminated, funding is decreased instead of being reallocated to needed care services. This formula does not provide the necessary incentives for improving or restructuring service delivery.

The Growing Out-of-Pocket Expenditures and the Impact on the Poor and Vulnerable Groups

The private health care sector is growing, but it is not always recognized, integrated, or well regulated. Private expenditures are estimated to represent 30–55 percent of all health spending in Russia (*World Health Report* 2002 [WHO]; IISP 2003; Beliaeva and Doctorovich 2001). Most private spending is out-of-pocket payment for pharmaceuticals by consumers (figure 11.5). Potent pharmaceuticals, including antibiotics, can often be purchased without a prescription in Russia (Nurgozhin and others 2001). It is estimated that over-the-counter medicines account for more than 60 percent of dispensing in Russia (Mossialos 1999).

The reliance on imports (70 percent) and limited public finances have meant that drug prices can be decisive in determining access to pharmaceuticals. There has been an attempt to institute price controls on both manufacturers' prices and mark-ups along the distribution chain.

Standard health benefits guaranteed for all Russian citizens include all inpatient and outpatient services except outpatient pharmaceuticals and services not considered medically necessary, such as dentistry and cosmetic surgery. The government has instituted social categories that are exempt from paying for certain outpatient drugs. These categories include pensioners 80 and older, veterans of wars, and Chernobyl victims. Nevertheless, charging for services, both officially and unofficially, has increased over the past several years in response to the cutbacks in public spending.

Figure 11.5. Public spending on pharmaceuticals has fallen, while out-of-pocket payments have been rising

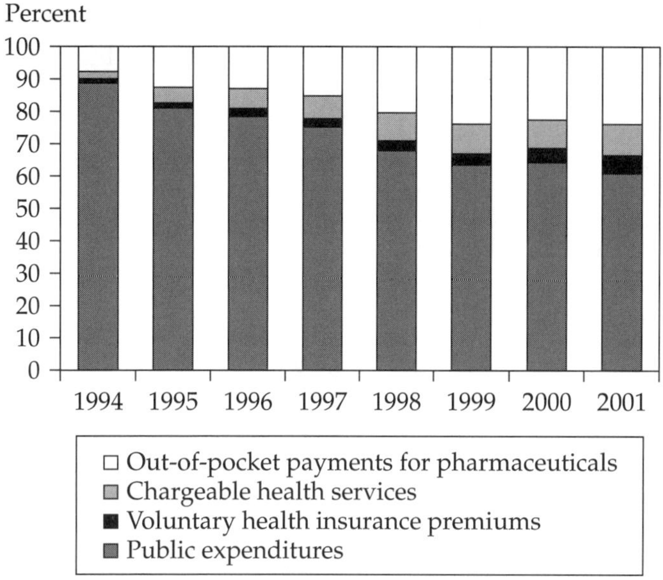

Sources: IISP (2003); *World Health Report 2001* (WHO).

The Household Budget Survey data reveal that the share of household revenues spent on health care has been increasing (IISP 2003). In 1994 health services represented 0.4 percent of total household expenses, and medical devices and personal hygiene represented 2.5 percent. By 2000 these values had increased to 0.9 percent and 3.5 percent, respectively. There are substantial differences across income groups. The highest decile in 2000 spent a much larger share of income (1.8 percent) on health services than the lowest decile (0.2 percent); in 2002 the highest decile spent 2.8 percent and the lowest decile 1.4 percent. These data suggest an increase in equity across income groups but also an increase in the burden of health expenditures. This pattern does not hold for some expenditures, however, such as pharmaceuticals, for which poor people spent a higher proportion in 2000 (4.1 percent for the lowest decile versus 3 percent for the highest decile).

The Household Budget Survey reporting tends to be lower than either the NOBUS or independent surveys. Perhaps the most detailed analysis of independent household out-of-pocket payments was carried out by the Institute for Social Studies (Moscow) and Boston University's School of

Public Health in 1998–99. This study covered 3,000 households across Russia (Boikov and others 2000). It found that, on average, each Russian household spent 14 percent of income on drugs and medical care: 7 percent on drugs, 3 percent on dental care, 3 percent on hospital expenses, and 1 percent on outpatient medical care. The lower the income of the respondents, the higher the percentage of income spent on drugs and medical care. The analysis divided households into four income groups. The lowest-income group spent 33 percent of income on health: 22 percent on drugs, 5 percent on dental care, 4 percent on hospital care, and 3 percent on outpatient care. The highest-income group spent only 9 percent of total income on health care: 4 percent on drugs and 5 percent on other medical services.

The low level of public sector funding and the bloated public sector infrastructure have combined to force providers to resort to charging for services, especially for specialized and surgical services, often within public institutions. This "shadow market" for services was estimated at $600 million in 2001 (Satarov 2002). Various nongovernmental surveys and studies in Russia estimate that 15–60 percent of patients using hospital services make shadow payments (Boikov and others 2000; Shishkin 2003). Payments are also made for other types of services, including outpatient services (4–38 percent), diagnostic services (21–45 percent), and dental care (80–84 percent). Some of these services, notably dental services, may not be covered by the government (IISP 2003).

Table 11.8. Wealthier people spend more on outpatient and hospital care than the poor (rubles)

	Outpatient care		*Hospital care*				
Item	*Official payment*	*Unofficial payment*	*Official payment*	*Unofficial payment*	*Additional drugs*	*Food*	*Other*
Mean	1,277	984	2,736	2,201	1,261	1,006	1,026
Consumption quintile							
1 (lowest)	904	838	2,255	1,903	927	756	827
2	984	787	2,274	2,432	1,158	608	739
3	1,362	890	2,945	1,987	1,222	1,028	664
4	1,103	1,096	2,841	2,036	1,355	928	1,006
5 (highest)	1,664	1,096	3,112	2,457	1,521	1,412	1,455
Location							
Urban	1,341	983	3,013	2,197	1,280	929	1,181
Rural	1,072	986	2,023	2,212	1,209	1,237	640

Source: Bank staff calculations based on data from NOBUS (Goskomstat 2003b).

The NOBUS survey found that about 35 percent of all households paid for health care or health services when seeking hospital care.[3] More than 95 percent report that the payment was out-of-pocket, with about 5 percent reporting that insurance, enterprises, or other institutions paid for the services. For both outpatient and inpatient services, higher consumption groups pay more for similar types of services and for both official and unofficial encounters (table 11.8). This could indicate that providers price discriminate or that upper income groups demand more.

Among the poor a higher percentage of consumption goes to medical services, across all categories of services (figure 11.6). Poorer groups consistently pay a higher percentage of consumption for all categories of services, in both inpatient and outpatient settings, as a percentage of both official and unofficial spending (figure 11.7). In some categories the percentage spent by the poor is almost equal to or greater than average consumption levels. For the bottom three quintiles, inpatient costs account for at least 50 percent of average consumption. For the lowest-income

Figure 11.6. The poor spend a higher share of consumption on all types of medical services

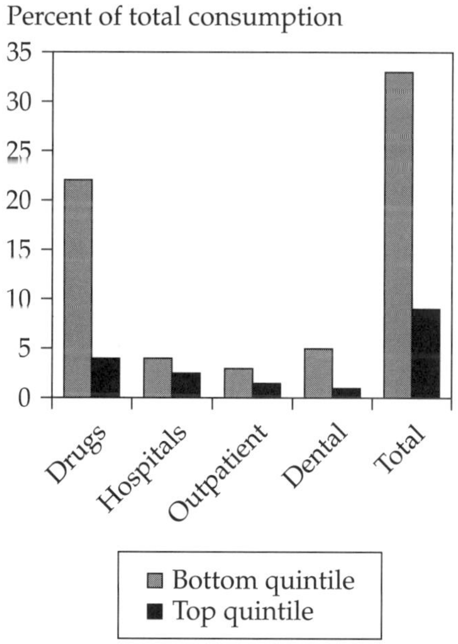

Source: Bank staff calculations based on data from NOBUS (Goskomstat 2003b).

Figure 11.7. Both official and unofficial payments for medical services represent a larger share of consumption for the poor than the nonpoor

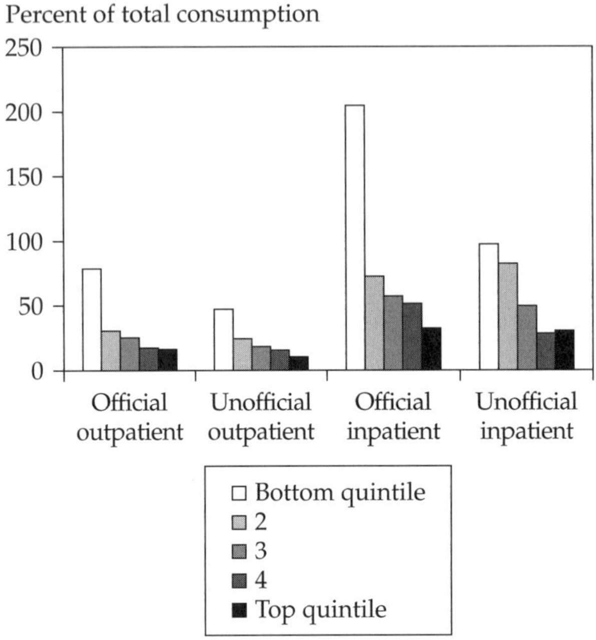

Source: Bank staff calculations based on data from NOBUS (Goskomstat 2003b).

quintile, expenditures on unofficial payments connected with inpatient care are twice average consumption. If health care costs exceed total average consumption, families may fall into poverty or deeper into poverty as a result of health care needs.

Across consumption groups, 50–60 percent of respondents indicated that they sought paid medical services because there were no free providers or because it was difficult to find the necessary specialist providers in their geographic area. This suggests that paid services are common and well established. Providers charge most patients across income groups and for all types of services.

Lack of access stems from lack of physicians and the high cost of services. Among people who do not seek care even when confronted with a health problem, about 20 percent report inability to pay as the reason (table 11.9). Nearly half of these people come from the two lowest-income

Table 11.9. Lack of specialists and inability to pay for services are the leading reasons why the poor do not seek care

	Consumption quintile						
Reason	*1 (lowest)*	*2*	*3*	*4*	*5 (highest)*	*Urban*	*Rural*
No doctors of medical specialty in area	34	23	18	15	10	25	75
Difficult to arrange a visit	15	24	18	22	21	86	14
Cannot afford necessary services	32	22	20	17	9	72	28
Other reasons	21	18	20	19	21	75	28

Source: Bank staff calculations based on data from NOBUS (Goskomstat 2003b).

quintiles, but some households in every consumption quintile report inability to pay as a reason for not seeking care. The lack of a specialist was cited three times as often in rural areas as in urban areas. Rural poor face not only availability issues but also travel and time costs relative to urban dwellers.

About 10 percent of respondents indicated that price affected their use of pharmaceuticals, either partially or entirely (table 11.10). More than 72 percent of all households indicated that care was followed completely.

Table 11.10. Problems with affordability of pharmaceuticals affect the treatment of the poor more than the nonpoor

	Consumption quintile				
Item	*1 (lowest)*	*2*	*3*	*4*	*5 (highest)*
Only prescriptions that are free	21	23	21	20	16
Partly not followed due to lack of money for drugs and procedures	21	24	21	19	14
Not followed at all due to lack of money	22	27	16	22	12
Not followed for other reasons	15	18	19	20	27

Source: Bank staff calculations based on data from NOBUS (Goskomstat 2003b).

The remainder did not follow the prescribed treatment completely or at all. The percentage of people who did not follow the prescribed treatment was higher in the lower quintiles (40–50 percent of households) and lower among the highest consumption quintile (26 percent of households).

Policy Recommendations

Public funding overall has declined over the past decade, and health financing reforms and decentralization policies have had unintended negative consequences. Russia is now grappling with sweeping reforms for the sector. No one unifying vision has yet emerged. Regardless of the model chosen, efforts are needed to improve health status and health outcomes and to better target Russia's poor and vulnerable groups. Doing so will require changes at the policy level along a number of different dimensions. Interventions specific to the poor and the impoverished (who fall into poverty due to health problems) are needed, in addition to improvements in the system as a whole. Three areas for change and intervention are recommended.

Reduce Out-of-Pocket Payments

The evidence is consistent: by any measure or survey, out-of-pocket payments are growing, hurting the poor and vulnerable groups disproportionately. Many people from lower-income groups are afraid to seek medical care.

Several policy changes could be developed to deal with this problem:

1. Begin to formalize informal payments through a standardized copayment system. All services need not be billable. Such a system need not be complicated or burdensome administratively.
2. Develop explicit protections from copayments for poor and medically vulnerable groups.
3. Inform and educate patients about their responsibilities for copayments under current law and their rights and entitlements to free guaranteed services.

These actions could result in greater transparency in revenues for health facilities, with some of the monies used to offset costs for those in need.

A fundamental issue is understanding who the poor and medically vulnerable are. The poor are not always well identified by the government or providers. Poorer groups that many believe are partially protected or exempt from paying for drugs or services report large out-of-pocket payments. Part of the issue is the targeting of exemptions. Exempt groups are mostly from the Soviet era and are based to a great degree on disease categories. There is a mismatch of the categorically exempt and the truly needy. For example, although the principle of encouraging access for those in need is exemplary, not every person in a specified disease category or other demographic category may need free pharmaceuticals all the time. In rural areas the Soviet-era targeting policy used school-based programs of nutrition, preventive measures, and routine care, but this model has been hurt by funding cuts. Once targeting improves, greater public funding may be needed. The Ivaschenko (2002) study, for example, shows the positive effect of publicly financed health services on life expectancy, which is particularly large for regions in which the incidence of poverty is higher.

Restructure the Health Care System to Improve Equity and Better Reach the Poor

Russia needs to revamp and restructure its health financing and delivery system. Major changes are needed to improve both efficiency and equity, as well as access to services. The following are priorities for change in the short term:

1. Increase the geographic equity of public health expenditures. Allocation based on population and criteria such as need and level of poverty could make possible a redistribution of funds and a cross-subsidization from richer regions to poorer ones and from the healthy to the sick. There is wide variation across regions in the current per capita amount budgeted for health care. Under current financing and budget arrangements, public expenditure on health reflects the historical norms and revenue-raising capacity of each region rather than the health needs of the population.
2. Improve pooling at the regional or federal level to drive efficiency gains and better target poor populations. In the short term, greater pooling and improved allocation could occur under the Territorial Insurance Funds. Pooling at the regional level creates larger risk pools than at the rayon level, thereby allowing for redistribution from the healthy to the sick. In addition, pooling at the regional level can help reduce fragmentation in funding streams, facilitate the rationalization process, and facilitate the reallocation of funds between health facilities and services to improve allocative efficiency to more cost-effective outpatient services. Pooling also adds leverage to the purchasing function, with a single larger purchaser able to strategically manage resources and contract selectively or according

to performance-based standards with health care providers, both public and private.

3. Unify and reconfigure the benefit package of free guaranteed services. Guaranteed services should equal available revenues, using improved cost data for services, and be split into three types of services. Fully covered services would be free to the patient at the point of service. Partially covered services would involve copayments made up to a yearly maximum per insured person. Other services, such as cosmetic surgery, would not be covered. The poor, vulnerable groups, and pensioners should be exempt from copayments.

The overall package of guaranteed services should also be reconfigured in three important ways:

- Introduce coverage of some drugs outside of the hospital in order to encourage patients to receive more services, especially day surgery, on an outpatient basis. Evidence from Estonia and the Kyrgyz Republic suggests that savings would accrue from this change (Langenbrunner and Odeyi 2003; Langenbrunner and others 2005).
- Restructure and add social service benefits for the poor, the elderly, and the vulnerable, including community-based services that allow the elderly and the disabled to stay at home as long as possible. A differentiated network of providers could offer services such as home social and nursing care, day care, medical aides, and old age and nursing home care. Some community hospitals could be turned into nursing homes. Recent changes in Chuvashiya Republic offer a good example of what is possible (World Bank 2004d).
- Autonomize the delivery system and create public trusts or corporations. This would move regional health facilities directly off budget and make them dependent on purchasing contracts. Facilities, in turn, would be accountable for certain services but would retain flexibility for the use of funding paid to them by the purchaser. Work on this transition in Russia is under way, supported by nonlending services provided by the World Bank. The government will need to ensure that Article 41 of the Constitution, which mandates free provision of care regardless of a facility's legal status, still works. Additional special bylaws and other regulations may be needed to address specific health sector issues as part of broader legislation on nonprofit organizations. The autonomization process provides an opportunity to facilitate optimization and rationalization through facility network mergers. The efficiency issue becomes internalized to the hospital management level.

International experience suggests that as providers merge and accounting becomes more transparent, the incidence of informal payments decreases, as it has in parts of the Czech Republic and Poland (Lewis 2000; Shahriari, Belli, and Lewis 2001). This can indirectly reduce the burden for the poor and reduce impoverishment by the nonpoor at the point of service.

Close Health Gaps by Adopting Public Health Interventions

The deteriorating health status requires closing the health gaps through public health policies and interventions to protect the poor and the vulnerable and to control risk factors. Such initiatives could include the following actions.

1. Increase the role of cross-sectoral policies.
2. Formulate and implement policies and strategies that include other sectors. Examples include transport policies on road safety; agriculture policies on food safety; economic development and trade policies for food and price incentives to encourage the consumption of more fruits and vegetables and less fatty meat; education policies that emphasize educating young adults on risk factors and how to control them; pragmatic policies to control the excessive consumption of alcohol, especially among lower-income groups; and focused health care access, preventive services, and nutritional supplement programs as part of larger rural development strategies
3. Adopt and implement policies to stimulate demand for cost-effective prevention practices by individuals.
4. Move toward full implementation of the Framework Convention on Tobacco Control, adopted by WHO member states in May 2003. This framework includes higher taxes on cigarettes and other tobacco products; bans and restrictions on smoking in public and work places; comprehensive bans on the advertising and promotion of all tobacco products, logos, and brand names; provision of better consumer information on the health risks of tobacco; warning labels on the health risks of tobacco; and help for smokers who want to quit.
5. Allocate sufficient public resources for HIV/AIDS control and lower the cost of antiretroviral therapy. Government responses have been weak and patchy to date, with emphasis on mass screening for HIV and relatively little emphasis on effective prevention among high-risk core transmitters and bridge populations. The government will need to reform the approach to the purchase of antiretroviral drugs to ensure better access to quality-assured, competitively priced

drugs. Lessons could be learned from Brazil and South Africa, where antiretroviral therapy costs one-sixth to one-seventh what it costs in Russia.

The current federal anti-HIV/AIDS program runs from 2002 to 2007. It may need to be revised to reflect the epidemic and address the unacceptably high cost of antiretroviral therapy, which severely limits access by lower-income groups to a new generation of therapy for HIV/AIDS management.

Notes

1. In the absence of rigorous epidemiological surveillance, the data must be treated with great caution.

2. The full report and simulation model are available at www.worldbank.org.ru.

3. There was no question in the NOBUS on payment for outpatient care or services, nor was there any question regarding payment for pharmaceuticals.

Part IV
Poverty Monitoring

Reliable data on poverty are crucial for sound and operational social policymaking. Federal and local programs that provide effective targeted social assistance are developed based largely on data from the Household Budget Survey. Chapter 12 highlights the main issues affecting poverty monitoring and analysis in Russia and provides recommendations for improving the Household Budget Survey program. The chapter emphasizes the need to expand the Household Budget Survey dataset and to allow public access to its micro data. It examines the new survey sample design, assesses the quality of data collection and processing, and suggests ways to increase response rates and improve adjustment methods. Implementation of the recommendations would increase the accuracy of poverty measurement, improve the comprehensiveness of monitoring, and allow for deeper analysis of poverty in Russia.

Chapter 12
Using the Household Budget Survey to Monitor Poverty

Efforts to enhance the monitoring and analysis of poverty in Russia should include work to improve the statistical infrastructure and develop systems for making the data available to a wide community of researchers. This chapter examines the main issues and offers recommendations for improving Household Budget Survey–based poverty monitoring.

The Data Base for Monitoring Poverty

Official poverty monitoring in Russia is based largely on data from the Household Budget Survey conducted by Goskomstat.[1] This survey has been conducted in Russia since 1952, making it one of the longest running household budget surveys in the world. The current design dates back to 1997 and includes about 49,000 households per quarter, with the same sample of households interviewed each quarter. This very large sample is necessary to provide data not only at the national level but also for each of the 89 subjects of the Russian Federation.

Academics and government agencies use the Russia Longitudinal Monitoring Survey (UNC, various years) data because of its open access; wide scope, which facilitates broad policy analysis; representativeness at the federal level; and transparent methodology. Many research and policy analysis articles are based on the Russia Longitudinal Monitoring Survey, and much of the knowledge of poverty and household behavior outside Russia is based on analysis using the Russia Longitudinal Monitoring Survey data. The Russia Longitudinal Monitoring Survey is not appropriate for regional monitoring of poverty for several reasons: its small sample size, which does not allow poverty analysis to be conducted at the regional level; the fact that it is conducted just once a year, typically in the fall, so that there is no coverage of seasonality; its dependence on external funding (it was not undertaken in 1999, when the depth of the crisis at the household level was felt); and its nonofficial status (its estimates are not used in official policymaking).

The joint project of the government of Russia, World Bank, and U.K. Department for International Development (DFID) for Enhancing Measurement, Monitoring, and Analysis of Poverty in Russia is focused on joint work with government agencies to enhance the official Household Budget Survey as an important component of the poverty monitoring system (box 12.1).

Box 12.1. Activities implemented during Stage I of the Enhancing Measurement, Monitoring, and Analysis of Poverty in Russia Project

The Enhancing Measurement, Monitoring, and Analysis of Poverty in Russia project seeks to improve the methodology of poverty measurement of the Household Budget Survey data, evaluate the administrative data system and make recommendations for its improvement, enhance the targeting of social programs, and facilitate open access to household datasets in compliance with Russian legislation and international recommendations. Activities implemented under the first stage of the project included the following:

- Recommendations on feasible welfare indicators for the Household Budget Survey were made based on examination of broader datasets from Russia.
- The welfare consistency of regional poverty lines was established.
- Household expenditure recording procedures based on personal diaries were improved.
- A training workshop for regional supervisors on interviewer management and dealing with nonresponses was sponsored.
- The structure of the United Kingdom's Field Surveys Division was examined.
- An improved sample design for the Household Budget Survey based on 2002 population census data was developed.
- The weighting and editing procedures for Household Budget Survey data were improved.
- New poverty and social indicator questions for inclusion in the Household Budget Survey were designed and piloted.
- Principles for open access to micro data were established.
- Two internal reports, one on the dynamics and profile of poverty, growth, and inequality in 1997–2000, the other on the regional dynamics of poverty, were produced.

Source: World Bank (2004e).

Broadening the Poverty Indicators

To provide an adequate base for measurement and monitoring, the Household Budget Survey dataset has to be expanded to include nonmonetary dimensions of poverty. Most of the poverty indicators currently available from the Household Budget Survey are monetary indicators. Complete monitoring of poverty also requires the measurement of nonmonetary indicators, including indicators of relative deprivation, subjective indicators, and indicators of social exclusion.

Identification of deprivation began during the July–September 2003 survey. A sample of 3,500 households was given a list of statements and asked to indicate which signalled poverty or severe poverty. Statements endorsed by 90 percent or more of the respondents were used to create a list of deprivation indicators that was to be added to the Household Budget Survey beginning in 2005. Examples of indicators include not being able to afford meat or fish at least twice a week, not having even crude furniture for daily use, and not being able to buy new clothing or footwear for children as they grow. Many of the indicators can be derived from questions already included in the Household Budget Survey or from minor modifications to them. However, these deprivation indicators have not been included in the Household Budget Survey so far.

The suggested survey instrument would probably include about the same number of subjective as objective indicators of poverty. Subjective indicators include whether people feel poor, what they consider to be the minimum income needed to make ends meet, whether they consider themselves to be better or worse off than a year ago, and what their expectations are for the year to come. An important consideration is who in the household will be asked to respond, since these questions are attitudinal and the responses are attributes of an individual rather than of the whole household. In a typical survey, the responses are likely to be primarily the opinions of women who are housewives. One possibility for randomizing responses to these questions is to ask them of the household member whose birthday comes next. Doing so would raise operational issues and cost, however.

The third group of new indicators would be nine questions on social exclusion. These questions cover issues such as access to employment, education, health care, and the quality and accessibility of water supplies.

A Household Budget Survey adjustment pilot is needed to test all these questions, in order to make sure that respondents understand the questions and that there is no adverse effect on other responses. The FSSS (former Goskomstat) planned to carry out a small-scale pilot before full implementation of the new survey instrument in 2005. However, due to budgetary constraints, Goskomstat has not been able to carry out the pilot, and the implementation of the new Household Budget Survey program has been delayed until at least the end of 2005.

Improving the Sample Design

The sample of the Household Budget Survey should be redesigned. The current sample design of the Household Budget Survey was introduced in 1997 and comprises 49,000 households. Once selected, households are retained indefinitely. This represents a large response burden and, over time, a deteriorating level of response, as some attrition occurs in each round of the survey. Although there is replacement of nonresponding households, there is no systematic rotation of households to minimize the response burden and to refresh the sample to take account of households in newly constructed areas. Another problem is that the design is now based on a sample frame from the 1994 micro-census. For all these reasons, the FSSS decided to redesign the sample beginning in 2005, using the 2002 population census as the frame. Unfortunately, given problems with the financing of the redesigned sample, this change has been postponed indefinitely.

No sample design will be optimal for all possible purposes for which Household Budget Survey data are used. The Household Budget Survey is not just a poverty survey: it also serves other important requirements, such as determining the weights for the consumer price index and national accounts. Potential conflicts may arise over giving priority to national estimates at the federal level or regional data, to annual or quarterly data, to cross-sectional or longitudinal analyses, to estimates of the total population or to subgroups. Decisions on all of these issues will have important consequences for the sample design. There are finite financial resources for the Household Budget Survey; the redesign needs to take account of the practicalities of data collection and of considerations such as interviewer workloads, interviewer travel, and the employment status of interviewers, who are permanent staff and cannot simply be dismissed if the volume of work in their area declines.

Consultants submitted a draft sample redesign proposal to the FSSS in November 2003. It includes a quarterly, two-stage probability, repeat sample of 24,500 households, in which the samples are separately selected each quarter, providing an annual sample of 98,000 households. This new design would reduce interviewer workload and double the effective annual sample, since the current design revisits the same households each quarter. The new design also proposes incorporating a systematic rotation, so that half of the households interviewed in the first quarter of one year are revisited to form half of the first quarter's sample the following year, half of the second quarter's sample is revisited in the second quarter of the next year, and so forth. This technique would increase the precision of the estimates of annual change.

The longitudinal aspects of the Household Budget Survey require consideration. At a later time, a separate panel sample of 7,000–8,000 households should be revisited each quarter for two or three years. In principle, there is no such thing as a longitudinal study of households, because household composition changes from wave to wave in a panel survey. This means that individuals need to be traced and interviewed in their new households, along with other members of these new households. Apart from the costs and practical difficulties of doing this, there are severe analytical complexities. Mobility rates in Russia are assumed to be so low that tracing individuals will not be a major problem. This assumption needs to be tested, however.

Response rates in the proposed new design should be higher than under the current Household Budget Survey. Response rates should be higher for the main sample, which will revisit each household just twice, with the two interviews a year apart, and for the panel (if implemented), which will retain households for just two or three years instead of indefinitely, as is currently done. The new design should reduce any conditioning effects, whereby respondent behavior is affected by being included in the survey.

The new design will lighten the workload of interviewers, reducing the number of interviews from 25 to 16 households per quarter in urban areas and from 20 to 12 in rural areas. This means that interviewers will interview just one household a week in rural areas and not much more than that in urban areas. Interviewers perform other duties, such as collecting diaries from households and coding, and the new sample design will take more time, as a much larger proportion of households will be interviewed for the first time. Establishing initial contact with such households requires more effort than revisiting existing sample households, for whom the best times to call may already be well known and for whom appointments may have been made during the previous visit. In addition, if personal diaries are used as the preferred method of collecting daily expenditure data, interviewers will need to contact each household member to enlist cooperation and explain what is needed. Whether these additional tasks will offset the 35–40 percent reduction in the number of households included in each interviewer's assignment needs to be carefully assessed through piloting.

Improving Data Quality

Several major efforts could be undertaken to improve the quality of statistical data. To increase response rates, incentive payments, interviewer training, and standardization procedures could be introduced and data recording instruments could be revised. The statistical data adjustment is focused on developing the appropriate editing systems and weighting procedures.

Improving Data Collection

Response rates for the Russian Household Budget Survey are currently about 80 percent, but the figure is misleading. Nonresponse is highest when households are included in the sample for the first time; for a panel survey the true nonresponse rate should be the sum of the initial nonresponse figure plus attrition at subsequent rounds of enquiry. When the sample was first selected in 1997, the response rate was about 63 percent. The response figure almost certainly has declined since then, as some households that initially responded refuse to participate in subsequent rounds. The effect of this is disguised to some extent, as newly selected households substitute for nonresponding households. Although this maintains the sample and hence the estimates of variance and sampling error, it does not wholly compensate for nonresponse bias.

In fact, the response rate may be low, particularly in urban areas. Russia is one of the few developed countries or transition economies that does not offer any kind of incentive payment, in cash or in kind, to cooperating households. In most countries, incentives are paid when households are asked to do anything other than simply answer questions (such as keep expenditure diaries). Incentives do not necessarily have to be cash payments. If resources are insufficient to pay more than a nominal amount, small gifts or even lottery tickets may be an economic and effective alternative. Incentive payments may increase response rates in two ways. First, households may be more willing to cooperate if they expect to be paid for their time and trouble. Second, interviewer confidence in trying to enlist respondent cooperation may be higher if they know they can offer some form of payment. Interviewer confidence is an important factor in obtaining good response rates and is one reason why more experienced interviewers are usually more successful than inexperienced ones. At a recent meeting in the Moscow region, interviewers voiced strong criticism of the fact that incentives are not offered.

Response rates could be improved by interviewer training that focuses on maximizing responses and management techniques that improve interviewer motivation and morale. Improved interviewer management increased response rates in the Georgian Household Budget Survey from 72 percent in the last half of 2001 to 88 percent by the end of 2002, and the rates were maintained during the first half of 2003. The situations in Georgia and the Russian Federation are not directly comparable, however. There is a huge difference in geographic size and the scale of the two surveys, and Georgia pays households to participate. Nevertheless, the Georgian experience supports the view that better interviewer management and training can yield substantial benefits in terms of improved response rates. In addition to higher response rates, training in Georgia has led to significant improvements in the quality of the data collected, with fewer missing data items and a reduction in expenditure/income imbalances.

Employing specialists in fieldwork management operations is likely to improve interviewer management. The survey organization within the FSSS is structured so that each survey (the Household Budget Survey, the Labor Force Survey, and so forth) is managed separately and administered by its own field force. Data collection might benefit if fieldwork operations of these surveys were unified. Unifying these efforts would:

- Increase concentration, expertise, and experience in fieldwork operations.
- Allow interviewers to gain more experience and expertise by working across a range of surveys.
- Increase efficiency in deploying interviewer resources close to their work areas, which would minimize travel time and allow interviewers to be used more intensively, especially in urban areas.
- Increase flexibility to provide cover for interviewers who become unavailable (because of illness, for example).

Russia's huge size and the large number of regional offices to which responsibility for operations is devolved make data collection difficult. Reliable and consistent data that are free from local bias require firm adherence to uniform procedures. Although data collection is notionally controlled from the center, it would be surprising if there were not significant departures from the laid down procedures among the 89 regional offices, which face a wide diversity of conditions. Central supervision over such a vast territory and large number of local offices constitutes a major and continuing challenge. At the interviewer management workshops held under the joint poverty project, it became apparent that different offices handle interviewer management differently. The desire for more standardization and more detailed recruitment and training materials and procedures from the center was frequently expressed.

The Russian Household Budget Survey uses two principal forms of data recording instruments: questionnaires and a diary in which households record day-to-day expenditures. The diary is kept for a two-week period each calendar quarter by one person on behalf of the whole household. This "family diary" system is fairly typical among budget surveys in transition economies. In contrast, such surveys in many other countries use personal diaries, completed by each adult household member (and children as young as 7 in some countries). The argument in favor of personal diaries is that they better capture expenditures of a personal nature, such as alcohol and tobacco, daily travel, personal toiletries, entertainment, and food eaten outside the home, for which family diaries may well underrecord expenditure. Personal diaries are better suited to modern societies, especially urban societies, where traditional household spending behavior, in which expenditure is largely undertaken or controlled by one person within the household, is less and less common.

Assessing the level of underreporting is important for establishing the reliability of the Household Budget Survey. To examine the extent of underreporting for each item and each type of household, an experiment was carried out during the third quarter of 2003. A sample of 3,500 Household Budget Survey households containing more than one person 14 or older was asked to complete personal diaries. The sample was a stratified random sample covering all federal districts, 44 subject areas, large cities, other urban settlements, and rural areas. Personal diaries yielded higher levels of expenditure than household diaries—about 6 percent higher in urban areas and 11 percent higher in rural areas. Use of personal diaries reduced response rates, however, and increased interviewer workload. Of the initial sample of 3,500 households, only 1,874 (53.5 percent) actually took part in the experiment. The coding load for interviewers rose 63 percent, and the number of personal interviews they conducted with household members rose 50–100 percent (by the interviewers' own estimates).

First-hand information from interviewers is valuable in assessing the effectiveness of Household Budget Survey information collection. As part of an evaluation process, in November 2003, 20 interviewers from Moscow and Moscow Oblast who had participated in the experiment were invited to attend a feedback meeting. They were generally opposed to the idea of personal diaries, which they claimed would substantially increase their workloads, since they would have to visit households more often and at less convenient hours to find people at home. In fact, the sample included only households with more than one person (when one-person households are included, it is likely that the proportion of households for which all diaries are completed will rise, although the proportion of total nonresponse may also rise). Moreover, the experiment was carried out on households already in the Household Budget Survey, which were therefore accustomed to the lower response burden of family diaries. With newly selected households under the sample redesign, it may be that the reception of personal diaries would be better. The interviewers' views on personal diaries seemed highly prejudiced by, and inseparable from, their views on response problems, especially the problems they perceived to arise from the lack of incentive payments.

Improving the Tools Used for Statistical Adjustment

Editing and weighting are two main tools used for statistical adjustment. Under the current system, data are edited to correct for inconsistent responses. They are then weighted to produce estimates for the total population from sample data (using base weights) and to adjust for nonresponses. There is no attempt to impute responses for missing items in surveys that were otherwise completed by households.

The review process and the proposals for alternative data editing systems were completed by the end of 2003. The recommendations were then tested: a new editing and imputation system based on the Canadian Census Edit and Imputation System (CANCEIS) was carried out using simulated questionnaires from three regions. Based on the results of the simulation test, Goskomstat decided to use CANCEIS for editing and weighting their data.

Creating Open Access to Micro Data

No official statistical agency has the in-house capacity and expertise to generate full analytic value from the data it collects. For this reason, micro data should be made available to a much wider community of researchers. This general thrust is evident in Article 1 of the UN Fundamental Principles of Official Statistics, which states that "official statistics provide an indispensable element in the information system of a democratic society, serving the government, the economy and the public with data about the economic, demographic, social and environmental situation. To this end, official statistics that meet the test of practical utility are to be compiled and made available on an impartial basis by official statistical agencies to honor citizens' entitlement to public information" (UN Statistical Commission 1994). However, Article 6 provides that "individual data collected by statistical agencies for statistical compilation, whether they refer to natural or legal persons, are to be strictly confidential and used exclusively for statistical purposes" (UN Statistical Commission 1994). Reconciling these two objectives is a challenge facing all national statistical offices, especially in the provision of access to micro data.

Currently, micro data from the Household Budget Survey are available only to FSSS staff. This means that research analysis based on micro data is limited to what the FSSS has the resources to carry out. The FSSS wants to open up access to household datasets to the extent possible under Russian law. According to Vladimir Sokolin, chairman of the FSSS, beginning in 2005 the FSSS plans to provide researchers with anonymous micro data of Household Budget Surveys (Sokolin 2003). A key objective of the joint World Bank-DFID-Russian poverty project is to assist the FSSS in this process, in accordance with international standards and recommendations.

Work on opening micro data to the general public covers the following issues:

1. *Acquisitions and deposits.* When deposited, datasets must be accompanied by meta data. The international standard—the Data Documentation Initiative—specifies the requirements for doing so. In the United Kingdom the archiving of data is carried out by an independent agency, the data archive (UKDA), but depositors retain ownership and copyright of their deposited material. Depositors are also responsible for ensuring that the micro data are made anonymous, in order to protect confidentiality.
2. *Users and access.* Terms and conditions of access need to be set out, including whether to charge for data. In the United Kingdom data are provided free of charge to academic users; other users are charged only for the cost of provision, not for the data themselves. Terms and conditions of access include the following:
   - Data may be used only for noncommercial research and teaching purposes.
   - Users must preserve at all times the confidentiality of information pertaining to individuals or households for information collected less than 100 years ago, and no attempt should be made to compromise confidentiality.
   - The original creators of the data, the depositors, and the copyright holders of the data must be acknowledged in all publications.
   - All publications must clearly state that the data creators bear no responsibility for further analyses or interpretation of the data.
   - The UKDA must receive two copies of any published work based on the datasets.
   - The UKDA must be notified of any errors in the data that are discovered.
3. *Preservation.* Although they are invisible to outside users, good preservation procedures are vital to the long-term storage of data. This entails not only physical conditions of storage but storage formats as well.
4. *Organizational structures.* Organizational structures range from fully centralized to completely decentralized. Each structure has advantages and disadvantages.

Although a new statistical law is expected to be passed in the next few years and provision for open access to micro data depends on its adoption, the FSSS has made a decision in principle to proceed with open access. The intent is to take action with development work in parallel with the legislative process so that the new facility will be available as soon as possible after the new law is enacted.

Nearly all the statistical enhancements designed to improve the quality and efficiency of the survey are scheduled to be incorporated into the mainstream survey. These changes improve fieldwork management procedures, improve and increase the efficiency of sample design, provide better adjustment methods, include questionnaires that provide for more comprehensive poverty measurement, and allow general access to the micro data.

Note

1. Goskomstat was renamed the Federal Service for State Statistics (FSSS) in the spring of 2004.

Appendix A
Price Indexes, Poverty Lines, and Incidence of Poverty, by Region and Territory

Table A.1. Spatial price indexes by region and territory, 2002

Territory code	*Region and territory name*	*Food*	*Nonfood*	*Total*
	Russian Federation	100	100	100
	Region 1	*160.2*	*149.8*	*155.7*
402	Taimyr Autonomous Region	170.7	152.3	162.8
7174	Yamalo-Nenetskiy Autonomous Region	149.8	141.6	146.3
7700	Chukotka Autonomous Region	225.2	205.1	216.6
	Region 2	*126.0*	*131.2*	*128.2*
1113	Nenetskiy Autonomous Region	164.9	134.5	151.9
4700	Murmansk Oblast	124.2	131.0	127.1
	Region 3	*121.5*	*131.2*	*125.7*
500	Primorie Territory	117.9	116.4	117.3
800	Khabarovsk Territory	112.4	137.0	123.0
1000	Amur Oblast	98.6	110.8	103.8
3021	Kamchatka Oblast (excluding Kariakskiy Autonomous Region)	155.0	163.6	158.7
3051	Kariakskiy Autonomous Region	241.3	188.6	218.7
4400	Magadan Oblast	150.7	145.9	148.6
6400	Sakhalin Oblast	134.9	160.6	145.9
9800	Sakha (Yakutia) Republic	138.8	146.3	142.0
9900	Evreiskaya Autonomous Oblast	105.1	103.5	104.4
	Region 4	*99.9*	*97.0*	*98.6*
100	Altay Territory	85.3	89.7	87.2
406	Evenkiyskiy Autonomous Region	166.8	119.4	146.5
409	Krasnoyarsk Territory (excluding Taimyr and Evenkiyskiy Autonomous Regions)	111.4	100.5	106.7
2523	Irkutsk Oblast (excluding Ust-Ordynskiy Buriatskiy Autonomous Region)	103.8	97.6	101.2
2555	Ust-Ordynskiy Buriatskiy Autonomous Region	102.1	95.4	99.2
3200	Kemerovo Oblast	96.6	95.5	96.1
5000	Novosibirsk Oblast	106.0	101.2	103.9
5200	Omsk Oblast	85.2	88.1	86.4

(continued)

Table A.1. *(continued)*

Territory code	*Region and territory name*	*Food*	*Nonfood*	*Total*
6900	Tomsk Oblast	98.9	104.4	101.3
7635	Chita Oblast (excluding Aginskiy Buriatskiy Autonomous Region)	112.1	109.9	111.2
7667	Aginskiy Buriatskiy Autonomous Region	99.0	99.9	99.4
8100	Buriatiya Republic	100.3	93.0	97.2
8400	Altay Republic	99.4	93.7	97.0
9300	Tuva Republic	103.0	94.7	99.5
9500	Khakassiya Republic	103.1	99.2	101.4
	Region 5	*104.9*	*105.8*	*105.3*
3700	Kurgan Oblast	93.0	96.8	94.6
6500	Sverdlovsk Oblast	106.4	109.0	107.5
7139	Tumen Oblast (excluding Khanty-Mansiyskiy and Yamalo-Nenetskiy Autonomous Regions)	107.4	105.7	106.7
7172	Khanty-Mansiyskiy Autonomous Region	123.7	138.7	130.1
7500	Chelyabinsk Oblast	98.1	91.5	95.3
	Region 6	*102.2*	*101.5*	*101.9*
1116	Arkhangelsk Oblast (excluding Nenetskiy Autonomous Region)	98.1	99.5	98.7
1900	Vologda Oblast	100.4	92.2	96.9
2700	Kaliningrad Oblast	100.3	109.1	104.1
4000	St. Petersburg City	108.4	110.3	109.2
4100	Leningrad Oblast	99.4	95.6	97.8
4900	Novgorod Oblast	91.4	95.8	93.3
5800	Pskov Oblast	92.9	84.7	89.4
8600	Karelia Republic	102.8	90.9	97.7
8700	Komi Republic	103.1	102.8	103.0
	Region 7	*102.5*	*101.9*	*102.3*
1400	Belgorod Oblast	88.7	84.8	87.0
1500	Briansk Oblast	92.4	84.8	89.1
1700	Vladimir Oblast	88.0	78.2	83.8
2000	Voronezh Oblast	88.7	87.0	87.9
2400	Ivanovo Oblast	87.5	93.3	90.0
2800	Tver Oblast	94.6	93.6	94.2
2900	Kaluga Oblast	93.4	86.4	90.4
3400	Kostroma Oblast	87.6	85.4	86.6
3800	Kursk Oblast	87.6	89.6	88.5
4200	Lipetsk Oblast	92.7	81.9	88.1
4500	Moscow City	132.5	144.9	137.8
4600	Moscow Oblast	103.2	101.0	102.3

Territory code	*Region and territory name*	*Food*	*Nonfood*	*Total*
5400	Orel Oblast	87.3	81.5	84.8
6100	Riazan Oblast	90.9	82.3	87.2
6600	Smolensk Oblast	96.4	80.0	89.4
6800	Tambov Oblast	85.2	85.8	85.5
7000	Tula Oblast	91.7	79.7	86.6
7800	Yaroslavl Oblast	94.2	87.4	91.3
	Region 8	*93.9*	*92.4*	*93.3*
2200	Nizhniy Novgorod Oblast	96.2	93.3	95.0
3300	Kirov Oblast	93.2	96.1	94.4
3600	Samara Oblast	104.7	107.3	105.8
5300	Orenburg Oblast	91.3	88.6	90.1
5600	Penza Oblast	82.5	90.8	86.1
5731	Perm Oblast (excluding Komi-Permyatskiy Autonomous Region)	99.3	98.6	99.0
5759	Komi-Permyatskiy Autonomous Region	91.5	83.4	88.0
6300	Saratov Oblast	92.0	99.8	95.3
7300	Ulianovsk Oblast	90.0	88.8	89.5
8000	Bashkortostan Republic	91.2	83.6	87.9
8800	Mariy El Republic	94.5	84.0	90.0
8900	Mordoviya Republic	95.4	89.8	93.0
9200	Tatarstan Republic	88.9	89.5	89.2
9400	Udmurtiya Republic	97.7	87.2	93.2
9700	Chuvashiya Republic	93.2	82.0	88.4
	Region 9	*91.0*	*93.4*	*92.0*
300	Krasnodar Territory	93.4	97.7	95.2
700	Stavropol Territory	93.9	95.7	94.7
1200	Astrakhan Oblast	92.4	93.3	92.8
1800	Volgograd Oblast	92.1	91.3	91.7
2600	Ingushetiya Republic	93.8	107.5	99.7
6000	Rostov Oblast	87.7	95.2	90.9
7900	Adygeia Republic	92.4	84.7	89.1
8200	Dagestan Republic	89.7	89.9	89.8
8300	Kabardino-Balkariya Republic	89.6	81.1	85.9
8500	Kalmykiya Republic	81.7	88.7	84.7
9000	Severnaya Osetiya Republic	88.5	81.2	85.3
9100	Karachaevo-Cherkessiya Republic	83.5	82.2	82.9

Source: Bank staff calculations based on data from Household Budget Survey 2002 (Goskomstat).

Table A.2. Average poverty line, by region and territory, 2002 (rubles per capita per month)

		Poverty line			*Higher poverty line*		
Territory code	*Region and territory name*	*Food*	*Nonfood*	*Total*	*Food*	*Nonfood*	*Total*
	Russian Federation	570	486	1,056	703	549	1,251
	Region 1	*1,061.1*	*737.7*	*1,798.8*	*1,307.0*	*831.7*	*2,138.8*
402	Taimyr Autonomous Region	1,112	743	1,854	1,369	837	2,206
7174	Yamalo-Nenetskiy Autonomous Region	1,000	692	1,693	1,232	780	2,012
7700	Chukotka Autonomous Region	1,452	1,047	2,499	1,789	1,183	2,972
	Region 2	*819.9*	*651.0*	*1,470.9*	*1,009.9*	*735.5*	*1,745.5*
1113	Nenetskiy Autonomous Region	1,078	650	1,729	1,328	733	2,062
4700	Murmansk Oblast	808	651	1,459	995	736	1,731
	Region 3	*691.5*	*633.5*	*1,325.0*	*851.7*	*715.2*	*1,566.9*
500	Primorie Territory	667	560	1,228	822	633	1,455
800	Khabarovsk Territory	646	664	1,310	796	749	1,545
1000	Amur Oblast	556	535	1,091	685	604	1,289
3021	Kamchatka Oblast (excluding Kariakskiy Autonomous Region)	898	800	1,697	1,106	903	2,008
3051	Kariakskiy Autonomous Region	1,379	929	2,308	1,698	1,049	2,747
4400	Magadan Oblast	855	724	1,579	1,053	818	1,871
6400	Sakhalin Oblast	772	788	1,560	951	890	1,841
9800	Sakha (Yakutia) Republic	786	687	1,474	968	774	1,743
9900	Evreiskaya Autonomous Oblast	597	514	1,110	735	580	1,315
	Region 4	*570.0*	*468.4*	*1,038.5*	*702.1*	*528.8*	*1,230.9*
100	Altay Territory	489	437	925	602	493	1,095
406	Evenkiyskiy Autonomous Region	947	580	1,528	1,167	654	1,821
409	Krasnoyarsk Territory (excluding Taimyr and Evenkiyskiy Autonomous Regions)	641	492	1,134	790	556	1,346
2523	Irkutsk Oblast (excluding Ust-Ordynskiy Buriatskiy Autonomous Region)	593	472	1,065	730	532	1,262
2555	Ust-Ordynskiy Buriatskiy Autonomous Region	581	444	1,025	716	500	1,215
3200	Kemerovo Oblast	547	464	1,012	674	524	1,199
5000	Novosibirsk Oblast	604	489	1,093	744	552	1,296
5200	Omsk Oblast	488	421	908	601	475	1,076
6900	Tomsk Oblast	563	510	1,073	693	576	1,269

Territory code	Region and territory name	Poverty line			Higher poverty line		
		Food	*Nonfood*	*Total*	*Food*	*Nonfood*	*Total*
7635	Chita Oblast (excluding Aginskiy Buriatskiy Autonomous Region)	637	522	1,159	785	589	1,374
7667	Aginskiy Buriatskiy Autonomous Region	560	455	1,015	690	512	1,202
8100	Buriatiya Republic	571	436	1,006	703	491	1,194
8400	Altay Republic	565	451	1,015	695	508	1,204
9300	Tuva Republic	585	437	1,022	721	492	1,213
9500	Khakassiya Republic	588	480	1,068	725	542	1,266
	Region 5	*593.3*	*515.2*	*1,108.5*	*730.7*	*582.1*	*1,312.9*
3700	Kurgan Oblast	524	476	999	645	538	1,183
6500	Sverdlovsk Oblast	599	535	1,134	738	605	1,343
7139	Tumen Oblast (excluding Khanty-Mansiyskiy and Yamalo-Nenetskiy Autonomous Regions)	609	513	1,122	750	579	1,329
7172	Khanty-Mansiyskiy Autonomous Region	704	662	1,367	867	746	1,614
7500	Chelyabinsk Oblast	557	446	1,003	686	504	1,190
	Region 6	*582.2*	*501.0*	*1,083.2*	*717.1*	*566.3*	*1,283.5*
1116	Arkhangelsk Oblast (excluding Nenetskiy Autonomous Region)	560	489	1,049	690	552	1,242
1900	Vologda Oblast	569	462	1,031	701	523	1,224
2700	Kaliningrad Oblast	568	527	1,095	699	596	1,295
4000	St. Petersburg City	621	541	1,162	765	611	1,377
4100	Leningrad Oblast	569	483	1,052	701	546	1,247
4900	Novgorod Oblast	515	480	995	634	544	1,178
5800	Pskov Oblast	523	426	950	644	483	1,128
8600	Karelia Republic	580	451	1,031	714	510	1,225
8700	Komi Republic	582	500	1,082	716	565	1,281
	Region 7	*581.8*	*502.9*	*1,084.7*	*716.6*	*568.8*	*1,285.5*
1400	Belgorod Oblast	509	415	923	627	469	1,095
1500	Briansk Oblast	521	416	936	642	470	1,112
1700	Vladimir Oblast	500	388	888	615	439	1,055
2000	Voronezh Oblast	502	424	926	618	480	1,098
2400	Ivanovo Oblast	491	463	954	605	524	1,129
2800	Tver Oblast	528	472	1,000	650	535	1,185
2900	Kaluga Oblast	526	431	957	648	487	1,136
3400	Kostroma Oblast	493	429	922	607	486	1,093
3800	Kursk Oblast	491	432	924	605	489	1,095
4200	Lipetsk Oblast	523	404	927	645	457	1,101
4500	Moscow City	756	711	1,467	932	804	1,735
4600	Moscow Oblast	589	499	1,088	725	564	1,289
5400	Orel Oblast	494	401	895	609	453	1,062
6100	Riazan Oblast	512	409	921	631	463	1,094
6600	Smolensk Oblast	543	395	938	669	447	1,116

		Poverty line			*Higher poverty line*		
Territory code	*Region and territory name*	*Food*	*Nonfood*	*Total*	*Food*	*Nonfood*	*Total*
6800	Tambov Oblast	484	429	913	596	486	1,082
7000	Tula Oblast	521	397	918	641	450	1,091
7800	Yaroslavl Oblast	528	437	965	650	495	1,145
	Region 8	*533.9*	*447.5*	*981.4*	*657.6*	*505.5*	*1,163.2*
2200	Nizhniy Novgorod Oblast	540	457	997	665	517	1,182
3300	Kirov Oblast	525	473	998	646	536	1,182
3600	Samara Oblast	602	525	1,126	741	592	1,333
5300	Orenburg Oblast	523	429	952	645	484	1,129
5600	Penza Oblast	467	442	909	575	501	1,076
5731	Perm Oblast (excluding Komi-Permyatskiy Autonomous Region)	567	478	1,045	698	540	1,238
5759	Komi-Permyatskiy Autonomous Region	511	395	906	629	446	1,075
6300	Saratov Oblast	523	491	1,014	644	555	1,200
7300	Ulianovsk Oblast	513	433	946	631	489	1,121
8000	Bashkortostan Republic	517	400	917	637	451	1,088
8800	Mariy El Republic	539	401	940	664	452	1,117
8900	Mordoviya Republic	548	447	995	675	506	1,181
9200	Tatarstan Republic	509	424	933	627	478	1,105
9400	Udmurtiya Republic	552	418	970	680	471	1,152
9700	Chuvashiya Republic	522	385	907	642	435	1,077
	Region 9	*517.6*	*437.5*	*955.1*	*637.6*	*493.7*	*1,131.3*
300	Krasnodar Territory	530	465	995	653	525	1,178
700	Stavropol Territory	532	448	980	655	506	1,161
1200	Astrakhan Oblast	526	451	976	647	509	1,156
1800	Volgograd Oblast	524	444	968	646	501	1,147
2600	Ingushetiya Republic	534	435	969	658	486	1,144
6000	Rostov Oblast	499	453	951	614	511	1,125
7900	Adygeia Republic	520	398	918	641	449	1,090
8200	Dagestan Republic	515	393	908	634	442	1,076
8300	Kabardino-Balkariya Republic	510	362	872	628	407	1,036
8500	Kalmykiya Republic	468	411	879	577	463	1,040
9000	Severnaya Osetiya Republic	505	364	869	622	410	1,032
9100	Karachaevo-Cherkessiya Republic	476	375	851	586	422	1,008

Source: Bank staff calculations based on data from Household Budget Survey 2002 (Goskomstat).

Table A.3. Incidence of poverty, by region and territory, 2002

			Poverty line			Higher poverty line			
Territory code	*Region and territory name*	*Sample size*	*Head-count (%)*	*Gap (%)*	*Severity (%)*	*Head-count (%)*	*Gap (%)*	*Severity (%)*	*Per capita consumption (rubles per month)*
	Russian Federation	194,118	19.6	5.1	2.0	29.0	8.1	3.3	2,159
	Region 1	*3,800*	*9.5*	*2.7*	*1.1*	*13.8*	*4.2*	*1.8*	*4,531*
402	Taimyr Autonomous Region	1,260	34.2	10.1	4.1	44.2	14.9	6.6	3,045
7174	Yamalo-Nenetskiy Autonomous Region	1,040	3.2	0.7	0.2	6.0	1.4	0.5	4,826
7700	Chukotka Autonomous Region	1,500	37.7	12.1	5.5	48.8	17.0	8.2	3,394
	Region 2	*3,100*	*12.3*	*3.0*	*1.1*	*20.6*	*5.1*	*2.0*	*2,867*
1113	Nenetskiy Autonomous Region	1,340	31.6	12.3	6.4	43.9	16.5	8.8	2,260
4700	Murmansk Oblast	1,760	11.4	2.5	0.9	19.5	4.6	1.6	2,895
	Region 3	*16,180*	*21.4*	*5.8*	*2.4*	*30.7*	*8.9*	*3.8*	*2,347*
500	Primorie Territory	2,520	24.2	6.5	2.6	35.3	10.1	4.3	1,949
800	Khabarovsk Territory	2,440	17.0	4.9	2.1	26.0	7.4	3.2	2,631
1000	Amur Oblast	1,900	20.8	5.4	2.0	29.6	8.4	3.4	1,846
3021	Kamchatka Oblast (excluding Kariakskiy Autonomous Region)	1,720	13.8	3.0	1.0	22.0	5.3	1.9	3,192
3051	Kariakskiy Autonomous Region	1,280	36.1	10.8	4.7	48.9	16.1	7.3	3,105
4400	Magadan Oblast	1,880	33.7	10.4	4.5	43.9	14.8	6.8	2,323
6400	Sakhalin Oblast	1,620	22.6	5.5	2.1	31.4	8.7	3.5	2,549
9800	Sakha (Yakutia) Republic	1,800	21.8	6.4	2.7	28.7	9.3	4.1	2,890
9900	Evreiskaya Autonomous Oblast	1,020	18.7	4.8	1.7	27.1	7.6	3.0	2,081
	Region 4	*31,578*	*20.8*	*5.6*	*2.3*	*30.1*	*8.7*	*3.7*	*1,831*
100	Altay Territory	2,980	18.8	4.3	1.5	29.0	7.3	2.7	1,759
406	Evenkiyskiy Autonomous Region	1,100	32.8	11.2	5.5	43.5	15.5	7.9	2,449
409	Krasnoyarsk Territory (excluding Taimyr and Evenkiyskiy Autonomous Regions)	2,860	12.3	2.8	1.0	19.9	4.9	1.8	2,283
2523	Irkutsk Oblast (excluding Ust-Ordynskiy Buriatskiy Autonomous Region)	2,800	15.0	3.5	1.2	23.4	6.0	2.2	2,273
2555	Ust-Ordynskiy Buriatskiy Autonomous Region	1,000	46.5	14.6	6.4	59.6	20.7	9.7	1,281
3200	Kemerovo Oblast	3,040	21.1	5.5	2.1	30.6	8.7	3.6	1,553
5000	Novosibirsk Oblast	2,740	25.2	6.8	2.6	35.7	10.5	4.4	1,615

			Poverty line			*Higher poverty line*			
Territory code	*Region and territory name*	*Sample size*	*Head-count %*	*Gap %*	*Severity %*	*Head-count %*	*Gap %*	*Severity %*	*Per capita consumption (rubles per month)*
5200	Omsk Oblast	2,600	20.7	6.2	2.9	28.3	9.1	4.2	1,675
6900	Tomsk Oblast	2,020	16.6	4.8	1.9	24.3	7.3	3.1	1,961
7635	Chita Oblast (excluding Aginskiy Buriatskiy Autonomous Region)	2,020	30.0	8.2	3.4	42.3	12.6	5.4	1,983
7667	Aginskiy Buriatskiy Autonomous Region	1,080	42.3	13.5	6.0	51.9	18.8	8.9	1,320
8100	Buriatiya Republic	2,120	31.9	9.6	4.4	42.7	13.9	6.5	1,370
8400	Altay Republic	1,558	31.6	9.0	3.8	42.6	13.4	6.0	1,459
9300	Tuva Republic	1,840	41.6	16.4	8.4	51.6	21.2	11.4	1,329
9500	Khakassiya Republic	1,820	22.4	6.1	2.5	32.6	9.4	4.0	1,759
	Region 5	*11,620*	*18.8*	*5.2*	*2.1*	*25.8*	*7.9*	*3.4*	*2,125*
3700	Kurgan Oblast	1,860	28.8	8.7	3.7	40.8	12.7	5.7	1,460
6500	Sverdlovsk Oblast	3,980	21.8	6.0	2.4	29.3	9.0	3.9	1,858
7139	Tumen Oblast (excluding Khanty-Mansiyskiy and Yamalo-Nenetskiy Autonomous Regions)	1,240	16.0	3.5	1.2	22.9	6.0	2.2	2,246
7172	Khanty-Mansiyskiy Autonomous Region	1,520	3.4	0.5	0.1	6.7	1.2	0.3	4,015
7500	Chelyabinsk Oblast	3,020	19.3	5.6	2.4	25.6	8.2	3.7	1,871
	Region 6	*19,240*	*11.7*	*2.9*	*1.1*	*19.6*	*4.8*	*1.9*	*2,133*
1116	Arkhangelsk Oblast (excluding Nenetskiy Autonomous Region)	1,820	11.3	2.5	0.9	18.2	4.3	1.6	2,067
1900	Vologda Oblast	2,020	14.8	3.9	1.5	22.1	6.3	2.5	2,067
2700	Kaliningrad Oblast	1,960	24.1	6.9	3.1	36.1	10.5	4.7	1,792
4000	St. Petersburg City	3,720	3.1	0.4	0.1	8.7	1.2	0.3	2,513
4100	Leningrad Oblast	2,040	14.1	3.2	1.1	25.3	5.6	2.0	1,837
4900	Novgorod Oblast	1,800	24.0	6.4	2.5	33.3	9.9	4.1	1,478
5800	Pskov Oblast	1,900	20.6	5.1	1.9	31.0	8.3	3.3	1,677
8600	Karelia Republic	1,700	12.3	2.7	1.0	19.4	4.8	1.8	2,158
8700	Komi Republic	2,280	15.9	4.8	2.1	23.9	7.1	3.2	2,171
	Region 7	*42,680*	*15.2*	*3.6*	*1.3*	*24.5*	*6.1*	*2.3*	*1,823*
1400	Belgorod Oblast	1,900	6.8	0.9	0.2	12.8	2.2	0.6	1,778
1500	Briansk Oblast	1,800	24.4	6.0	2.2	38.4	10.0	3.9	1,407
1700	Vladimir Oblast	2,200	15.2	2.9	0.9	25.5	5.7	1.9	1,582
2000	Voronezh Oblast	2,760	23.7	6.0	2.2	34.0	9.6	3.9	1,404
2400	Ivanovo Oblast	1,620	25.4	6.1	2.4	36.1	9.9	4.0	1,475
2800	Tver Oblast	2,720	21.2	5.1	1.8	31.6	8.3	3.2	1,715
2900	Kaluga Oblast	1,820	10.3	2.0	0.7	18.8	3.9	1.3	1,886
3400	Kostroma Oblast	1,920	23.9	6.3	2.4	35.9	10.0	4.1	1,336
3800	Kursk Oblast	1,980	24.0	5.5	1.8	36.0	9.3	3.4	1,288
4200	Lipetsk Oblast	1,780	12.4	2.8	0.9	20.0	4.8	1.8	1,942
4500	Moscow City	5,520	8.6	1.5	0.4	17.0	3.2	1.0	2,454

			Poverty line			*Higher poverty line*			
Territory code	*Region and territory name*	*Sample size*	*Head-count %*	*Gap %*	*Severity %*	*Head-count %*	*Gap %*	*Severity %*	*Per capita consumption (rubles per month)*
4600	Moscow Oblast	4,040	16.8	4.8	2.0	24.9	7.4	3.2	1,780
5400	Orel Oblast	2,000	12.7	2.9	1.0	22.0	5.1	1.9	1,716
6100	Riazan Oblast	2,020	17.5	4.3	1.6	27.5	7.1	2.8	1,584
6600	Smolensk Oblast	1,800	19.5	4.2	1.4	30.3	7.5	2.7	1,302
6800	Tambov Oblast	2,200	20.0	4.5	1.5	29.6	7.6	2.8	1,510
7000	Tula Oblast	2,300	8.8	1.4	0.4	18.8	3.3	0.9	1,633
7800	Yaroslavl Oblast	2,300	11.9	3.1	1.3	19.2	5.0	2.1	1,836
	Region 8	*38,420*	*21.4*	*5.6*	*2.2*	*31.4*	*8.9*	*3.6*	*1,621*
2200	Nizhniy Novgorod Oblast	3,320	21.5	5.5	2.1	32.2	8.9	3.6	1,531
3300	Kirov Oblast	2,500	18.9	5.4	2.1	28.0	8.2	3.5	1,863
3600	Samara Oblast	3,460	20.3	5.8	2.5	28.2	8.7	3.8	1,896
5300	Orenburg Oblast	2,580	13.4	2.4	0.7	23.1	4.9	1.5	1,893
5600	Penza Oblast	1,900	16.8	4.0	1.4	27.3	6.8	2.6	1,591
5731	Perm Oblast (excluding Komi-Permyatskiy Autonomous Region)	3,340	20.0	5.2	2.0	30.2	8.2	3.4	1,727
5759	Komi-Permyatskiy Autonomous Region	1,160	43.4	12.1	4.6	55.7	18.1	7.7	1,249
6300	Saratov Oblast	3,080	26.0	7.8	3.5	35.6	11.3	5.2	1,598
7300	Ulianovsk Oblast	2,040	28.8	8.4	3.5	39.0	12.4	5.5	1,349
8000	Bashkortostan Republic	3,700	20.1	4.9	1.8	29.3	8.0	3.1	1,585
8800	Mariy El Republic	1,900	38.7	11.9	5.1	50.9	17.1	7.9	1,347
8900	Mordoviya Republic	1,760	30.0	8.1	3.2	44.8	12.9	5.3	1,427
9200	Tatarstan Republic	3,760	20.4	5.0	1.9	30.8	8.2	3.2	1,509
9400	Udmurtiya Republic	1,920	21.0	4.7	1.6	30.1	8.0	3.0	1,773
9700	Chuvashiya Republic	2,000	19.9	5.2	2.0	32.9	8.7	3.4	1,193
	Region 9	*27,500*	*28.9*	*7.9*	*3.2*	*40.0*	*12.0*	*5.1*	*1,428*
300	Krasnodar Territory	3,620	25.2	6.9	2.8	36.7	10.6	4.5	1,500
700	Stavropol Territory	2,740	29.8	7.1	2.5	41.3	11.5	4.5	1,481
1200	Astrakhan Oblast	1,800	25.4	6.5	2.4	34.5	10.2	4.1	1,797
1800	Volgograd Oblast	3,080	23.1	5.7	2.1	35.0	9.3	3.6	1,515
2600	Ingushetiya Republic	960	46.7	13.6	5.9	58.2	19.5	8.9	1,549
6000	Rostov Oblast	3,720	21.2	5.2	1.9	31.4	8.5	3.4	1,468
7900	Adygeia Republic	1,860	22.0	5.4	2.0	31.8	8.8	3.5	1,768
8200	Dagestan Republic	2,460	55.6	18.1	8.1	68.6	24.9	12.0	886
8300	Kabardino-Balkariya Republic	1,900	41.7	12.5	5.4	50.5	17.9	8.3	1,143
8500	Kalmykiya Republic	1,820	36.4	11.8	5.4	45.8	16.3	7.9	1,247
9000	Severnaya Osetiya Republic	1,920	25.6	6.7	2.4	35.0	10.5	4.2	1,323
9100	Karachaevo-Cherkessiya Republic	1,620	18.2	4.4	1.5	26.6	7.1	2.7	1,535

Source: Bank staff calculations based on data from Household Budget Survey 2002 (Goskomstat).

Appendix B
Inequality Measures

Regional Inequality Measures (Gini)

Following Kakwani (1980), the unweighted Gini for regional average Gross Regional Product (GRP) is computed as follows:

$$G_U = \left(\frac{1}{2\overline{y}_U}\right)\frac{1}{n(n-1)}\sum_i^n\sum_j^n |y_i - y_j| ,$$

where y_i and y_j are the incomes per capita of region i and j, respectively; n is the number of regions; and $\overline{y}_u$ is the unweighted mean of the per capita GRPs. G varies from 0 for perfect equality to 1 for perfect inequality.

The weighted Gini index weights each difference in per capita GRPs by the respective population proportions:

$$G_W = \left(\frac{1}{2\overline{y}}\right)\sum_i^n\sum_j^n |y_i - y_j|\frac{p_i p_j}{P^2} ,$$

where $\overline{y}$ is the national mean per capita GDP; p_i and p_j are the populations of regions i and j, respectively; P is the national population; and n is the number of regions. G_w varies from 0 for perfect equality to $P/p_i - 1$ for perfect inequality. If p_i is small relative to P—that is, if the region with a small proportion of the population produced all GRP—then the value for perfect inequality would approach 1.

Theil Index Decomposition

Let y_i be income of the ith household (out of the population of n households). The Theil entropy index, T, is defined by

$$T = \frac{1}{n}\sum_i^n \frac{y_i}{\mu}\log\frac{y_i}{\mu} ,$$

where μ is mean income.

The Theil mean log deviation index T_0 is given by

$$T = \frac{1}{n}\sum_{i}^{n}\log\frac{\mu}{y_i}$$

This inequality can be divided into components B (between-region inequality) and W_g (within-region inequality), where W and W_0 represent the sum of the contribution to overall inequality due to the inequality within each region, and B and B_0 represent the sum of the contribution to national inequality due to inequality between mean incomes μ_g for regions $g = 1, \ldots, G$. Assume that the weight of the gth region in the population is given by w_g, that the income share is given by v_g, and that T_{0g} and T_g are correspondingly the Theil mean log deviation and the Theil entropy indexes for region g. Then the following basic formula for decomposing both Theil indexes into the within-region (first term) and between-region (second term) components holds:

$$T = W_g + B = \sum_{g=1}^{G} v_g T_g + \sum_{g=1}^{G} v_g \log\frac{v_g}{w_g}, \quad T_0 = W_{0g} + B_0 = \sum_{g=1}^{G} w_g T_{0g} + \sum_{g=1}^{G} w_g \log\frac{w_g}{v_g}.$$

Inequality can be decomposed for any other groupings, not only regions, provided that the population can be partitioned into mutually exclusive groups (urban and rural residence, level of education, age group, employment status, and so forth).

Appendix C
A Tale of Two Regions

The dozen richest and dozen poorest regions of Russia (based on GRP per capita) include two regions in European Russia that are similar in climate and location: Ivanovo Oblast, with a per capita GRP of about 26,000 rubles in 2002, and Samara Oblast, with a per capita GRP of about 73,000 rubles (table C.1). Understanding why the per capita GRP in the two regions is so different may shed some light on the economic and political roots of regional inequality in Russia.

Ivanovo was as well (or better) placed at the outset of the transition as Samara: it is closer to the capital (300 kilometers instead of 1,000) and is smaller and therefore easier to govern (1 million inhabitants as opposed to 3 million). Both regions have predominantly urban populations (80 percent) and well-educated workforces (12 percent of the population in each *oblast* has higher education). Ivanovo was praised as the main textile industrial center of Russia (it produced half of national textile production) and a "city of brides" (due to the fact that it employed mostly women). Samara, with its large chocolate factories and breweries, had an image as a "sweets" and "beer" city. Before the transition (1985), the two regions had strikingly similar living standards, with an average per capita income of 185 rubles per month and similar levels of wages, employment, and enrollment in higher education. Housing stock per capita and enrollment rates in preschool education were higher in Ivanovo, but Samara had more doctors per capita.

By 2002 these two regions had moved far apart. Average monthly wages were $85 in Ivanovo and $140 in Samara, and Ivanovo had significant unemployment. Samara attracted several large investors (Nestlé, General Motors), while Ivanovo was struggling to attract even one and had a low and deteriorating investment rating. Samara was one of the largest contributors to the federal budget (2.9 percent of consolidated budget revenues), while Ivanovo was relying on federal transfers to balance its budget. Though social indicators of access to health and education remained similar, Ivanovo experienced one of the largest population losses in Central Russia (11 percent between 1989 and 2002), while Samara's population held steady. Ivanovo acquired a reputation as a "rust belt" region, with industrial production that had few export markets (only 5 percent of output was exported), while Samara became renowned as "Detroit on the Volga" and exported more than a quarter of its industrial output.

A key difference between the regions was the composition of their outputs. Samara relied on two sectors that were positively affected by transition: automobile production and oil production and processing. Despite the economic crisis, car purchases in the CIS skyrocketed. While the stock of known oil resources in Samara would barely cover Russia's annual oil output, its position on the main oil transport road from Siberia and its own resource base created favorable conditions for developing oil processing. In contrast, Ivanovo was stuck with an uncompetitive, outdated textile industry that suffered large negative external shocks owing to the opening to the international markets. It inherited some heavy industry plants that were losing their customers due to the transition recession.

Corruption and criminality (notorious mafia gangs surrounding automobile production and marketing) were countervailing factors working against Samara's success. As a result, despite being ranked by the Ministry of Economy and Trade as one of the top three regions in terms of production potential, an independent Expert Investment Rating Agency (2002) ranked Samara as having only "average potential/moderate risk," quite close to Ivanovo's "low potential/moderate risk" rating.

Political factors were also important. Ivanovo was a Communist Party stronghold, but it suffered from instability and often changed regional governments. Together with constant interference in the operation of key businesses, this hurt the region's image among potential investors. In contrast, for more than 10 years Samara was governed by the same person—Konstantin Titov, an independent, reform-minded politician with strong ties to business circles and connections to central authorities. Titov's role in the privatization and subsequent bankruptcy deal of the largest car manufacturer was particularly prominent. Manipulating foreign trade regulations on car imports in favor of domestically produced cars made the regional administration famous. Although Titov was a controversial figure, his influence on the economic development of the region is now deemed to have been positive.

GRP per capita is an important determinant of poverty, but it is not the only factor. Despite having very different GRP per capita levels, Ivanovo's poverty rate (25 percent in 2002, according to the recommended methodology), while one of the highest in European Russia, is surprisingly close to Samara's (20 percent) (table C.2). However, the Gini index of inequality in Ivanovo was 0.25, while in Samara it was 0.33 (table C.3). Although small in absolute value, the actual difference in inequality between the two regions is quite large, given that the whole range of inequality for Russian regions is 0.24–0.40. The high inequality in Samara might be the missing part of the picture explaining why, despite economic success in terms of GRP per capita, Samara did not manage a significant poverty reduction.

The per capita GRP differences between Ivanovo and Samara illustrate that huge contrasts between regions reported in the national accounts data are, to a large extent, an illusion: actual living standards (as evidenced by similar poverty rates) vary much less. The issue for policymakers is not to arrest the tendency for regional differentiation but to ensure that economic development is beneficial for the population and the poor in every region.

This appendix is based on *Regions of Russia* (Goskomstat, various years), the Expert Investment Rating Agency database, and data from the Ministry of Economy and Trade.

Table C.1. Economic indicators by region, 1997–2002

Region and territory name	*Population (thousands)*	*GRP per capita (rubles in 2002 prices)*			*Disposable resources (rubles per capita in 2002 prices)*			*Consumption (rubles per capita in 2002 prices)*		
	2002	*1997*	*1999*	*2002*	*1997*	*1999*	*2002*	*1997*	*1999*	*2002*
Russian Federation[a]	144,060	53,226	52,607	65,249	37,402	20,116	33,675	24,824	15,685	25,904
Center										
Belgorod Oblast	1,511	33,579	36,025	43,482	37,921	20,416	28,773	28,186	15,911	24,258
Briansk Oblast	1,379	24,375	23,533	29,969	24,374	14,537	24,885	19,498	12,411	19,042
Vladimir Oblast	1,524	28,977	29,392	34,970	24,414	14,217	23,168	18,379	12,236	19,909
Voronezh Oblast	2,379	33,782	33,424	37,054	26,799	17,403	25,347	18,467	12,356	20,039
Ivanovo Oblast	1,148	24,388	22,025	25,668	23,682	11,616	20,025	18,423	10,634	17,279
Kaluga Oblast	1,042	33,498	32,326	38,593	26,692	16,625	26,656	20,124	14,025	22,719
Kostroma Oblast	737	33,802	33,843	37,415	22,491	13,884	22,317	17,844	11,827	17,402
Kursk Oblast	1,235	31,185	32,102	37,806	28,932	16,435	25,037	20,957	14,164	19,127
Lipetsk Oblast	1,213	47,933	47,338	58,622	30,950	18,917	31,871	22,237	15,216	24,534
Moscow Oblast	6,618	45,431	46,652	56,032	27,577	17,164	30,328	22,310	14,945	26,875
Orel Oblast	860	31,941	34,633	45,159	31,682	19,646	29,565	22,529	15,507	21,848
Riazan Oblast	1,228	38,202	37,671	44,554	24,677	13,603	25,295	19,714	11,855	22,268
Smolensk Oblast	1,049	34,804	40,114	44,805	36,969	13,526	22,036	19,237	11,796	20,076
Tambov Oblast	1,178	24,281	26,268	33,286	22,454	18,062	24,704	17,406	14,652	20,062
Tver Oblast	1,471	33,410	35,773	39,956	25,054	13,494	27,864	18,688	11,618	21,798
Tula Oblast	1,676	35,930	34,625	40,508	28,090	15,031	24,962	22,396	13,445	21,591
Yaroslavl Oblast	1,368	51,386	51,776	63,650	30,975	17,865	30,903	23,608	15,053	24,578
Moscow City	10,383	143,242	142,714	192,622	122,530	46,031	66,799	61,328	31,422	50,609
North West										
Karelia Republic	716	47,107	48,490	58,108	34,443	21,715	38,517	24,651	16,584	29,760
Komi Republic	1,018	83,200	79,520	91,506	41,452	31,827	44,092	25,156	18,557	32,534
Arkhangelsk Oblast	1,336	47,117	50,528	63,384	31,189	20,493	37,930	22,085	15,972	27,655
of which Nenetskiy Autonomous Region	42	—	—	398,562	—	22,182	54,071	—	16,776	35,782
Vologda Oblast	1,270	53,053	57,909	65,068	40,926	19,407	38,429	25,629	15,519	27,608
Kaliningrad Oblast	955	34,113	32,969	43,032	29,448	23,331	27,300	22,885	14,688	24,118
Leningrad Oblast	1,669	40,154	42,787	60,979	24,766	17,130	25,988	19,894	14,557	22,645
Murmansk Oblast	893	71,926	73,359	76,154	55,972	44,200	59,894	34,249	25,085	37,344
Novgorod Oblast	694	35,895	40,445	45,905	26,128	18,073	28,296	19,316	14,534	21,693
Pskov Oblast	761	26,587	28,981	32,366	22,515	14,233	28,579	17,834	12,229	21,811
St. Petersburg City	4,661	57,616	57,947	78,911	35,726	23,320	40,617	27,925	19,935	34,105

Region and territory name	Population (thousands)	GRP per capita (rubles in 2002 prices)			Disposable resources (rubles per capita in 2002 prices)			Consumption (rubles per capita in 2002 prices)		
	2002	1997	1999	2002	1997	1999	2002	1997	1999	2002
South										
Adygeia Republic	447	17,139	17,433	18,800	22,819	13,703	27,530	18,930	12,134	22,630
Dagestan Republic	2,577	11,616	10,872	16,470	13,249	7,777	12,452	10,177	7,345	11,593
Ingushetiya Republic	467	9,168	6,982	8,227	18,784	—	14,503	13,233	—	14,295
Kabardino-Balkariya Republic	902	16,607	18,193	26,074	18,463	10,989	17,801	14,640	9,922	14,466
Kalmykiya Republic	292	32,737	27,804	46,151	19,530	10,497	18,297	14,794	8,847	15,773
Karachaevo-Cherkessiya Republic	440	18,010	17,503	23,953	24,346	15,532	23,876	20,470	13,027	19,541
Severnaya Osetiya Republic	710	14,874	16,992	23,602	21,961	15,117	22,043	17,468	13,317	18,101
Krasnodar Territory	5,125	35,159	38,825	45,757	25,392	14,433	26,267	17,959	11,677	21,029
Stavropol Territory	2,735	25,415	25,028	31,255	29,731	14,888	26,538	19,993	11,343	19,874
Astrakhan Oblast	1,005	30,338	34,307	44,584	22,895	17,032	33,527	17,405	13,456	24,904
Volgograd Oblast	2,699	36,523	32,469	41,586	26,445	13,817	26,051	19,110	11,073	21,505
Rostov Oblast	4,404	23,414	24,799	33,415	26,482	16,067	25,968	19,723	13,862	21,601
Volga										
Bashkortostan Republic	4,104	46,791	44,649	52,345	30,033	19,600	31,474	19,267	14,206	23,054
Mariy El Republic	728	27,041	25,899	25,945	19,911	12,653	18,597	14,505	11,127	15,685
Mordoviya Republic	889	22,027	21,412	27,371	25,253	13,456	22,435	19,270	11,904	18,277
Tatarstan Republic	3,779	57,111	56,413	69,289	28,343	16,019	28,388	20,210	13,893	21,847
Udmurtiya Republic	1,570	47,096	44,647	52,955	32,701	21,389	31,744	22,707	14,494	21,822
Chuvashiya Republic	1,314	28,543	26,122	30,324	22,243	11,757	25,884	16,791	10,101	19,410
Kirov Oblast	1,504	34,296	33,821	35,730	30,288	15,936	28,160	21,512	12,906	22,318
Nizhniy Novgorod Oblast	3,524	44,882	44,316	55,874	34,837	15,380	27,840	26,652	12,844	23,393
Orenburg Oblast	2,179	43,183	40,615	47,267	29,876	17,008	28,631	19,824	13,760	23,231
Penza Oblast	1,453	27,490	27,147	30,874	23,416	13,179	24,815	18,916	11,298	20,211
Perm Oblast	2,820	58,929	59,177	60,920	33,332	19,922	37,029	21,001	15,809	26,293
of which Komi-Permyatskiy Autonomous Region	136	—	—	21,505	—	8,545	17,107		7,290	14,071
Samara Oblast	3,240	65,740	62,320	73,474	38,561	22,755	41,260	24,467	16,913	26,505
Saratov Oblast	2,668	34,178	31,868	39,230	30,463	15,266	24,540	20,366	12,777	21,542
Ulianovsk Oblast	1,383	32,433	31,383	35,239	25,303	14,796	22,751	19,375	12,639	18,772
Ural										
Kurgan Oblast	1,019	30,764	28,603	31,483	38,581	14,739	24,692	20,243	11,951	18,960
Sverdlovsk Oblast	4,486	46,039	43,104	54,851	42,834	18,147	32,695	30,089	14,708	25,969
Tumen Oblast	3,265	233,796	231,804	294,042	73,215	41,812	80,914	45,040	27,227	48,443
of which Khanty-Mansiyskiy Autonomous Region	1,433	—	—	405,985	—	53,252	102,851	—	34,048	55,765
of which Yamalo-Nenetskiy Autonomous Region	507	—	—	550,997	—	67,528	113,496	—	37,426	67,845
Chelyabinsk Oblast	3,604	49,096	44,171	50,884	37,381	20,229	32,891	26,425	16,174	23,184
Siberia										
Altay Republic	203	26,323	24,872	31,278	27,215	13,057	22,954	20,978	11,693	19,016
Buriatiya Republic	981	32,992	33,532	39,822	24,306	14,769	22,614	17,686	12,346	19,501
Tuva Republic	306	17,740	18,116	22,057	21,745	11,100	21,977	16,068	9,637	17,968
Khakassiya Republic	546	45,806	41,473	44,890	31,112	20,298	31,628	22,642	15,879	23,855
Altay Territory	2,607	23,461	23,343	29,010	25,232	15,443	27,774	19,424	12,753	20,691

Region and territory name	Population (thousands)	GRP per capita (rubles in 2002 prices)			Disposable resources (rubles per capita in 2002 prices)			Consumption (rubles per capita in 2002 prices)		
	2002	1997	1999	2002	1997	1999	2002	1997	1999	2002
Krasnoyarsk Territory	2,966	69,531	68,392	79,565	39,183	26,935	46,576	27,500	18,775	31,914
of which Taimyr Autonomous Region	40	—	—	71,585	—	39,725	55,958	—	30,960	37,175
of which Evenkiyskiy Autonomous Region	18	—	—	48,339	—	27,782	35,525	—	21,299	30,528
Irkutsk Oblast	2,582	57,746	52,813	57,945	32,863	23,035	38,166	23,782	17,857	28,914
of which Ust-Ordynskiy Buriatskiy Autonomous Region	135	—	—	28,110	—	13,821	16,900	—	11,968	14,423
Kemerovo Oblast	2,899	43,184	42,979	49,883	31,649	18,328	28,917	22,532	15,205	23,004
Novosibirsk Oblast	2,692	36,423	36,152	48,295	38,539	15,987	27,683	22,448	13,386	22,485
Omsk Oblast	2,079	37,843	33,276	43,739	32,090	15,700	31,644	18,065	13,974	24,312
Tomsk Oblast	1,046	60,431	58,056	77,360	38,277	20,562	37,433	25,899	16,530	26,596
Chita Oblast	1,156	34,220	32,602	38,974	29,879	14,739	28,123	22,881	12,696	22,641
of which Aginskiy Buriatskiy Autonomous Region	72	—	—	22,704	—	10,393	20,803	—	8,797	16,100
Far East										
Sakha (Yakutia) Republic	949	108,761	109,103	121,072	50,552	34,797	50,996	31,623	24,100	38,188
Primorie Territory	2,071	47,452	47,454	48,757	35,847	19,984	32,478	27,950	17,094	25,733
Khabarovsk Territory	1,436	53,670	54,926	70,742	36,940	24,345	47,610	26,571	19,437	33,217
Amur Oblast	903	45,966	42,671	51,613	43,928	17,251	27,902	22,614	14,573	23,599
Kamchatka Oblast	359	84,294	71,920	70,657	80,506	34,968	54,401	36,224	25,439	41,333
of which Kariakskiy Autonomous Region	25	—	—	144,224	—	34,537	41,819	—	29,367	38,598
Magadan Oblast	183	133,252	104,069	114,536	57,080	28,901	39,936	38,909	22,445	36,051
Sakhalin Oblast	547	85,718	98,096	103,089	43,361	28,024	50,904	32,437	20,678	37,943
Evreiskaya Autonomous Oblast	191	31,206	28,460	34,813	—	19,215	34,219	—	14,569	25,081
Chukotka Autonomous Region	54	157,867	111,153	220,265	—	33,543	49,592	—	32,127	44,640
Highest	10,383	233,796	231,804	550,997	122,530	67,528	113,496	61,328	37,426	67,845
Lowest	18	9,168	6,982	8,227	13,249	7,777	12,452	10,177	7,290	11,593

Sources: Regions of Russia (Goskomstat, various years); *Social Status and Living Standards of Russian Population* (Goskomstat, various years), and Bank staff calculations based on data from Household Budget Survey 1997–2002 (Goskomstat).

Note: For consistency over time, this and all subsequent tables report summary statistics at the regional level inclusive of smaller regions for 1999 and 2002. For example, data for Kamchatka Oblast include the Kariakskiy Autonomous Region for GRP per capita for 2002 and for disposable resources and consumption for 1999 and 2002; population data also include smaller constituent regions in a larger one. Regional CPI indexes were used for deflation.

a. Figure excludes the Chechen Republic, for which data were not available.

— Not available.

Table C.2. Poverty indexes by region, 1997–2002 (percent of population with corresponding welfare index below the poverty line)

Region and territory name	*Consumption (using recommended methodology)*[a]			*Disposable resources and official constant poverty line*[b]			*Money incomes and official current poverty line*[c]		
	1997	*1999*	*2002*	*1997*	*1999*	*2002*	*1997*	*1999*	*2002*
Russian Federation[d]	24.7	35.9	19.6	45.1	58.9	45.1	25.0	37.6	30.7
Official all-Russia[e]	—	—	—	—	—	—	20.8	28.7	25.0
Center									
Belgorod Oblast	6.3	24.5	6.8	26.3	45.6	27.0	18.9	26.9	25.0
Briansk Oblast	24.3	40.6	24.4	45.2	56.9	45.0	18.6	45.0	33.8
Vladimir Oblast	20.9	40.0	15.2	45.1	62.3	43.8	24.3	40.8	36.7
Voronezh Oblast	26.4	48.1	23.7	49.7	57.8	47.9	24.0	33.8	33.8
Ivanovo Oblast	31.3	54.3	25.4	58.6	79.8	61.6	27.0	64.9	67.4
Kaluga Oblast	19.5	35.3	10.3	39.2	55.1	42.4	22.8	47.0	40.1
Kostroma Oblast	30.8	45.1	23.9	48.9	59.7	46.9	19.8	38.1	37.5
Kursk Oblast	27.0	31.1	24.0	53.1	57.6	58.6	22.6	35.0	35.9
Lipetsk Oblast	20.9	27.9	12.4	35.0	45.1	27.6	17.7	25.9	25.8
Moscow Oblast	19.9	46.0	16.8	51.2	61.4	51.7	22.7	27.6	28.6
Orel Oblast	18.8	26.0	12.7	35.8	44.1	36.3	21.7	35.9	31.4
Riazan Oblast	28.4	44.1	17.5	49.6	62.0	42.9	21.2	52.4	31.1
Smolensk Oblast	29.5	44.3	19.5	36.7	65.6	52.1	18.4	27.2	26.2
Tambov Oblast	30.6	29.8	20.0	55.1	52.4	42.4	21.2	27.9	26.8
Tver Oblast	29.9	51.6	21.2	51.1	65.8	46.5	23.1	67.4	41.0
Tula Oblast	16.4	37.7	8.8	36.5	58.9	34.9	16.6	31.2	22.1
Yaroslavl Oblast	22.8	41.8	11.9	39.8	53.7	34.6	18.5	27.7	21.4
Moscow City	2.1	23.1	8.6	24.3	37.4	30.4	16.1	23.3	21.0
North West									
Karelia Republic	16.4	29.5	12.3	39.7	49.2	40.8	19.6	26.2	20.0
Komi Republic	27.3	42.2	15.9	45.4	58.5	43.6	16.7	22.1	21.5
Arkhangelsk Oblast of which Nenetskiy	21.9	38.0	11.3	51.4	65.8	45.5	25.3	49.5	28.8
Autonomous Region	—	64.8	31.6	—	83.3	51.6	—	—	31.5
Vologda Oblast	17.5	35.2	14.8	31.8	49.7	35.9	19.9	37.3	23.3
Kaliningrad Oblast	30.5	45.4	24.1	54.8	65.1	56.4	24.5	37.4	40.2
Leningrad Oblast	24.2	34.4	14.1	53.6	65.9	49.0	24.3	51.5	41.9
Murmansk Oblast	18.3	34.7	11.4	42.1	42.9	32.4	16.8	19.8	24.5
Novgorod Oblast	32.1	39.4	24.0	51.4	53.5	48.1	17.8	24.0	31.8
Pskov Oblast	30.8	44.3	20.6	53.5	64.0	44.2	28.6	51.2	31.8
St. Petersburg City	12.4	21.7	3.1	48.4	54.9	34.6	22.9	33.2	21.1
South									
Adygeia Republic	23.5	40.7	22.0	49.0	59.5	40.2	40.2	54.8	35.6
Dagestan Republic	66.4	71.3	55.6	79.9	87.0	85.2	53.9	67.2	47.9
Ingushetiya Republic	59.5	—	46.7	86.9	—	89.7	76.9	95.1	87.6
Kabardino-Balkariya Republic	46.6	51.6	41.7	62.1	73.0	61.6	39.8	46.6	29.4
Kalmykiya Republic	42.3	59.8	36.4	63.6	81.5	66.9	46.0	78.1	57.4

Region and territory name	*Consumption (using recommended methodology)*[a]			*Disposable resources and official constant poverty line*[b]			*Money incomes and official current poverty line*[c]		
	1997	*1999*	*2002*	*1997*	*1999*	*2002*	*1997*	*1999*	*2002*
Karachaevo-Cherkessiya Republic	22.8	33.2	18.2	55.3	61.6	46.5	41.0	64.6	38.8
Severnaya Osetiya Republic	26.2	33.9	25.6	45.1	45.7	41.0	33.9	31.2	24.9
Krasnodar Territory	35.5	55.9	25.2	48.4	64.5	47.0	24.2	35.3	32.7
Stavropol Territory	29.7	55.0	29.8	50.5	63.6	52.4	34.8	45.2	39.1
Astrakhan Oblast	34.0	42.7	25.4	56.6	64.0	47.3	27.8	42.9	26.2
Volgograd Oblast	33.1	54.5	23.1	48.5	63.9	47.6	24.1	58.1	31.5
Rostov Oblast	29.6	41.0	21.2	50.5	54.3	46.4	19.4	25.3	26.9
Volga									
Bashkortostan Republic	29.1	40.7	20.1	49.3	54.9	40.9	25.2	30.3	23.1
Mariy El Republic	38.1	53.7	38.7	62.3	71.8	65.1	52.1	69.0	54.7
Mordoviya Republic	31.7	52.3	30.9	52.2	69.0	55.1	38.6	68.1	43.6
Tatarstan Republic	26.0	39.7	20.4	48.5	59.4	46.7	17.9	24.1	24.0
Udmurtiya Republic	16.1	37.7	21.0	37.2	52.0	36.9	24.6	49.5	31.8
Chuvashiya Republic	35.6	57.4	19.9	52.6	71.7	39.2	28.8	68.2	42.3
Kirov Oblast	23.1	45.2	18.9	39.3	58.8	41.2	30.8	56.6	36.3
Nizhniy Novgorod Oblast	15.0	46.0	21.5	45.7	67.0	43.7	17.3	38.0	22.9
Orenburg Oblast	28.6	38.7	13.4	50.3	56.7	42.3	22.9	35.6	33.3
Penza Oblast	26.1	48.8	16.8	55.4	67.6	41.6	38.0	68.7	39.4
Perm Oblast	24.2	39.8	20.0	41.3	54.5	44.2	18.3	25.6	24.1
of which Komi-Permyatskiy Autonomous Region	—	76.2	43.4	—	80.4	71.0	—	37.5	70.4
Samara Oblast	20.4	39.9	20.3	43.2	55.8	43.9	18.3	23.4	28.4
Saratov Oblast	29.8	48.2	26.0	46.9	62.2	52.5	32.1	43.0	38.5
Ulianovsk Oblast	32.0	47.1	28.8	47.2	59.0	50.0	17.1	31.4	43.1
Ural									
Kurgan Oblast	37.8	56.3	28.8	35.8	67.2	53.7	42.6	56.5	47.8
Sverdlovsk Oblast	14.9	51.6	21.8	35.0	57.4	42.8	23.1	35.6	24.9
Tumen Oblast	21.0	25.7	16.0	30.4	70.6	39.5	13.4	17.8	16.1
of which Khanty-Mansiyskiy Autonomous Region	—	17.0	3.4	—	36.8	20.5	—	—	11.8
of which Yamalo-Nenetskiy Autonomous Region	—	18.8	3.2	—	30.9	13.6	—	—	7.6
Chelyabinsk Oblast	14.5	32.6	19.3	45.4	55.4	39.6	23.3	32.0	30.2
Siberia									
Altay Republic	36.4	54.0	31.6	53.4	72.9	57.8	39.2	61.0	37.8
Buriatiya Republic	39.6	51.7	31.9	60.9	73.5	63.7	44.3	50.5	39.1
Tuva Republic	49.7	70.0	41.6	75.7	90.2	68.2	62.4	78.6	49.9
Khakassiya Republic	21.2	38.1	22.4	54.6	65.4	45.9	27.6	45.0	33.4
Altay Territory	25.4	45.0	18.8	45.4	60.4	40.7	45.7	56.4	38.9
Krasnoyarsk Territory	20.2	37.4	12.3	38.9	50.5	34.2	19.7	25.1	25.6
of which Taimyr Autonomous Region	—	49.6	34.2	—	77.9	56.4	—	—	31.8
of which Evenkiyskiy Autonomous Region	—	44.3	32.8	—	95.3	82.6	—	—	67.8

Region and territory name	*Consumption (using recommended methodology)*[a]			*Disposable resources and official constant poverty line*[b]			*Money incomes and official current poverty line*[c]		
	1997	*1999*	*2002*	*1997*	*1999*	*2002*	*1997*	*1999*	*2002*
Irkutsk Oblast	22.9	30.8	15.0	42.3	49.9	38.9	27.3	29.9	33.9
of which Ust-Ordynskiy Buriatskiy Autonomous Region	—	49.9	46.5	—	77.5	79.0	—	—	82.7
Kemerovo Oblast	24.4	42.2	21.1	40.3	59.4	54.0	17.9	27.9	23.5
Novosibirsk Oblast	27.3	53.6	25.2	32.7	68.4	52.0	39.3	61.1	44.7
Omsk Oblast	31.8	39.0	20.7	40.4	65.0	44.9	23.4	38.5	24.3
Tomsk Oblast	17.9	37.9	16.6	38.2	53.0	40.5	19.8	27.2	23.3
Chita Oblast	29.9	59.0	30.0	64.9	82.8	62.1	61.2	88.8	57.3
of which Aginskiy Buriatskiy Autonomous Region	—	70.7	42.3	—	95.1	80.8	—	—	74.5
Far East									
Sakha (Yakutia) Republic	29.6	37.1	21.8	46.5	59.4	50.6	28.3	33.2	23.8
Primorie Territory	22.8	41.4	24.2	49.5	68.2	57.4	28.6	39.8	46.6
Khabarovsk Territory	27.4	40.5	17.0	49.1	64.1	43.6	24.1	28.2	28.6
Amur Oblast	27.5	47.1	20.8	31.5	70.7	60.2	27.9	44.9	47.7
Kamchatka Oblast	52.1	43.3	13.8	47.1	72.8	52.4	25.9	33.6	35.5
Kariakskiy Autonomous Region	—	53.4	36.1	—	81.8	82.0	—	—	47.7
Magadan Oblast	23.4	50.7	33.7	46.6	68.2	66.8	25.9	46.3	25.5
Sakhalin Oblast	26.3	49.6	22.6	58.8	66.1	54.3	32.8	36.5	33.3
Evreiskaya Autonomous Oblast	—	55.4	18.7	—	75.7	48.3	—	—	38.7
Chukotka Autonomous Region	—	52.1	37.7	—	91.5	80.6	—	—	43.9
Maximum	66.4	76.2	55.6	86.9	95.3	89.7	76.9	95.1	87.6
Minimum	2.1	17.0	3.1	24.3	30.9	13.6	13.4	17.8	7.6

Sources: Social Status and Living Standards of Russian Population (Goskomstat, various years) and Bank staff calculations based on data from Household Budget Survey 1997–2002 (Goskomstat).

— Not available.

a. Consumption indicator based on Household Budget Survey (methodology proposed in Gibson and Poduzov 2003) and regionally consistent poverty line (methodology proposed in Kakwani and Sajaia 2003); see chapter 1.

b. Disposable resources indicator for Household Budget Survey constructed by Goskomstat; 2002 official poverty lines by regions deflated back to 1997 by Goskomstat (expert estimates).

c. Model estimate produced by Goskomstat based on regional money balances of personal incomes and current official poverty lines.

d. Sum of regions.

e. Official poverty counts at the level of the Russian Federation are obtained from a separate model that is not consistent with the regional models. As a result, the sum of poverty in Russian regions is always greater than the official published estimate of poverty for the country as a whole. The official poverty line changed in 2000, limiting the time comparability of figures relying on official poverty lines.

Table C.3. Inequality by region, 1997–2002 (Gini indexes)

Region and territory name	Consumption per capita			Disposable resources per capita		
	1997	*1999*	*2002*	*1997*	*1999*	*2002*
Russian Federation[a]	0.346	0.340	0.330	0.412	0.386	0.388
Official all-Russia[b]	—	—	—	0.444	0.422	0.419
Center						
Belgorod Oblast	0.310	0.252	0.239	0.398	0.342	0.264
Briansk Oblast	0.305	0.303	0.298	0.348	0.333	0.367
Vladimir Oblast	0.278	0.285	0.260	0.330	0.321	0.297
Voronezh Oblast	0.299	0.330	0.319	0.407	0.416	0.363
Ivanovo Oblast	0.320	0.285	0.248	0.379	0.304	0.283
Kaluga Oblast	0.271	0.295	0.257	0.325	0.311	0.282
Kostroma Oblast	0.296	0.285	0.264	0.340	0.315	0.296
Kursk Oblast	0.339	0.276	0.313	0.438	0.323	0.405
Lipetsk Oblast	0.332	0.295	0.287	0.388	0.323	0.362
Moscow Oblast	0.253	0.323	0.317	0.292	0.336	0.355
Orel Oblast	0.343	0.274	0.293	0.407	0.327	0.351
Riazan Oblast	0.323	0.321	0.304	0.373	0.348	0.328
Smolensk Oblast	0.329	0.310	0.277	0.421	0.353	0.305
Tambov Oblast	0.324	0.294	0.285	0.374	0.360	0.335
Tver Oblast	0.279	0.295	0.303	0.368	0.324	0.375
Tula Oblast	0.304	0.294	0.249	0.347	0.320	0.284
Yaroslavl Oblast	0.331	0.351	0.287	0.402	0.384	0.335
Moscow City	0.359	0.368	0.340	0.421	0.400	0.364
North West						
Karelia Republic	0.301	0.297	0.336	0.357	0.345	0.407
Komi Republic	0.341	0.375	0.378	0.454	0.517	0.420
Arkhangelsk Oblast	0.269	0.297	0.292	0.358	0.354	0.376
of which Nenetskiy Autonomous Region	—	0.372	0.388	—	0.393	0.432
Vologda Oblast	0.323	0.301	0.329	0.454	0.343	0.403
Kaliningrad Oblast	0.339	0.334	0.342	0.383	0.521	0.377
Leningrad Oblast	0.272	0.254	0.241	0.308	0.289	0.284
Murmansk Oblast	0.303	0.343	0.282	0.389	0.454	0.373
Novgorod Oblast	0.324	0.295	0.324	0.393	0.335	0.380
Pskov Oblast	0.316	0.304	0.328	0.360	0.331	0.410
St. Petersburg City	0.265	0.265	0.261	0.308	0.291	0.291
South						
Adygeia Republic	0.293	0.289	0.388	0.336	0.312	0.422
Dagestan Republic	0.338	0.335	0.283	0.401	0.339	0.312
Ingushetiya Republic	0.430	—	0.292	0.429	—	0.306
Kabardino-Balkariya Republic	0.362	0.312	0.314	0.397	0.335	0.363
Kalmykiya Republic	0.353	0.317	0.322	0.391	0.325	0.379

Region and territory name	*Consumption per capita*			*Disposable resources per capita*		
	1997	*1999*	*2002*	*1997*	*1999*	*2002*
Karachaevo-Cherkessiya Republic	0.355	0.288	0.294	0.387	0.346	0.360
Severnaya Osetiya Republic	0.305	0.301	0.285	0.357	0.321	0.327
Krasnodar Territory	0.306	0.353	0.324	0.376	0.389	0.377
Stavropol Territory	0.334	0.320	0.320	0.447	0.389	0.436
Astrakhan Oblast	0.307	0.342	0.384	0.363	0.399	0.465
Volgograd Oblast	0.324	0.319	0.324	0.383	0.363	0.373
Rostov Oblast	0.331	0.338	0.313	0.380	0.357	0.339
Volga						
Bashkortostan Republic	0.336	0.332	0.346	0.438	0.405	0.414
Mariy El Republic	0.304	0.318	0.314	0.369	0.340	0.351
Mordoviya Republic	0.321	0.327	0.299	0.379	0.347	0.339
Tatarstan Republic	0.356	0.366	0.320	0.414	0.380	0.398
Udmurtiya Republic	0.265	0.301	0.300	0.360	0.407	0.377
Chuvashiya Republic	0.313	0.347	0.288	0.366	0.360	0.323
Kirov Oblast	0.296	0.305	0.291	0.369	0.332	0.334
Nizhniy Novgorod Oblast	0.328	0.310	0.338	0.375	0.356	0.366
Orenburg Oblast	0.356	0.314	0.291	0.449	0.346	0.348
Penza Oblast	0.298	0.279	0.284	0.344	0.309	0.335
Perm Oblast	0.331	0.347	0.366	0.423	0.383	0.450
of which Komi-Permyatskiy Autonomous Region	—	0.340	0.288	—	0.360	0.337
Samara Oblast	0.311	0.357	0.326	0.415	0.419	0.450
Saratov Oblast	0.331	0.328	0.327	0.307	0.366	0.351
Ulianovsk Oblast	0.318	0.339	0.313	0.371	0.362	0.335
Ural						
Kurgan Oblast	0.399	0.323	0.309	0.423	0.366	0.373
Sverdlovsk Oblast	0.305	0.335	0.315	0.377	0.357	0.338
Tumen Oblast	0.365	0.373	0.363	0.437	0.467	0.463
of which Khanty-Mansiyskiy Autonomous Region	—	0.372	0.349	—	0.446	0.462
of which Yamalo-Nenetskiy Autonomous Region	—	0.342	0.349	—	0.419	0.413
Chelyabinsk Oblast	0.310	0.320	0.301	0.411	0.359	0.380
Siberia						
Altay Republic	0.353	0.298	0.309	0.412	0.319	0.353
Buriatiya Republic	0.348	0.337	0.328	0.409	0.374	0.362
Tuva Republic	0.385	0.361	0.386	0.452	0.392	0.422
Khakassiya Republic	0.287	0.331	0.313	0.346	0.382	0.367
Altay Territory	0.308	0.335	0.295	0.362	0.365	0.362

Region and territory name	*Consumption per capita*			*Disposable resources per capita*		
	1997	*1999*	*2002*	*1997*	*1999*	*2002*
Krasnoyarsk Territory	0.345	0.330	0.324	0.403	0.382	0.409
of which Taimyr Autonomous Region	—	0.386	0.359	—	0.411	0.406
of which Evenkiyskiy Autonomous Region	—	0.365	0.357	—	0.386	0.389
Irkutsk Oblast	0.342	0.315	0.345	0.406	0.358	0.396
of which Ust-Ordynskiy Buriatskiy Autonomous Region	—	0.328	0.280	—	0.376	0.333
Kemerovo Oblast	0.329	0.352	0.314	0.389	0.380	0.360
Novosibirsk Oblast	0.324	0.311	0.307	0.367	0.339	0.340
Omsk Oblast	0.341	0.343	0.375	0.400	0.363	0.434
Tomsk Oblast	0.314	0.325	0.310	0.416	0.391	0.419
Chita Oblast	0.376	0.314	0.333	0.431	0.344	0.383
of which Aginskiy Buriatskiy Autonomous Region	—	0.362	0.309	—	0.406	0.381
Far East						
Sakha (Yakutia) Republic	0.383	0.344	0.361	0.444	0.415	0.421
Primorie Territory	0.317	0.293	0.313	0.356	0.312	0.364
Khabarovsk Territory	0.316	0.327	0.330	0.371	0.368	0.420
Amur Oblast	0.317	0.335	0.295	0.410	0.366	0.357
Kamchatka Oblast	0.310	0.329	0.297	0.429	0.409	0.366
Kariakskiy Autonomous Region	—	0.333	0.302	—	0.378	0.338
Magadan Oblast	0.334	0.387	0.399	0.409	0.453	0.424
Sakhalin Oblast	0.319	0.321	0.355	0.379	0.380	0.415
Evreiskaya Autonomous Oblast	—	0.394	0.288	—	0.500	0.372
Chukotka Autonomous Region	—	0.395	0.333	—	0.421	0.353
Maximum	0.430	0.395	0.399	0.454	0.521	0.465
Minimum	0.253	0.252	0.239	0.292	0.289	0.264

Sources: Social Status and Living Standards of Russian Population (Goskomstat, various years) and Bank staff calculations based on data from Household Budget Survey 1997–2002 (Goskomstat).

— Not available.

a. Figure for the Russian Federation is based on Household Budget Survey data corrected for regional price differences using as spatial price deflators the experimental poverty line for consumption-based measure and the official 2002 poverty line with expert-based deflated values for 1999 and 1997 for disposable resource measure.

b. The official method for compiling the national level inequality index does not take into account regional differences in the cost of living.

Appendix D
Trends in Real Wages

Table D.1. Real wage trends by industry, 1998–2002 (1997 = 100)

Sector	*1998*	*1999*	*2000*	*2001*	*2002*
Industry	91	81	123	121	110
Agriculture	83	75	117	119	116
Forestry	84	84	116	117	126
Construction	85	74	126	123	109
Transport	87	82	122	109	115
Communications	86	77	113	118	118
Wholesale and retail sales, catering	88	77	109	119	114
Information services	89	79	139	100	129
Geology and geodesy	92	77	140	127	102
Utilities	85	68	117	117	114
Health, sports, and social services	86	71	117	123	137
Education	84	71	117	121	139
Culture	88	70	120	128	130
Science	91	86	134	124	118
Credit and finance	98	90	128	141	116
Management	85	75	118	111	124
Total	87	78	119	121	117

Source: Bank staff calculations based on data from Goskomstat (2003a).

Figure D.1. Average nominal hourly wage, by industry, 1996–2002

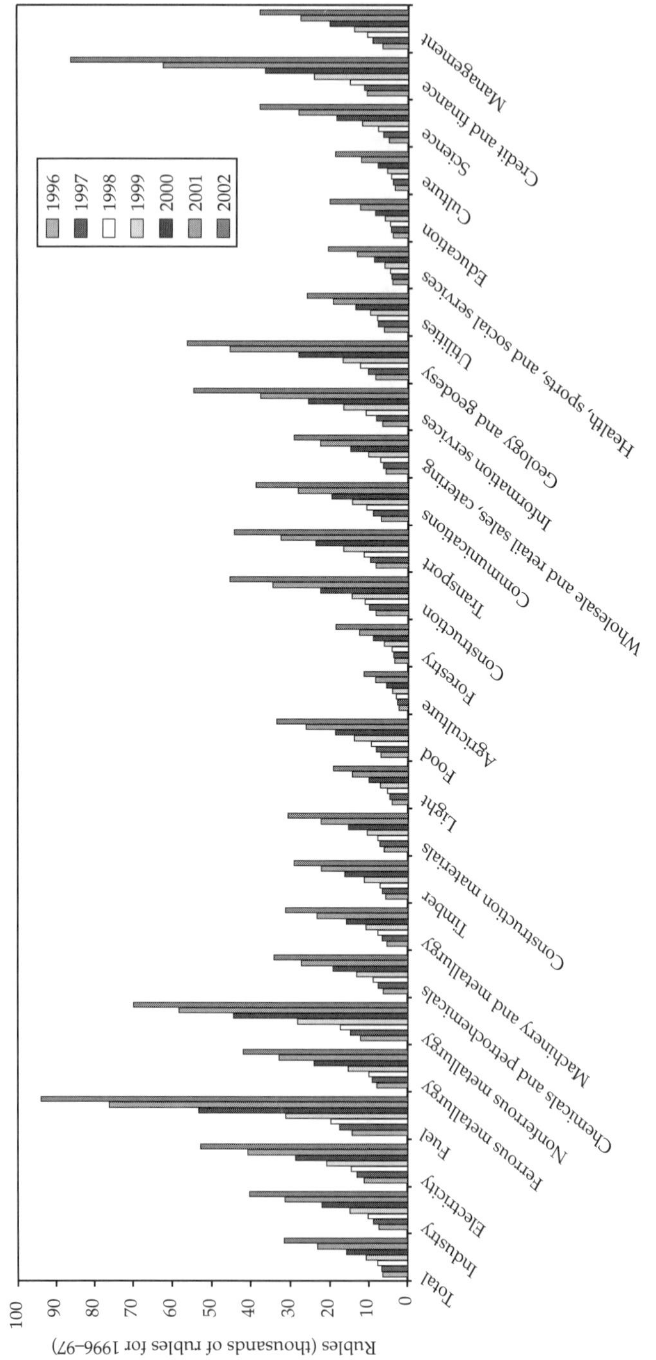

Source: Goskomstat (2003a).

Appendix E
The Poverty Growth Curve and Poverty Equivalent Growth Rates

Two additional concepts—the poverty growth curve and poverty equivalent growth rates—confirm that the growth that occurred in the Russian Federation between 1997 and 2002 was pro-poor.

The Poverty Growth Curve

Suppose μ is the mean welfare and $L(p)$ its Lorenz curve, then $\mu L(p)$ is the generalized Lorenz curve. When the entire generalized Lorenz curve shifts upward, the new distribution has second-order dominance over the old distribution. In this respect, the generalized Lorenz curve may also be called the second-order dominance curve. Atkinson (1987) provides a useful link between second-order dominance and changes in poverty. Using his theorem, it can be shown that when the entire generalized Lorenz curve shifts upward (downward), poverty unambiguously decreases (increases). This result holds for a general class of additive decomposable poverty measures (except the headcount ratio) and all poverty lines.

The poverty growth curve is defined as the growth rate of the mean welfare of the bottom p percent of the population when the individuals are ranked by their per capita welfare. Denoting this curve by $g(p)$ yields

$$g(p) = \Delta Ln(\mu_p) \tag{1}$$

where μ_p is the mean income or consumption of the bottom p percent of the population. Using the definition of the Lorenz curve yields

$$g(p) = \Delta Ln(\mu\ L(p)) \tag{2}$$

from which it follows that $g(p)$ varies with p and ranges from 0 to 100. From Atkinson's theorem, if $g(p) > 0$ ($g(p) < 0$) for all p, then poverty has decreased (increased) unambiguously between two periods.

Equation (2) can also be written as

$$g(p) = g + \Delta Ln(L(p)) \tag{3}$$

where $g = \Delta Ln(\mu)$ is the growth rate of the mean income of the whole society. Note that when $p = 100$, $g(p) = g$ because $\Delta L(p) = 0$ at $p = 100$.

From equation (3) it follows that if $g(p) > g$ for all $p < 100$, then growth is pro-poor, because the entire Lorenz curve shifts upward ($L(p) > 0$ for all p). If $0 < g(p) < g$ for all $p < 100$, then growth reduces poverty but is accompanied by an increase in inequality ($L(p) < 0$ for all p). This situation may be characterized as trickle-down growth: growth reduces poverty, but the poor receive proportionally fewer benefits than the nonpoor. If $g(p) < 0$ for all $p < 100$ and g is positive, growth is immiserizing (increases poverty) (Bhagwati 1988).

The poverty growth curve is depicted for different years in figures E.1–E.6. If the entire curve lies in the positive (negative) quadrant, poverty has unambiguously decreased (increased). The ordinate of the curve when $p = 100$ is equal to the growth of the mean welfare of the society. Growth will be unambiguously pro-poor if the entire poverty curve lies above the last point (when $p = 100$).

Figure E.1 shows that the entire curve falls in the negative quadrant, implying that poverty increased during the 1998 crisis. The fact that the entire curve lies below the last point means that Russia's crisis hurt the poor proportionally more than the nonpoor.

Figure E.2 shows that the entire poverty growth curve also fell in the negative quadrant in 1999, indicating that poverty continued to increase in the postcrisis period in 1999. An interesting change took place in 1999, however: the entire curve is above the last point. This implies that the poor were hurt proportionally less than the nonpoor. A decrease in the unemployment rate helped the poor proportionally more than the nonpoor, particularly

Figure E.1. Poverty growth curve, 1997–98

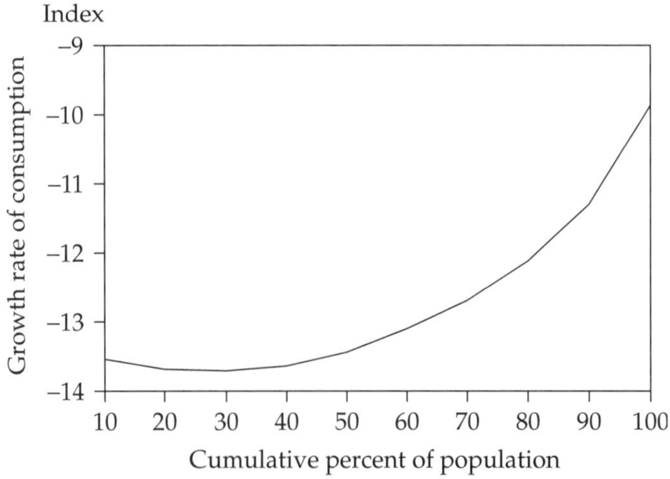

Figure E.2. Poverty growth curve, 1998–99

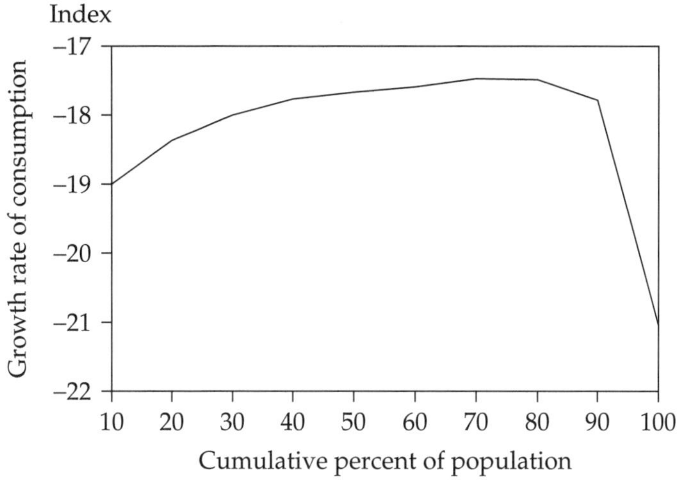

when the economy was coming out of recession. During 1999 the unemployment rate dropped very sharply, but real wages fell even more sharply. Falling real wages increased poverty, but a sharp increase in employment helped the poor proportionally more than the nonpoor.

During 2000 unemployment continued to decline and the real wage increased very sharply. Consequently, poverty declined sharply. This is evident from figure E.3, which shows that the entire poverty growth curve falls in the positive quadrant. More important, the curve falls

Figure E.3. Poverty growth curve 1999–2000

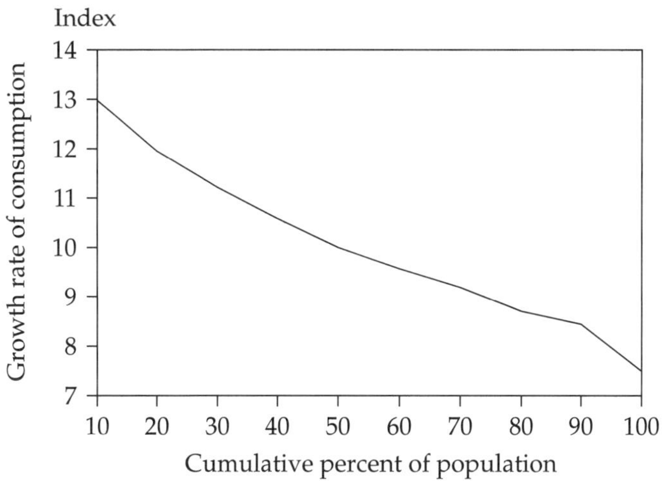

Figure E.4. Poverty growth curve, 2000–01

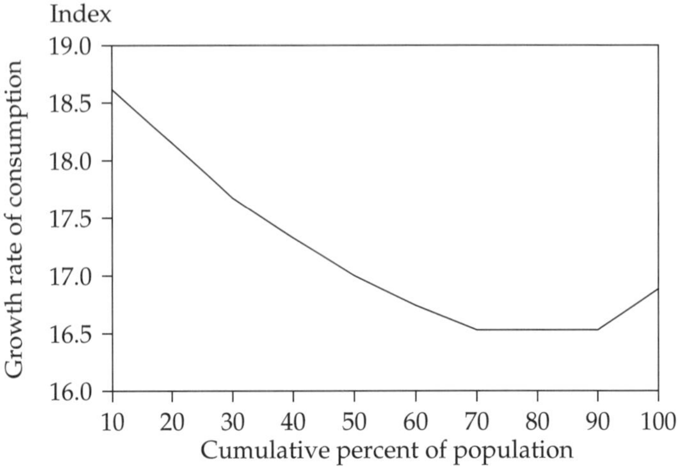

steeply, indicating that growth was highly pro-poor: the poor benefited proportionally more than the nonpoor.

During 2001 the real wage continued to increase sharply, but the rate of decline in unemployment slowed. The real wage increased about 19 percent, but unemployment declined from 9.3 percent in 2000 to 8.9 percent in 2001. Poverty again declined sharply, but the poverty growth curve did not decline monotonically, increasing at the 90th percentile (figure E.4).

Figure E.5. Poverty growth curve, 2001–02

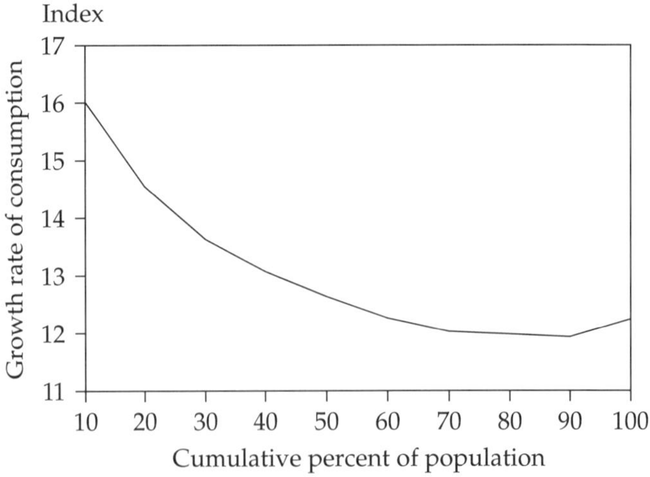

Figure E.6. Poverty growth curve, 1997–2002

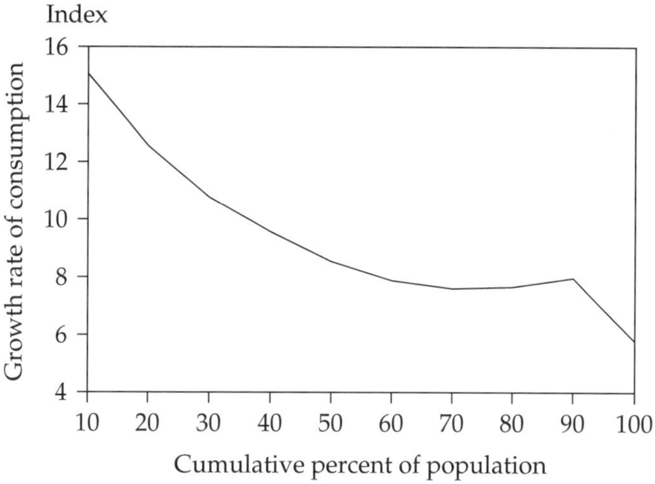

Although one cannot conclude that growth is pro-poor for all poverty lines, growth is pro-poor until the percentage of poor is less than or equal to 50 percent. A similar picture emerges from figure E.5. Figure E.6 depicts the cumulative dynamic, implying that poverty decreased between 1997 and 2002 despite the 1998 crisis.

The Poverty Equivalent Growth Rate

Maximizing growth alone will not necessarily lead to the maximum reduction in poverty. Poverty reduction depends on two factors. The first is the magnitude of the economic growth rate: the larger the growth rate, the greater the poverty reduction. The second is the distribution of the benefits of growth: the larger the share of benefits of growth that go to the poor, the greater the poverty reduction. Kakwani and Son (2003) developed a measure of pro-poor growth derived from the idea of a poverty equivalent growth rate (PEGR), which takes into account not only the magnitude of growth but also how much of the benefits of growth the poor receive. They demonstrated that the proportional reduction in poverty is a monotonically increasing function of the PEGR: the larger the PEGR, the greater the proportional reduction in poverty.[1] Thus maximizing the PEGR leads to the greatest reduction in poverty.

The PEGR that satisfies the monotonic relation with poverty reduction is therefore not only a necessary but also a sufficient condition for poverty reduction. The PEGR is derived for a class of additively decomposable poverty measures, including the Foster-Greer-Thorbecke (1984) and the

Table E.1. Poverty equivalent growth rates, 1998–2002 (percent)

Period	Actual growth rate	Poverty equivalent growth rate: Headcount	Gap ratio	Severity
Lower poverty line				
1998	–9.4	–13.2	–13.1	–13.0
1999	–19.0	–15.7	–16.1	–16.4
2000	7.9	9.4	11.1	12.0
2001	18.5	18.4	19.2	19.7
2002	13.0	13.4	15.1	16.5
1997–02	6.0	9.5	12.6	14.7
Higher poverty line				
1998	–9.3	–12.7	–13.0	–13.0
1999	–19.0	–15.7	–16.0	–16.3
2000	8.0	8.9	10.6	11.5
2001	18.3	17.8	18.7	19.3
2002	13.0	12.6	14.3	15.6
1997–02	6.0	7.5	11.0	13.2

Source: Bank staff calculations based on data from Household Budget Survey 1998–2002 (Goskomstat).

Watts (1968) poverty measures. These measures are the average of the growth rates at each percentile weighted by various poverty measures (table E.1).

The PEGR is the effective growth rate for poverty reduction. If the PEGR is higher than the actual growth rate, we can say that growth is favoring the poor proportionally more than the nonpoor. Between 1997 and 2002, the actual average annual growth rate of consumption was 6 percent, but the annual PEGR for the headcount ratio was 9.5 percent. The equivalent growth for poverty reduction was 3.5 percentage points higher than the actual growth rate because growth favored the poor. The gain in growth rate was 8.7 percentage points when poverty is measured by the severity index. This implies that growth was even more favorable to the ultrapoor than to the poor.

Note

1. Ravallion and Chen (2003) have proposed a pro-poor growth index based on the Watts measure (Watts 1968). The pro-poor growth indexes used here—namely, poverty equivalent growth rates—are more general, covering the entire class of additive poverty measures, including headcount, poverty gap, severity of poverty, and the Watts index.

Appendix F
Overview of Social Protection Programs in the Russian Federation

Program	*Eligibility*	*Benefit*	*Financing/administration*
Pension (labor)	Women 55 and older, men 60 and older, disabled people, and survivors (spouse or dependents of the deceased)	Monthly cash benefit	Contributory; three-pillar system (pay-as-you-go, funded, and voluntary); financed by the social tax paid to the Social Insurance Fund, administered by the Pension Fund
Unemployment benefit	Officially registered unemployed	Monthly cash benefit for up to 12 months. Beneficiaries receive 75 percent of the previous wage for the first three months of unemployment, 60 percent for the next four months, and 45 percent for the next five months. The benefit has minimum (20% of Minimum Standard of Living) and maximum thresholds.	Noncontributory; financed from general revenues, administered by the Employment Services
Sick leave compensation	Employed people temporarily unable to work	Monthly cash benefit for limited period of time	Contributory; financed by a tax paid to the Social Insurance Fund, administered by enterprises
Maternity leave	Employed mothers 70 days before and 70 days after delivery (110 days after delivery of more than one child)	Monthly cash payment	Contributory; financed by a tax paid to the Social Insurance Fund, administered by enterprises
Social pension	Women 60 and older, men 65 and older, and people with disabilities (including those disabled since childhood) who are ineligible for labor pension and have no other source of income	Monthly cash benefit	Noncontributory; financed from general revenues, administered by the Pension Fund

Program	*Eligibility*	*Benefit*	*Financing/administration*
Housing allowance	Income tested, based on share of family budget spent on housing and utility services norms	Monthly housing subsidy	Noncontributory; financed by federal and local budgets (federally mandated), administered by local governments
Social assistance benefits	Income based	One-time or monthly benefit in cash or in kind	Noncontributory; financed by regional and local budgets
Child allowance	Children from families with per capita income below the regional subsistence minimum	Monthly cash benefit until child reaches 16 (18 if in school)	Noncontributory; financed by the federal budget., administered by the Ministry of Labor and Social Protection
Early pregnancy registration benefit	Pregnant women (up to 12 weeks of gestation) at registration for prenatal care	One-time cash payment	Noncontributory; financed by the Social Insurance Fund for the employed and by local governments for the unemployed, administered by enterprises and the local social protection administration
Birth grant	Newborn children	One-time cash benefit	Noncontributory; financed by the Social Insurance Fund for the employed and by local governments for the unemployed, administered by enterprises and the local social protection administration
Child care allowance	Mothers (employed and unemployed) until child is 18 months old	Monthly cash benefits	Noncontributory; financed by the Social Insurance Fund for the employed and by local governments for the unemployed, administered by enterprises and the local social protection administration
Privileges and subsidies	Various categories of individuals and families; merit or needs based	Discounted or free goods and services (food, transportation, housing and utilities, recreation and rehabilitation, health services, preschool, training, and so forth)	Noncontributory; financed by federal, regional, and local budgetary and nonbudgetary funds and enterprises, administered by local governments and enterprises
Social work and care services	Vulnerable children and youth and their families, adults, and the elderly	Counseling services, rehabilitation, day care, temporary shelters, psycho-social support	Noncontributory; financed by regional and local governments, administered by the local government
Residential care in institutions	Children deprived of parental care, poor children, children and adults with disabilities, frail elderly	Long-term placement in residential care	Noncontributory; financed by regional and local governments, administered by the local government

Source: Bank staff assessment.

Appendix G
Methodology for Constructing the Benchmark Scenario and Making Welfare Inferences

Ten different possible components of the housing cost are distinguished (table G.1). The number in the first column of table G.1 is used as a subscript for various variables (for example, e_i refers to recorded expenditures on the ith component, where i can be 1–10, depending on the component to the price per unit of the p_ith component, and so forth).

The housing costs for a household reflect the bill it receives from the companies that provide services, its own expenditures on housing or utility-related services, or a combination of both (which is usually the case). Rules were applied to determine which households receive bills (or part of bills) and which do not. These rules are item dependent, as explained below.

The standard bill, B, is calculated as follows:

$$\begin{aligned} B &= B(q_m, n, q_8, p_1, \ldots, p_8) \\ &= (p_1 + p_5)q_m + (p_2 + p_3 + p_4 + p_6 + p_7)n + p_8 q_8 \end{aligned} \qquad (1)$$

where q_m refers to the surface of the dwelling in square meters, n to the number of people living in the dwelling, and q_i to the quantity of utility i consumed. The most important feature of equation (1) is that the bill is

Table G.1. Components of the housing cost

Subscript	*Description*
1	Maintenance
2	Cold water
3	Sewerage
4	Hot water
5	Central heating
6	Gas
7	Garbage collection
8	Electricity
9	Wood, firewood, peat, bituminous coal
10	Other housing-related expenditures

Source: Decoster and Puzanov (2004).

only partially related to quantities consumed: for maintenance and heating, the surface is taken into account; electricity consumption (q_8) is metered. For hot and cold water, sewerage, garbage collection, and gas, the bill is not related to consumption but to the number of people in the household.

Calculating the bill in equation (1) requires the following information: the eight different prices, the surface of the dwelling (q_m), the number of people in the household (n), and electricity consumption (q_8). The surface of the dwelling and the number of people are easily obtained, as they are recorded in the Household Budget Survey. For electricity, recorded expenditures (e_8) were used as part of the bill. Price information was collected for all regions.

It would have been useful to introduce some intraregional differentiation in the prices, as there is evidence that utility prices in large cities, smaller towns, and rural areas differ significantly. However, the information to determine whether a household in the budget survey lives in the capital or not was not available. Hence the analysis was carried out with the prices of utilities (and the cost coverage percentages) at the regional level.

The housing cost is the combination of the components of bill *B* and additional expenditures (for example, spending on coal and wood). *C* denotes the housing cost before deductions and allowances, *HC* denotes the housing cost after deductions and allowances.

Table G.2. Variables in the Household Budget Survey related to housing costs

Item	*Name in this report*	*Name in the Budget Survey*
1	Maintenance	471 Rent for main housing
2	Cold water	531 Cold running water
3	Sewerage	521 Servicing sewerage
4	Hot water	591 Hot running water
5	Central heating	592 Central heating
6	Gas	561 Gas
7	Garbage collection	511 Garbage collection
8	Electricity	551 Electric power
9	Coal	571 Kerosene
		572 Other kinds of liquid fuel
		581 Firewood, cuts
		582 Bituminous and brown coal, coal briquettes
		583 Peat and other kinds of fuel
10	Other expenditures	541 Other kinds of housing services
11	Rent for second housing	472 Rent for second housing

Source: Decoster and Puzanov (2004).

The micro data used to calculate distributional effects of changes in the housing policy come from the fourth quarter of the 2000 Household Budget Survey, which includes very detailed expenditure information on 54,744 households in 88 regions (all Russia's regions except the Chechen Republic) (table G.2). The survey also contains information on the type of home a household lives in (for example, a single-unit apartment or a stand-alone house) and which amenities the household has (central heating, hot and cold water, gas, and so forth). All of the variables in table G.2 except rent for second housing are included in the housing cost calculation.

There are several reasons to assess the impact of reforms on the housing sector by means of a benchmark situation that is not (exclusively) based on recorded expenditures in the budget survey.

First, expenditures are assumed to be recorded after deductions, privileges, and allowances have been attributed. Since the purpose here is to study the effect of deductions and allowances across the income distribution, the analysis needs to start from housing costs before deductions. The easiest and most consistent way to do this is simply to calculate the gross bill for all households judged to receive bills.

A second reason to construct a benchmark has to do with the poor quality of the recorded expenditures in the survey. The percentage of households that do not record expenditures on one of the items in table G.3 but do have access to the amenity is high. One reason why this is the

Table G.3. Households that do not record expenditures but do report using an amenity

		Average monthly expenditures on rent for main housing (rubles)	
Amenity	*Percentage of households that use the amenity but do not record expenditures*	*Households with zero expenditures*	*Household with nonzero expenditures*
Cold water	27.4	72	31
Sewerage	65.1	49	33
Hot water	39.8	52	35
Central heating	42.6	52	33
Gas	18.9	45	31

Source: Decoster and Puzanov (2004).

case could be bad recording. Another is the fact that households may not decompose their bill into the different components but record the whole bill under the same item (probably "rent for main housing"). Table G.3 seems to confirm this hypothesis: on average, households that dispose of an amenity but do not record expenditures for it have substantially larger expenditures on rent for main housing than do households that record expenditures for the related item.

A third reason to construct a benchmark is that doing so allows a sounder comparison between the situation before and after the price change. To compare the situation after the price reform with a well-defined situation before the reform, it is better to work with imputed housing costs for all households. The difference is significant. Based on recorded expenditures, the average household spends 5.2 percent of its budget on housing; based on an imputed housing cost (after deductions and allowances are taken into account), the figure is 9.4 percent.

Criteria for Assessing the Impact of Reforms

To assess the distributional consequences of policy changes, households or individuals need to be ordered from poor to rich based on some criterion, referred to here as the living standard. This standard is based on expenditures rather than income. In calculating it, durable expenditures were taken out,[1] home production and in-kind income were added, expenditures were divided by the number of people living in the household, and regional price differences were corrected for using the poverty lines for 2000 constructed by Kakwani and Sajaia (2003).

One additional adjustment was made, related to the specific setting of this report. Expenditures for housing are only partly linked to quantities consumed. This makes the usual practice of assessing the welfare impact of a price change by means of a price index used to deflate nominal expenditures less appropriate. This deflation procedure effectively transforms nominal expenditures into a quantity index, which can be interpreted as a welfare indicator, but it is built on the assumption that quantities change in response to higher prices. This is not the case for most housing cost components, certainly not in the short run. Therefore an alternative route was used to depict the welfare effect of changing prices. Under this approach, changes in the prices of utilities leading to a change in housing costs must be fully matched by changes in nonhousing expenditures, since a budget constraint must be satisfied. Hence an increase in the housing bill of, say, 200 rubles a month has to be compensated for by a decrease in monthly nonhousing expenditures of 200 rubles. Therefore the change in housing costs can itself be considered a measurement of the welfare change.

This approach amounts to constructing the following welfare indicator for the household, denoted by ls^h (for living standard), as follows:

$$ls^h = \frac{E^h - e^h_{durables} - e^h_{hous} + y_{kind}}{P^h \cdot n^h} \tag{2}$$

where E^h denotes the total expenditures of household h in the budget survey; $e^h_{durables}$ denotes the expenditures of household h in the budget survey on durable items; e^h_{hous} denotes the expenditures of household h in the budget survey on housing costs; y_{kind} denotes the in-kind income of household h in the budget survey;[2] P^h denotes a price index for the region in which household h lives, calculated as the ratio between the poverty line for the region and the population weighted average poverty line for the whole Russian Federation; and n^h denotes the number of people living in household h.

The ordering of individuals from poor to rich, poverty and distributional analysis is based on this "nonhousing" welfare concept. To calculate the incidence of poverty, the poverty lines provided by Kakwani and Sajaia (2003) are adjusted slightly by taking out housing expenditures. To do so—in the spirit of Kakwani and Sajaia, who augmented a food poverty line with nonfood expenditures—this study used the subset of households whose living standard, including housing expenditures, was between 10 percent below and 10 percent above the Kakwani and Sajaia poverty line. Average expenditures on housing, as recorded in the budget survey, were calculated for this subset and then subtracted from the poverty line to obtain nonhousing poverty lines in the broader Goskomstat region classification of seven federal districts.

Assumptions Used to Construct a Benchmark Scenario

Not every household receives a bill. If a household is not connected to the system or lives in a remote rural area in a stand-alone house, it probably receives no bill for gas, garbage collection, or even central heating. Hence it would be erroneous to simply impute housing costs for all households in the sample on the basis of equation (1). Instead, rules were established to determine when a household was liable for a bill and for which part (table E.4).

For maintenance and garbage collection, the criterion is based on the type of house the household lives in. This variable is categorized into seven classes in the Household Budget Survey. Here, households living in a single unit or communal apartment, a hostel, or a semi-basement apartment are assumed to receive bills for these two items. This group makes up 78 percent of the sample. For people living in stand-alone

Table G.4. Criteria used to determine whether housing cost was calculated from the bill formula or from recorded expenditures

Item	*Criterion used*	*Percentage of households for which bill was calculated*	*Percentage of households for which recorded expenditures were used*
Maintenance	Type of house	78.0	22.0
Cold water	Presence of amenity	84.7	15.3
Sewerage	Presence of amenity	81.2	18.8
Hot water	Presence of amenity	80.1	19.9
Central heating	Presence of amenity	89.3	10.7
Gas	Presence of amenity	76.1	23.9
Garbage collection	Type of house	78.0	22.0
Electricity	Expenditures	0.0	100.0
Coal	Expenditures	0.0	100.0
Other	Expenditures	0.0	100.0

Source: Decoster and Puzanov (2004).
Note: For amenities, missing values were interpreted as absence of the amenity, except for central heating and hot water, where missing values were interpreted as presence of the amenity, in order to make the percentages in the table more consistent with information from other sources.

houses (17.7 percent) or in part of a house (4.3 percent), recorded expenditures are used. For cold and hot water, sewerage, central heating, and gas, the presence of the amenity is used to determine whether to use expenditures or the bill component in the housing cost formula. For electricity, coal, and other housing-related expenditures (items 8, 9, and 10 in table G.4), expenditures recorded in the survey are added to housing costs.

One final adjustment was made for heating. For the 10.7 percent of the sample (7,402 households) that does not have central heating, additional checks on energy-related expenditures were conducted. For households that do not have gas connections and report spending zero on coal or other fuels (22.2 percent of the subsample), expenditures on coal were imputed based on the region and the size of the home.[3] For households that do dispose of a gas connection, their expenditures on gas are taken into account if these expenditures exceed their gas bill (37.6 percent of the subsample). If their expenditures on gas are lower than the gas bill (35.3 percent of the subsample), this amount is inflated by the ratio of expenditures on gas to the bill for gas calculated for the first group.

These adjustments lead to a gross housing cost, denoted by C. The final step consists in moving from gross to net housing costs, by applying deductions and allowances. *Deductions* refer to the reduction in housing costs obtained by households that are "privileged." *Allowances* refer to the reduction in housing costs obtained under the terms of the housing allowance program. The housing allowance program provides a reduction in housing costs on the basis of a maximum social rent concept, which determines housing cost on the basis of equation (1), with normatively determined surface in squared meters varying with the number of people in the household and normatively determined electricity consumption. Formally,

$$\begin{aligned} MSR_{n=1} &= B(q_m = a_1, n, q_8 = a_4, p_1, \ldots, p_8) \\ MSR_{n=2} &= B(q_m = a_2, n, q_8 = a_4 \cdot n, p_1, \ldots, p_8) \\ MSR_{n\geq 1} &= B(q_m = a_3 \cdot n, n, q_8 = a_4 \cdot n, p_1, \ldots, p_8) \end{aligned} \tag{3}$$

where a_1 to a_4 are policy parameters with the following interpretation: a_1 denotes the normatively determined surface for single people, a_2 denotes the normatively determined surface for couples, a_3 denotes the normatively determined surface per capita for households with at least three people, and a_4 denotes the normatively determined consumption of electricity per capita in KwH, which equals 50 in the benchmark situation. The parameters a_1, a_2, and a_3 vary by region, with average values of 32, 42, and 19 square meters, respectively.

The maximum social rent is allocated to the household, but it decreases with income and cannot become negative:

$$A = \max(0, MSR - tY) \tag{4}$$

where A denotes the allowance, MSR denotes maximum social rent, Y denotes the total disposable income of the household, and t denotes the rate of decrease of the allowance with income, or the maximum allowable budget share for housing costs.

Households living in a dwelling that exactly corresponds to the one normatively determined ($C = HC$) will have a net housing cost of tY. It is important to note that Y is taken directly from the budget survey—variable *doxodsn* (household money income) in the Goskomstat terminology—and is thus not directly related to the expenditure-based welfare concept. Yet this concept probably comes closer to the one observed and used by the administration to calculate the allowance (equation (4)). Parameter t varies by region. The average in 2000 was 0.1733.

The role of maximum social rent is clear when the household lives in a dwelling that exceeds the normatively determined space parameters a_1, a_2, and a_3. Since the allowance is not paid as a cash benefit but is provided as a reduction in the housing bill, households that live in apartments that are smaller than the normatively determined size do not fully exploit the benefit of the allowance program. Therefore, where a household occupies less space than normatively determined, some regions replace the actual space with the normatively determined one in the calculation of the bill; others use the actual space. In the model used here, the actual surface space is always used to calculate the bill and the norms are used to calculate the maximum social rent.[4]

The most common privilege is the reduction of 50 percent of gross housing costs. Since the survey does not provide enough detailed information to implement other possible cases (for example, a deduction of 100 percent), the model simplifies the system of privileges in the benchmark situation to this 50 percent reduction. The policy parameter for the deductions due to privileges is denoted as a_5. Hence net housing costs, *HC*, are equal to

$$HC = (1 - a_5)C, \tag{5}$$

where a_5 is set at 0.5 in the benchmark situation.

The two deductions (being privileged and receiving a housing allowance) cannot be combined in the simulations. The characteristic of being privileged is exogenously determined, whereas the allowance is endogenous (that is, it depends on the housing costs calculated in the model). Unfortunately, the Household Budget Survey does not provide clear and unambiguous information about whether the household includes privileged members. In contrast, the allowance can be calculated. Reasonable assumptions were made to discriminate between the two cases on the basis of the question in the budget survey that asks whether the household received discounts on housing costs and the calculation of the allowance based on household-specific information (table G.5).

If the calculated allowance is zero and the household reports not having received a discount on housing costs (case 1), the household is assumed not to be privileged. For these households, the gross housing cost and the net housing costs are equal. Case 2 includes the 17 percent of all households that have at least one privileged member. The assignment to this subset rests on the observation that the calculated allowance is zero but the household still reports having received discounts on housing costs. For these households, equation (5) is applied. In case 4 a positive allowance is calculated for the household and the household reports that it received discounts on housing costs. In this case the allowance is used to calculate the difference between gross and net housing costs. In the benchmark situation, 7.3 percent of all households fit this case and hence take up the allowance. Case 3 contains households that are eligible for an allowance but report they have not benefited from a discount on housing

Table G.5. Determining whether a household is privileged or receives an allowance

Case	*Does the household receive discounts on housing cost?*	*Is the calculated allowance strictly positive?*	*Status*	*Percentage of households in the benchmark situation*
1	No	No	Household is not privileged and receives no allowance	54.8
2	Yes	No	At least one member in the household is privileged	17.0
3	No	Yes	The household is not privileged, is eligible for an allowance, but did not receive it	20.9
4	Yes	Yes	The household is not privileged, is eligible for an allowance, and did effectively use it	7.3

Source: Decoster and Puzanov (2004).

costs. Their failure to take up the allowance may reflect lack of information, the stigma attached to it, or the fact that the allowance is too low relative to the costs of applying for it.[5] In the benchmark case, these households are treated as if they did not receive any discount on housing costs.

Notes

1. First best would have been to estimate a user cost for ownership of durables, but this was not feasible within the timeframe of this project. Moreover, recent experience of durables' user cost imputation on Russia Longitudinal Monitoring Survey data shows that compared to omitting durables exenditure altogether, the impact is limited (Decoster and Verbina 2003).

2. This is a net concept, which adds in home production and the estimated value of benefits received in kind (based on the estimate provided by Goskomstat) and subtracts food that is provided free of charge.

3. This measure was calculated only for the seven broad regions used by Goskomstat.

4. There are indications that the allowance program would cost 15 percent less if allowances were calculated based on actual space occupied instead of using the norms when the actual space is less than the norm.

5. The level of the allowance does not seem to differ much between groups 3 (56.4 rubles) and 4 (53.3 rubles).

References

Asvall, J., and R. Alderslade. 2002. "Europe." In *Critical Issues in Global Health*, ed. C. Koop, C. Pearson, and M. Schwarz, 37–46. San Francisco: Jossey-Bass.

Atkinson, A. 1987. "On the Measurement of Poverty." *Econometrica* 55 (4): 749–64.

Barro, R., and X. Sala-i-Martin. 1991. "Convergence across States and Regions." *Brookings Papers of Economic Activity* 1: 107–58.

Beliaeva, N., and A. Doctorovich. 2001. "National Health Accounts: Types and Suppliers of Health Care Goods and Services." *Economics of Healthcare* (Russia) 11–12: 37–49.

Bhagwati, J. 1988. *Protectionism (Ohlin Lectures)*. Cambridge, MA: MIT Press.

Boikov, I., F. Feeley, I. Sheiman, and S. Shishkin. 2000. "Survey of Household Spending in Russian Federation." Boston University.

Boldrin, M., and F. Canova. 2001. "Inequality and Convergence: Reconsidering European Regional Policies." *Economic Policy* 16 (32): 207–53.

Bourguignon, F. 1979. "Decomposable Income Inequality Measures." *Econometrica* 47 (4): 901–20.

Brown, D., and J. Earle. 2002. "Job Reallocation and Productivity Growth under Alternative Economic Systems and Policies: Evidence from the Soviet Transition." William Davidson Institute Working Paper No. 514, Ann Arbor, MI.

Burdiak, A., L. Ovcharova, D. Popova, and R. Popova. 2005. "Income of the Population: Structural and Dynamic Analysis." In *Incomes and Social Services: Inequality, Vulnerability, Poverty* (in Russian), ed. L. Ovcharova. Moscow: IISP, State University–Higher School of Economics.

Canning, M., P. Moock, and T. Heleniak. 1999. "Reforming Education in the Regions of Russia." World Bank Technical Paper No. 457, Washington, DC.

Carluer, F., and E. Sharipova. 2001. "Regional Convergence in Russia? Or When Economic Geography Confirms Macroeconomic Analysis." June. Russian-European Center for Economic Policy Working Paper, Moscow.

Castañeda, T., and K. Lindert (with B. de la Brière, L. Fernandez, C. Hubert, O. Larrañaga, M. Orozco, and R. Viquez). 2005. "Designing and Implementing Household Targeting Systems: Lessons from Latin America and the United States." Social Protection Discussion Paper Series No. 0526, World Bank, Washington, DC.

Center for Economic Analysis of the Government of Russia. Various years. "Average Capacity Utilization in Industrial Enterprises." Moscow.

Central Bank of Russia. Various years. *Bulletin of Banking Statistics*. Moscow: Central Bank of Russia.

Commander, S., A. Tolstopiatenko, and R. Yemtsov. 1999. "Channels of Redistribution: Inequality and Poverty in the Russian Transition." *Economics of Transition* 7 (2): 411–47.

Commander, S., and R. Yemtsov. 1995. "Russian Unemployment: Its Magnitudes, Characteristics, and Regional Dimension." World Bank Policy Research Working Paper No. 1426, Washington, DC.

Commission on Macroeconomics and Health. 2002. *Final Report*. Geneva.

Deaton, A. 2001. "Counting the World's Poor: Problems and Possible Solutions." *World Bank Research Observer* 16 (2): 125–47.

Deaton, A., and S. Zaidi. 2002. "A Guide to Aggregating Consumption Expenditures, Living Standards Measurement Study." World Bank Working Paper No. 135, Washington, DC.

Decoster, A., and A. Puzanov. 2004. "The Distributional Effect of the Transition to Full Cost Coverage and the Introduction of a Housing Allowance Program in Russia." January. World Bank, Washington, DC.

Decoster, A., and I. Verbina. 2003. "Who Pays Indirect Taxes in the Russian Federation?" WIDER Discussion Paper 2003/58, World Institute for Development Economics Research, Helsinki.

Deininger, K., and L. Squire. 1996. "A New Data Set Measuring Income Inequality." *World Bank Economic Review* 10 (3): 565–91.

Dolinskaya, I. 2002. "Transition and Regional Inequality in Russia: Reorganization or Procrastination?" IMF Working Paper No. 169, Washington, DC.

EBRD (European Bank for Reconstruction and Development), and World Bank. 1999. "The BEEPS Interactive Dataset." Available at http://info.worldbank.org/governance/beeps2002/.

———. 2002. "The BEEPS II Interactive Dataset: Enterprise Survey in Transition." Available at http://info.worldbank.org/governance/beeps2002/.

Expert Investment Rating Agency (Russia). 2002. "Investment Ratings of Russian Regions." Available at http://www.raexpert.ru/ratings/regions/.

Fakhrutdinova, L. 2002. "The Anatomy of Wage Differential: Analysis for Russia." Master's thesis. Department of Economic History and World Economy, New Economic School, Moscow.

Federal AIDS Center. 2004. "Statistical Database on HIV/AIDS in Russia." Available at http://www.hivrussia.org/index.php?where=2#.

Fedorov, L. 2002. "Regional Inequality and Regional Polarization in Russia, 1990–1999." *World Development* 30 (3): 443–56.

Field, M., and J. Twigg, eds. 2000. *Russia's Torn Safety Nets: Health and Social Welfare During the Transition*. New York: St. Martin's Press.

Förster, M., D. Jesuit, and T. Smeeding. 2002. "Regional Poverty and Income Inequality in Central and Eastern Europe: Evidence from the Luxembourg Income Study." Paper presented at the WIDER-Cornell-LSE Conference on Spatial Inequality and Development, London, June 28–30.

Foster, J., J. Greer, and E. Thorbecke. 1984. "A Class of Decomposable Poverty Measures." *Econometrica* 42 (3): 761–66.

Gibson, J., and A. Poduzov. 2003. "Assessing Welfare Indicators for Poverty Measurement in Russia." Background paper prepared for the World Bank, Russia Poverty Program, Washington, DC.

Gimpelson, V. 2004. "Temporary Employment in Russia: Data, Scale, Dynamics and Prevalence." Working Paper No. 3/2004/02. State University, Higher School of Economics, Moscow.

Gimpelson, V., R. Kapeljushnikov, and L. Khakhulina. 2003. "New Labor Code: Has It Brought Change?" (in Russian). *Public Opinion Monitoring* 2 (64): 41–50.

Goskomstat. 1999. "Results of the Household Budget Survey." *Statistical Bulletin* 11 (61). Moscow: Goskomstat.

———. 2001–03. *Education in Russia*. Moscow.

———. 2003a. *Labor and Employment in Russia*. Moscow.

———. 2003b. *NOBUS: The Survey of Household Welfare and Participation in Federal Programs*. Moscow.

———. 2003c. *Russia in Figures*. Moscow.

———. Various years (a). *Household Budget Survey*. Moscow.

———. Various years (b). *Labor Force in Russia*. Based on results of Labor Force Surveys. Moscow.

———. Various years (c). *Regions of Russia*. Moscow.

———. Various years (d). *Russian Statistical Yearbook*. Moscow.

———. Various years (e). *Social Status and Living Standards of Russian Population*. Moscow.

Government of Russia. 2003. "Program of the Socioeconomic Development of the Russian Federation over the Medium-Term, 2003–2005." Moscow.

Grishina, E. 2003. "The Effect of Tariff Reduction and Trade Liberalization on Wages in Russia." Master's thesis. New Economic School, Moscow.

Gupta, S., M. Verhoeven, and E. Tiongson. 2003. "Public Spending on Health Care and the Poor." *Health Economics* 12 (8): 685–96.

Hamilton, E., S.G. Banerjee, and M. Lomaia. 2004. "Exploring Housing Subsidies for Households in Russia." World Bank, Europe and Central Asia Infrastructure and Energy Services Unit, Washington, DC.

Hanson, P., and M. Bradshaw. 2000. *Regional Economic Change in Russia*. Cheltenham: Edward Elgar.

Heleniak, T. 2003. "The 2002 Census in Russia: Preliminary Results." *Eurasian Geography and Economics* 44 (6): 430–42.

Hovhannisyan, S., E. Tragakes, S. Lessof, H. Aslanian, and A. Mkrtchyan. 2001. *Health Care Systems in Transition: Armenia.* European Observatory on Health Care Systems, Copenhagen.

IISP (Independent Institute for Social Policy). 2002. "Poverty and Privileges: Myths and Reality." Moscow.

———. 2003. "Informal Out-of-Pocket Payments for Health Care." Moscow.

ILO (International Labour Organization). 2003. *Report II: Household Income and Expenditure Statistics.* Proceedings of the 17th International Conference of Labor Statisticians, Geneva, November 24–December 3.

IMEMO (Institute of World Economy and International Relations). Various years. *Russian Economic Barometer*. Moscow.

Interstate Statistical Committee of the CIS. Various years. *Statistics of the CIS. Statistical Bulletin.* Moscow.

Ivaschenko, O. 2003. "Mortality in Russian Regions: Do Poverty and Low Public Health Spending Kill?" World Bank, Poverty Reduction and Economic Management Unit, Europe and Central Asia Region, Washington, DC.

Jensen, J., T.F. Rutherford, and D.G. Tarr. 2004a. "Economy-Wide and Sector Effects of Russia's Accession to the WTO." August. World Bank, Washington, DC. Available at http://www.worldbank.org/trade/russia-wto.

———. 2004b. "The Impact of Liberalizing Barriers to Foreign Direct Investment in Services: The Case of Russian Accession to the World Trade Organization." June. World Bank, Washington, DC. Available at http://www.worldbank.org/trade/russia-wto.

Kakwani, N. 1980. *Income Inequality and Poverty: Methods of Estimation and Policy Applications*. New York: Published for the World Bank by Oxford University Press.

Kakwani, N., and Z. Sajaia. 2003. "Poverty Line in Russia: Issues, Methodology and Recommendations." University of New South Wales, School of Economics, and the World Bank, Poverty Reduction and Economic Management Unit, Europe and Central Asia Region, Washington, DC.

Kakwani, N., and H. Son. 2003. "Poverty Equivalent Growth Rate." Paper prepared for the conference on well-being held by the World Institute for Development Economics Research (WIDER), Helsinki.

———. 2004. "New Poverty Thresholds for Russia." University of New South Wales, School of Economics, and the World Bank, Poverty Reduction and Economic Management Unit, Europe and Central Asia Region, Washington, DC.

Kanbur, R. 2003. "The Policy Significance of Inequality Decompositions." Cornell University, Ithaca, NY.

Kapeljushnikov, R. 2003. "Wage-Setting Mechanisms in Russian Industry." Working Paper No. 3/2003/07. State University, Higher School of Economics, Moscow.

Karnitski, G. 1997. *Health Care Systems in Transition: Belarus*. European Observatory on Health Care Systems, Copenhagen.

Kimura, F., M. Ando, and T. Fujii. 2003a. "Estimating the Ad Valorem Equivalent of Barriers to Foreign Direct Investment in the Telecommunications Services Sectors in Russia." World Bank, Washington, DC. Available at http://www.worldbank.org/trade/russia-wto.

———. 2003b. "Estimating the Ad Valorem Equivalent of Barriers to Foreign Direct Investment in the Maritime and Air Transportation Service Sectors in Russia." World Bank, Washington, DC. Available at http://www.worldbank.org/trade/russia-wto.

———. 2003c. "Estimating the Ad Valorem Equivalent of Barriers to Foreign Direct Investment in Financial Services Sectors in Russia." World Bank, Washington, DC. Available at http://www.worldbank.org/trade/russia-wto.

Klugman, J., J. Micklewright, and G. Redmond. 2002. "Poverty in the Transition: Social Expenditures and the Working-Age Poor." Innocenti Working Paper No. 91, Florence, Italy.

Kochar, A. 2000. "Savings." In *Designing Household Survey Questionnaires for Developing Countries*, ed. M. Grosh and P. Glewwe, 183–209. Washington, DC: World Bank.

Kolenikov, S., and A.F. Shorrocks. 2003a. "Regional Poverty in Russia: Is It Geography or Economics That Matters?" Paper presented at the WIDER Conference on Spatial Inequality in Asia, Tokyo, March 28–29.

——. 2003b. "A Decomposition Analysis of Regional Poverty in Russia." WIDER Discussion Paper No. 2003/74, World Institute for Development Economics Research, Helsinki.

Lane, J. 2003. "Statistical Confidentiality and Access to Micro Data." *Proceedings of the Seminar Session of the 2003 Conference of European Statisticians*. New York and Geneva: United Nations Economic Commission for Europe.

Langenbrunner, J., J. Kutzin, E. Orosz, and M. Wiley. 2005. "Purchasing and Paying Providers." In *Purchasing to Improve Health Systems Performance*, ed. J. Figueras, R. Robinson, and E. Jakubowski, 236–64. Berkshire, UK: Open University Press.

Langenbrunner, J., and O. Odeyi, eds. 2003. *Health, Nutrition, and Population in Europe and Central Asia: A Decade of Experience: Lessons Learned, Implications for the Future*. Washington, DC: World Bank.

Lewis, M. 2000. "Who Is Paying for Health Care in Eastern Europe and Central Asia?" Study prepared for the World Bank, Human Development Sector Unit, Europe and Central Asia Region, Washington, DC.

Lock, K., E. Andreev, V. Shkolnikov, and M. McKee. 2002. "What Targets for International Development Policies Are Appropriate for Improving Health in Russia?" *Health Policy and Planning* 17 (3): 257–63.

Lukyanova, A. 2003. "Wage Differentiation and the Phenomenon of the Working Poor in Russia." State University, Higher School of Economics, Moscow.

Malyutina, S., M. Bobak, S. Kurilovitch, V. Gafarov, G. Simonova, Y. Nikitin, and M. Marmot. 2002. "Relation between Heavy and Binge Drinking and All-Cause and Cardiovascular Mortality in Novosibirsk, Russia: A Prospective Cohort Study." *Lancet* 360 (944): 1448–54.

Markusen, J., T. Rutherford, and D.G. Tarr. 2000. "Foreign Direct Investment in Services and the Domestic Market for Expertise." World Bank Policy and Research Working Paper No. 2143, Washington, DC.

Martini, A., A. Ivanova, and S. Novosyolova. 1996. "The Income and Expenditure Survey of Belarus: Design and Implementation." *Statistics in Transition* 2 (7): 1063–84.

McKay, A. 2000. "Should the Survey Measure Total Household Income?" In *Designing Household Survey Questionnaires for Developing Countries*, ed. M. Grosh and P. Glewwe, 315–38. Washington, DC: World Bank.

Men, T., P. Brennan, P. Boffeta, and D. Zaridze. 2003. "Russian Mortality Trends for 1991–2001: Analysis by Cause and Region." *British Medical Journal* 327 (7421): 964–70.

Milanović, B. 1998. "Income, Inequality, and Poverty During the Transition from Planned to Market Economy." World Bank Regional and Sectoral Studies, Washington, DC.

———. 2003. "Social Transfers, Inequality." In *Siromaštvo i Reforma Finansijske Podrske Siromašnima* (*Poverty and Reform of Financial Assistance to the Poor*), ed. B. Bogićević, G. Krstić, B. Mijatović, and B. Milanović, 45–72. Beograd: Goragraf.

Ministry of Finance of the Russian Federation. 2001. *Reports on Execution of Budgets for 1997–2001*. Moscow.

Mistiaen, J., and M. Ravallion. 2003. "Survey Compliance and the Distribution of Income." World Bank Policy Research Working Paper No. 2956, Washington, DC.

Moffitt, R. 2002. "The Temporary Assistance for Needy Families Program." NBER Working Paper No. 8749, National Bureau of Economic Research, New York.

Morozov, Alexander. 2004. "Overview of Public Spending on Education, Health, and Social Protection Sectors in Russia." World Bank, Poverty Reduction and Economic Management Unit, Europe and Central Asia Region, Washington, DC.

Mossialos, E. 1999. "The Pharmaceutical Sector in Russia." Paper prepared for the U.S. Agency for International Development by the Boston University Legal Reform Project.

Mroz, T.A., L. Henderson, M. Bontch-Osmolovskii, and B.M. Popkin. 2002. "Monitoring Economic Conditions in the Russian Federation: The Russia Longitudinal Monitoring Survey 1992–2001." Report prepared for the U.S. Agency for International Development by the Carolina Population Center, University of North Carolina, Chapel Hill.

Notzon, F., Y. Komarov, S. Ermakov, C. Sempos, J. Marks, and E. Tempos. 1998. "Causes of Declining Life Expectancy in Russia." *Journal of the American Medical Association* 279 (10): 793–800.

Nurgozhin, T., M. Pavin, G. Hafner, F. Yusupov, S. Khusanbaev, and R. Laing. 2001. "The Pharmaceutical Study in Ferghana Oblast, Uzbekistan." Technical report prepared by Abt Associates for USAID.

Park, A., and S. Wang. 2001. "China's Poverty Statistics." *China Economic Review* 12 (3): 384–98.

Plavinski, S., S. Plavinskaya, and A. Klimov. 2003. "Social Factors and Increase in Mortality in Russia in the 1990s: Prospective Cohort Study." *British Medical Journal* 326 (7401): 1240–42.

Poletaev, A. 2003. "Labour Market and Economic Efficiency." Working Paper No. 3/2003/06, State University, Higher School of Economics, Moscow.

Posarac, A., and S. Rashid. 2003. "Non-Income Dimensions of Poverty in Russia: Human Capital, Labor Markets, Social Protection." World Bank, Human Development Department, Europe and Central Asia Region, Washington, DC.

Prokofieva, L. 2003. "Measurement of Poverty and Social Exclusion: Russian Experience in Applying Nonmonetary Indicators." Background paper prepared for the World Bank, Russia Poverty Program, Washington, DC.

Rashid, M., and A. Posarac. 2002. "Non-Income Dimensions of Poverty in Russia: Human Capital, Labor Markets, Social Protection." World Bank, Human Development Unit, Europe and Central Asia Region, Washington, DC.

Ravallion, M. 2001. "Measuring Aggregate Welfare in Developing Countries: How Well Do National Accounts and Surveys Agree?" World Bank Working Paper No. 2665, Washington, DC.

———. 2004. "Competing Concepts of Inequality in the Globalization Debate." World Bank Policy Research Working Paper No. 3243, Washington, DC.

Ravallion, M., and S. Chen. 2003. "Measuring Pro-Poor Growth." *Economics Letters* 78 (1): 93–99.

Ravallion, M., and M. Lokshin. 2003. "On the Utility Consistency of Poverty Lines." World Bank Policy Research Working Paper No. 3157, Washington, DC.

Rimashevskaya, N. 1999. "Impoverishment of the Russian Population and Social Exclusion: Findings of a Special Survey." *Narodonaseleniye (Population)* 2 (4).

Roshtchina, Y. 2004. "Education and Poverty Interface." World Bank, Human Development Unit, Europe and Central Asia, Washington, DC.

Roshtchina, Y., M. Drugov, and O. Kuzina. 2001. "Access to Tertiary Education in Russia: Social Factors of Inequity in Access, Motivation and Demand." Independent Institute for Social Policy, Moscow.

Ruehl, C., V. Pokrovsky, and V. Vinogradov. 2002. "The Economic Consequences of HIV in Russia." World Bank, Washington, DC. Available at http://www.worldbank.org.ru.

Rutherford, T., D. Tarr, and O. Shepotylo. 2004. "Household and Poverty Effects from Russia's Accession to the WTO." Background paper prepared for the World Bank, Russia Poverty Program, Washington, DC.

Sabirianova, K. 2003. "Skill-Biased Transition: The Role of Markets, Institutions, and Technological Change." IZA Discussion Paper No. 893, Institute for the Study of Labor, Bonn, Germany.

Satarov, G. 2002. "Diagnosis of the Russian Corruption: Sociological Analysis." INDEM Foundation, Moscow.

Sen, A. 1985. *Commodities and Capabilities*. Amsterdam: North-Holland.

Shahriari, H., P. Belli, and M. Lewis. 2001. "Institutional Issues in Informal Health Payment in Poland: Report on the Qualitative Part of the Study." Study prepared for the World Bank, Health, Nutrition, and Population Reproductive Health Thematic Group, Washington, DC.

Shankar, R., and A. Shah. 2001. "Bridging the Economic Divide within Nations: A Scorecard on the Performance of Regional Development

Policies in Reducing Regional Income Disparities." World Bank Policy Research Working Paper No. 2717, Washington, DC.

Shishkin, S. 2000. "Issues of Health Care Financing in Russia." SPIDER Working Paper Series No. 16, Stockholm University and St. Petersburg State University.

Shishkin, S., ed. 2003. *Informal Out-of-Pocket Payments for Health Care in Russia*. Moscow: Moscow Public Science Foundation and Independent Institute for Social Policy.

Shorrocks, A.F. 1980. "The Class of Additively Decomposable Inequality Measures." *Econometrica* 48 (3): 613–25.

Shorrocks, A.F., and K. Stanislav. 2001. "Poverty Trends in Russia During the Transition." United Nations University/World Institute for Development Economics Research, Helsinki.

Shorrocks, A.F., and G. Wan. 2004. "Spatial Decomposition of Inequality." UNU/WIDER Discussion Paper No. 2004/01, United Nations University/World Institute for Development Economics Research, Helsinki.

Sokolin, V. 2003. "Confidentiality of Statistical Data: The Russian Federation." In *Statistical Confidentiality and Access to Microdata. Proceedings of the Seminar Session of the 2003 Conference of European Statisticians*, 53–58. New York and Geneva: United Nations Economic Commission for Europe.

State Institute of Statistics–Turkey. 2002. "Household Income and Consumption Expenditure Survey." Ankara.

State Institute of Statistics–Turkey, and World Bank. 2005. *Turkey: Joint Poverty Assessment Report*. Washington, DC: World Bank.

State University, Higher School of Economics and Institute of Statistical Research and Knowledge Economy. 2002. "Education Economics Monitoring Survey." Moscow.

Statistics Canada. 1999. "National Population Health Survey 1998/1999." Available at http://cansim2.statcan.ca/.

Tesliuc, E., and E. Zotova. 2004. "Improving the Targeting of Social Protection in Russia." Background paper for the World Bank, Russia Poverty Program, Washington, DC.

Tragakes, E., and S. Lessof. 2003. *Health Care Systems in Transition: Russian Federation*. European Observatory on Health Care Systems, Copenhagen.

UN Statistical Commission. 1994. "Fundamental Principles of Official Statistics." UN Economic and Social Council, 1994, Report of the Special Session of the Statistical Commission, New York, April 11–15.

UNCTAD (United Nations Conference on Trade and Development). 2001. *World Investment Report*. Geneva: UNCTAD.

UNDP (United Nations Development Programme). 2003. *Human Development Report 2002/2003 for the Russian Federation: The Role of the State in Economic Growth and Socio-Economic Reform*. New York: UNDP.

UNESCO (United Nations Educational, Scientific and Cultural Organization). 2000–2002. "Education and Literacy Database." Available at http://www.uis.unesco.org/pagesen/ed.htm.

UNC (University of North Carolina). Various years. "The Russia Longitudinal Monitoring Survey." Carolina Population Center, University of North Carolina, Chapel Hill.

VCIOM (Russian Public Opinion Survey Center). 2003. Survey data. Moscow.

Wagstaff, A. 2002. "Poverty and Health Sector Inequalities." *Bulletin of the World Health Organization* 80 (2): 97–105.

Watts, H. 1968. "An Economic Definition of Poverty." In *Understanding Poverty*, ed. Daniel P. Moynihan, 316–29. New York: Basic Books.

Westlund, H., A. Granberg, and F. Snickars. 2000. *Regional Development in Russia*. Cheltenham: Edward Elgar.

World Bank. 1995. "Poverty in Russia: An Assessment." Human Resources Division, Europe and Central Asia Country Department III, Washington, DC.

———. 1996. *Fiscal Management in Russia*. Washington, DC: World Bank.

———. 1998. "Russian Federation: Housing and Utility Services. Policy Priorities for the Next Stage of Reforms." Poverty Reduction and Economic Management Unit, Europe and Central Asia Region, Washington, DC.

———. 1999. "Russia: Targeting and the Long-Term Poor." Poverty Reduction and Economic Management and Human Development Networks, Europe and Central Asia Region, Washington, DC.

———. 2000a. *Making Transition Work for Everyone: Poverty and Inequality in Europe and Central Asia*. Washington, DC: World Bank.

———. 2000b. *World Development Report 1999/2000: Entering the 21st Century*. New York: Oxford University Press.

———. 2001. *World Development Report 2000/2001: Attacking Poverty*. New York: Oxford University Press.

———. 2002a. "Russian Federation: Child Welfare Outcomes During the 1990s. The Case of Russia." Human Development Sector Unit, Europe and Central Asia Region, Washington, DC.

———. 2002b. *World Development Indicators*. Washington, DC: World Bank.

———. 2003a. "Russia: Development Policy Review." Poverty Reduction and Economic Management Unit, Europe and Central Asia Region, Washington, DC.

———. 2003b. "Russian Economic Report No. 6." Russia Country Department, Moscow.

———. 2003c. *World Development Indicators*. Washington, DC: World Bank.

———. 2003d. *World Development Report 2004: Making Services Work for Poor People*. Washington, DC: World Bank and Oxford University Press.

———. 2004a. "From Transition to Development: A Country Economic Memorandum for the Russian Federation." Poverty Reduction and Economic Management Unit, Europe and Central Asia Region, Washington, DC.

———. 2004b. *The Modernization of Education in Russia: Outstanding Issues*. Washington, DC: World Bank.

———. 2004c. "Russian Economic Report No. 7." Russia Country Department, Moscow.

———. 2004d. "Russian Federation Health Sector Mission: Mission Report/Aide Memoire." Human Development Unit, Europe and Central Asia Region, Washington, DC.

———. 2004e. "Russia's Poverty Program: Project Progress Report." June. Europe and Central Asia Region, Poverty Reduction and Economic Management Unit, Washington, DC.

WHO (World Health Organization). Various years. *World Health Reports*. Geneva: WHO.

———. 2003. "MDG Proposal Report for Improving Baseline Information." Moscow.

———. 2004. "Health for All Database." Geneva.

Yemtsov, R. 2003. "Quo Vadis Inequality and Poverty Dynamics across Russian Regions." WIDER Discussion Paper No. 2003/67, World Institute for Development Economics Research, Helsinki.

Zhuravskaya, E.V. 2000. "Market-Hampering Federalism: Local Incentives for Reform in Russia." Russian-European Center for Economic Policy, Moscow.

Index

D

E

F

H

I

J

K

L

M

N

O

P

R

S

Y

Z